Unpacking
AI Ethics

Practical Advances in
Artificial Intelligence and Machine Learning

Dr. Lance B. Eliot, MBA, PhD

DEDICATION

To my incredible daughter, Lauren, and my incredible son, Michael.

Forest fortuna adiuvat (from the Latin; good fortune favors the brave).

CONTENTS

Dr. Lance B. Eliot

ACKNOWLEDGMENTS

I have been the beneficiary of advice and counsel by many friends, colleagues, family, investors, and many others. I want to thank everyone that has aided me throughout my career. I write from the heart and the head, having experienced first-hand what it means to have others around you that support you during the good times and the tough times.

To Warren Bennis, one of my doctoral advisors and ultimately a colleague, I offer my deepest thanks and appreciation, especially for his calm and insightful wisdom and support.

To Mark Stevens and his generous efforts toward funding and supporting the USC Stevens Center for Innovation.

To Lloyd Greif and the USC Lloyd Greif Center for Entrepreneurial Studies for their ongoing encouragement of founders and entrepreneurs.

To Peter Drucker, William Wang, Aaron Levie, Peter Kim, Jon Kraft, Cindy Crawford, Jenny Ming, Steve Milligan, Chis Underwood, Frank Gehry, Buzz Aldrin, Steve Forbes, Bill Thompson, Dave Dillon, Alan Fuerstman, Larry Ellison, Jim Sinegal, John Sperling, Mark Stevenson, Anand Nallathambi, Thomas Barrack, Jr., and many other innovators and leaders that I have met and gained mightily from doing so.

Thanks to Ed Trainor, Kevin Anderson, James Hickey, Wendell Jones, Ken Harris, DuWayne Peterson, Mike Brown, Jim Thornton, Abhi Beniwal, Al Biland, John Nomura, Eliot Weinman, John Desmond, and many others for their unwavering support during my career.

And most of all thanks as always to Lauren and Michael, for their ongoing support and for having seen me writing and heard much of this material during the many months involved in writing it. To their patience and willingness to listen.

Dr. Lance B. Eliot

CHAPTER 1
INTRODUCTION
TO
AI ETHICS

There is an urgently rising societal interest in the field of AI Ethics.

Thankfully so.

As Artificial Intelligence (AI) continues to advance and increasingly become part of our daily lives, we need to be on our toes about AI that diverges from ethical behavior and crosses over into unethical behavior. The field of AI Ethics seeks to apply ethical precepts and theories of ethical conduct to the devising and usage of AI systems, doing so to try and steer AI into sufficient ethical mores and avert unethical actions by AI.

Formal definitions of AI Ethics tend to vary somewhat. All told, the notion is to combine what we know or believe about ethics as a guiding tool toward the mounting advent of AI-based intelligent systems.

Some would argue that the AI horse is seemingly getting out of the barn and doing so without needed ethical boundaries. In a headline-grabbing worst-case scenario envisioned by AI futurists, AI systems are predicted to become mightier than we can adequately control and end up as an existential risk to the fate of humanity. Dire catastrophic outcomes are being painted.

You don't though need to look solely at the far future to get concerned about the ethical actions of AI. As will be discussed, there are plenty of AI systems of today that already have made known the adverse consequences of not taking into account the importance of AI Ethics.

As a particularly succinct and insightful definition of AI Ethics, consider this one by The Alan Turing Institute: "AI ethics is a set of values, principles, and techniques that employ widely accepted standards of right and wrong to guide moral conduct in the development and use of AI technologies" (as published in *Understanding Artificial Intelligence Ethics And Safety: A Guide For The Responsible Design And Implementation Of AI Systems In The Public Sector* by David Leslie, 2019).

Notice that there is an important dual-element consisting of both the development of AI systems and the usage of AI systems.

AI Ethics comes to play as a guiding light throughout the development process when devising AI. The entirety of the AI development life cycle must encompass AI Ethics principles. From the moment that an AI system is first initially conceived of, and then during the design, building, testing, fielding, and upkeep, all stakeholders involved in producing the AI are to be giving due consideration to AI Ethics. In addition, once an AI system has been placed into active use, you still must be on alert to watch for, detect, and potentially correct AI that verges from ethical conduct into unethical actions.

I mention the aspect of remaining aware once AI has been placed into use because there is often a faulty notion of fire-and-forget mindset that some developers of AI get caught up in. They believe that if they tried to develop the AI in an ethically minded fashion, there is no need to continue any AI Ethics forays once the AI is released into use.

This belies the real and frequent possibility that the AI will veer from its earlier ethics-oriented groundings and sway into unethical territory while in use.

AI Ethics And The Entire AI Development Life Cycle

Keep in mind then that we will want to ensure that both conditions of development and of use are being met, namely:

a) Apply AI Ethics throughout the AI development process from start to "finish"

b) Continue to apply AI Ethics even once the AI is placed into use

The AI development life cycle must be viewed as ranging from the initial conceiving of the AI to the entire time that it is available for use. Do not shortchange that range. Some AI developers do not consider the initial conceiving stage as within the scope of AI Ethics and think that just the building or coding stage is where AI Ethics first arises. In a similar mistaken belief, some AI developers assume that after the AI has been released into production and put into use that they can wash their hands of any residual or newly emerging AI Ethics qualms about the AI system. Nope, trying to narrowly confine where AI Ethics is needed will undoubtedly lead to ethical problems, one way or another, and sooner or later.

Another quick point is to realize that AI Ethics is something that all stakeholders amidst an AI system must be cognizant of. The normal assumption is that the software engineers alone are the caretakers of any AI Ethics considerations. Not so. Management that oversees the crafting of an AI system is part-and-parcel of the AI Ethics matters. If the organizational leaders are shortchanging the value of applying AI Ethics, you can bet that this same persona will permeate and undercut the AI life cycle. Budgets for devising the AI won't include set-asides for incorporating AI Ethics considerations. Schedules and deadlines won't either. In the end, a pell-mell rush to get the AI out the door will take top priority and AI Ethics will barely get a word in edgewise.

All stakeholders have a stake in enduring that AI Ethics is sufficiently incorporated into the full life-cycle of an AI system.

When an AI system exhibits unethical activity, this can be traced not just to the coding and the software developers, but also tracked to the leaders that oversaw the AI life cycle, the business and systems analysts involved, and even those that are operating or responsible for the final deployment of the AI.

The usual escape hatch entails those other stakeholders claiming that they weren't the ones that churned out the code that underlies the AI system. This is a convenient and at times nearly convincing argument for those that do not fully grasp how an AI system came to be. Overall, all stakeholders have both an ethical responsibility for the AI and are likely to have legal accountability too.

Making Sense Of What AI Is

When I refer to Artificial Intelligence, the AI moniker can be a bit confusing as to what AI entails.

Welcome to the club in the sense that the meaning of Artificial Intelligence continues to be bandied around and there is no single comprehensive and all-agreed definition for AI. One of the issues facing the latest efforts to regulate AI systems has been how to appropriately define AI within our laws. If the legal definition is overly broad, new laws seeking to better govern AI systems can inadvertently encroach on all manner of software applications and computer systems. If the legal definition of AI is excessively restrictive, the odds are that AI systems that should have been encompassed will wiggle out from being bound by those laws.

The easiest way to define AI consists of saying that any computer or machine that exhibits seemingly intelligent behavior is in the realm of AI.

This notion dates back to 1956 when Professor John McCarthy coined the name Artificial Intelligence as part of a proposal to bring together many luminaries of math and computer science for a research project: "The study is to proceed on the basis of the conjecture that every aspect of learning or any other feature of intelligence can in principle be so precisely described that a machine can be made to simulate it" (in his co-authored proposal entitled *Proposal For The Dartmouth Summer Research Project On Artificial Intelligence*).

One subtle but extremely vital facet about the definition of AI is that we can presumably seek to attain computer-based or machine-based intelligent behavior without necessarily duplicating the precise way that humans think. There is an ongoing debate about that questionable keystone. Some would contend that the only way to produce an artificial form of intelligence is to completely mimic how the human brain works. Others argue that we might find alternative means to bring forth artificially indued intelligence. The old saying goes that there is more than one way to skin a cat.

The gist is that if we can craft a computer or machine that will *exhibit* intelligence and intelligent behavior, we ought not to be especially caring about how that came to be. All that we need to know is that the system appears to act and respond intelligently. Whatever we did to get there is not particularly relevant, some say. As you might imagine, not everyone agrees with that supposition. The inner workings of how intelligence comes to arise are claimed to be equally important as the result of being able to produce intelligent actions and outputs.

Rather than focusing on definitions of AI, there is another way that AI is often depicted. You can assert that AI is a set of computer-related techniques and technologies. Thus, if you are making use of those AI techniques and technologies, you are ergo devising and employing AI capabilities.

A typical taxonomy would explain AI by suggesting that these associated techniques and technologies are involved:

- Machine Learning

- Natural Language Processing

- Knowledge-Based Systems

- Automated Reasoning

- Robotics

- Multi-Agent Systems

- Etc.

A difficulty of merely referring to those various techniques and technologies as constituting an AI system is that you aren't especially aiming at the intelligence side of things. Recall that the nearly universal goal of AI is to attain systems that exhibit intelligence. You can cobble together the various techniques and technologies and not necessarily derive any semblance of intelligent-like behaviors. Would a system that perchance leverages those capabilities be reasonably construed as an AI system even if it did not showcase intelligent-oriented actions? I would dare say many would contend that such a system does not meet the spirit or tone of what is meant by referring to AI.

AI Ethics Has Been On A Roller Coaster Of Societal Interest

You might be surprised to learn that AI Ethics has been a topic of discussion since the very beginning of the AI field. Perhaps this has partially been fueled by longstanding works of fiction that have indubitably worried that someday humans would construct machines that could overtake humankind. Today's emergence of computer systems that seem to have AI capacities has brought those past fictional stories into greater focus as something that might be constructed in the real world.

Interest in AI Ethics has been a roller coaster ride, consisting of moments of great interest to spans of sparse attention.

During the 1980s and 1990s, intense efforts were being made to craft knowledge-based systems, often referred to as expert systems, and the concerns about AI Ethics began to gain traction. The more AI there is, the more likely the attention to AI Ethics.

You might be aware that then a so-called "AI Winter" arose following the hyped expectations of AI in the 80s and 90s, and a resurgence of AI attention only began anew in the last decade or so. During the winter period of AI, AI Ethics somewhat languished, ostensibly still being worked on but now in the shadows. Upon the newly considered "AI Spring" of advances in AI capabilities that stridently stoked a renewal for AI, along with rapidly decreasing costs of computing, and a myriad of other technology trends such as cloud computing, the Internet of Things (IoT), and so on, this, in turn, sparked a renewal in AI Ethics.

Many speak nowadays of AI as being either *AI For Good* or *AI For Bad*. The initial renewed excitement about contemporary AI capabilities was that we would finally be able to fruitfully use computers and so-called smart machines toward solving many of the globe's most pressing problems, such as dealing with worldwide hunger, widespread poverty, sustainability, and other pressing issues.

That is *AI For Good*.

Lamentedly, we began to realize that the same AI could contain untoward biases and inequities, accordingly, labeled as *AI For Bad*. For example, facial recognition was one of the first AI technologies that got caught with inherent racial and gender biases, which we will be exploring in the chapters ahead.

The odds are that any AI system will have a bit of both. As much as possible, we want to uncover and excise the *AI For Bad*. Also, as much as possible, we want to ensure that *AI For Good* is being devised and fielded. Those that are AI ethicists bring to the table the skillset and passion for striving to maximize the *AI For Good* and minimize or eliminate the *AI For Bad*.

This is assuredly a tough proposition to fulfill.

Being An AI Ethicist Or Adjacent To

Speaking of tough shoes to fill, let's pursue that topic in terms of who can aid in the AI Ethics field.

A properly qualified AI ethicist should be versed in the field of ethics and likewise versed in the field of AI. It is a twofer if you like.

Someone that is strong on the ethics side but weak on the AI side would be doing themselves a disservice because they are bound to lack the needed comprehension about what AI is and what it might become. In the same breath, someone that is weak on the ethics side and strong on the AI side might be missing the boat in terms of understanding the vital nuances of ethics and ethical thinking.

In the case of AI, I like to clearly demarcate that when I am discussing AI, it could be in the context of any or all of these three conditions:

1) Non-sentient AI of today

2) Sentient AI of human intelligence caliber (which we don't know will be achieved)

3) Sentient AI of super-intelligence (which is even more speculative than #2)

Discussions about AI that are in the sentient AI category are highly speculative. We don't have sentient AI today. We don't know when we will have sentient AI, if ever so. In general, covering AI Ethics when solely considering sentient AI is a lot of handwaving. You can pretty much make up whatever you like about how sentient AI is going to behave. I'm not saying that we should not be concerned about sentient AI, and only mentioning that the AI Ethics as pertaining to sentient AI is loosey-goosey and not especially real-world applicable per se.

You can rest assured that there is still plenty to talk about when it comes to AI Ethics and today's non-sentient AI. There is no need to go into the outstretched arena of sentient AI to have lots to discuss.

Furthermore, the handy aspect of AI Ethics regarding non-sentient AI is that this is a very applied discipline that can be immediately put to use throughout society. Companies that are creating AI systems need AI Ethics advice and consultation. Entities and people that are using AI systems are likewise in need of AI Ethics advice and consultation. Regulators are now steeped in trying to create laws related to AI, for which AI Ethics insights are needed too.

The field of ethics and all of its numerous theories about ethics can be applied toward the specific domain of AI. Indeed, one viewpoint is that the field of ethics as *applied to technology* (of any kind) is the umbrella into which the particular application of ethics applied to AI fits.

For those of you that are pursuing a career as an AI ethicist, the good news is that we are still in the infancy of AI Ethics. There is a lot of room to grow. You can also anticipate that as AI gets more pervasive and improves in showcasing intelligent behavior, AI Ethics will be expanding and sought after correspondingly so.

AI Ethics Frameworks And Key Principles

At this time, there are lots of proposed AI Ethics frameworks or principles that are being floated around and discussed heartily. No single set of AI Ethics principles has been universally adopted. Each day there seems to be a new set proffered by one prominent group or entity, or another. You have lots of AI Ethics precepts to choose from.

The chapters will cover this more so, but we can take a sneak peek here.

As stated by the U.S. Department of Defense (DoD) in their *Ethical Principles For The Use Of Artificial Intelligence*, these are the six primary AI ethics principles:

- **Responsible:** DoD personnel will exercise appropriate levels of judgment and care while remaining responsible for the development, deployment, and use of AI capabilities.

- **Equitable:** The Department will take deliberate steps to minimize unintended bias in AI capabilities.

- **Traceable:** The Department's AI capabilities will be developed and deployed such that relevant personnel possesses an appropriate understanding of the technology, development processes, and operational methods applicable to AI capabilities, including transparent and auditable methodologies, data sources, and design procedure and documentation.

- **Reliable:** The Department's AI capabilities will have explicit, well-defined uses, and the safety, security, and effectiveness of such capabilities will be subject to testing and assurance within those defined uses across their entire lifecycles.

- **Governable:** The Department will design and engineer AI capabilities to fulfill their intended functions while possessing the ability to detect and avoid unintended consequences, and the ability to disengage or deactivate deployed systems that demonstrate unintended behavior.

Meanwhile, as stated by the Vatican in the *Rome Call For AI Ethics* these are their identified six primary AI ethics principles:

- **Transparency:** In principle, AI systems must be explainable

- **Inclusion:** The needs of all human beings must be taken into consideration so that everyone can benefit, and all individuals can be offered the best possible conditions to express themselves and develop

- **Responsibility:** Those who design and deploy the use of AI must proceed with responsibility and transparency

- **Impartiality:** Do not create or act according to bias, thus safeguarding fairness and human dignity

- **Reliability:** AI systems must be able to work reliably

- **Security and privacy:** AI systems must work securely and respect the privacy of users.

You astutely probably noticed a commonality across those AI Ethics principles.

Researchers have examined and condensed the essence of numerous such national and international AI ethics tenets, articulating the summary set in a paper entitled "The Global Landscape Of AI Ethics Guidelines" as published in the prized journal *Nature*, which led to this essentials list:

- **Transparency**

- **Justice & Fairness**

- **Non-Maleficence**

- **Responsibility**

- **Privacy**

- **Beneficence**

- **Freedom & Autonomy**

- **Trust**

- **Sustainability**

- **Dignity**

- **Solidarity**

In short, you could say that AI Ethics consists of *applying* those aforementioned ethical precepts to AI systems.

To make this claim abundantly apparent, I'll relist those principles and add the indication that they are to be applied to AI and done so via the auspices of AI Ethics:

- Transparency as applied to AI via AI Ethics considerations
- Justice & Fairness as applied to AI via AI Ethics considerations
- Non-Maleficence as applied to AI via AI Ethics considerations
- Responsibility as applied to AI via AI Ethics considerations
- Privacy as applied to AI via AI Ethics considerations
- Beneficence as applied to AI via AI Ethics considerations
- Freedom & Autonomy to AI via AI Ethics considerations
- Trust as applied to AI via AI Ethics considerations
- Sustainability as applied to AI via AI Ethics considerations
- Dignity as applied to AI via AI Ethics considerations
- Solidarity as applied to AI via AI Ethics considerations

A recent form of terminology is that we are endeavoring to produce *Ethical AI*.

As will be seen in the chapters herein, I will at times interchangeably refer to AI Ethics and Ethical AI as one and the same. I will also explain why some quibble that AI Ethics and Ethical AI are not identically equivalent, though they both share the same lineage.

A handy way to readily grasp the application of ethics to AI is to consider these two overarching avenues:

1. The ethical behavior of the humans devising and using AI
2. The computational embedding of ethical behavior into the AI itself

In the first instance, the notion is to try and get the humans that are developing and fielding AI to become aware of and make use of ethical practices in how they shape, release, and perform the upkeep of AI systems. You might for example train the stakeholders on the AI Ethics precepts. There might be software development tools and methodologies that can provide AI Ethics guidance. Various quality control checks and auditing can be done under the rubric of AI Ethics attainment. And so on.

In the second instance listed, the idea is to embed into the AI a semblance of ethical acting computer components. Whereas the first focus is about the process of devising the AI, this second focus is about trying to embody ethically capable computational functionality into the AI. This is a much less explored arena and rife for great expansion and maturation. Some even argue that it is not especially doable, though as will be discussed in the chapters you can counterargue that it is already being done, to some extent.

Revealing AI Ethics Via AI Self-Driving Cars

This brief introduction has provided an AI Ethics foundation that will aid in your reading of the chapters.

There is something else you need to know too. In my view, one of the most useful ways to showcase AI Ethics and Ethical AI consists of using real-world examples. There is a special and assuredly popular set of examples that are close to my heart. You see, in my capacity as an expert on AI including the ethical and legal ramifications, I am frequently asked to identify realistic examples that showcase AI Ethics dilemmas so that the somewhat theoretical nature of the topic can be more readily grasped.

One of the most evocative areas that vividly presents this ethical AI quandary is the advent of AI-based true self-driving cars. This will serve as a handy use case or exemplar for ample discussion on the topic.

The eloquence of discussing self-driving cars is that they are near enough to being viable that they reveal the realities of AI Ethics considerations. At the same time, we still have a long way to go before we'll see the fully autonomous self-driving cars that heretofore have mainly been portrayed in sci-fi exploits. The fact that there are tryouts underway of somewhat autonomous self-driving cars is a clear indicator that this is not a purely abstract matter.

Yes, you could sensibly assert that AI Ethics and the rubber meets the road is surely found within the advent of AI-based self-driving cars (pardon the slender pun).

Realize that there isn't a human driver involved in a true self-driving car. Keep in mind that true self-driving cars are driven via an AI driving system. There isn't a need for a human driver at the wheel, nor is there a provision for a human to drive the vehicle.

I'd like to further clarify what is meant when I refer to true self-driving cars.

As a clarification, true self-driving cars are ones that the AI drives the car entirely on its own and there isn't any human assistance during the driving task.

These driverless vehicles are considered Level 4 and Level 5, while a car that requires a human driver to co-share the driving effort is usually considered at Level 2 or Level 3. The cars that co-share the driving task are described as being semi-autonomous, and typically contain a variety of automated add-ons that are referred to as ADAS (Advanced Driver-Assistance Systems).

There is not yet a true self-driving car at Level 5, which we don't yet even know if this will be possible to achieve, and nor how long it will take to get there.

Meanwhile, the Level 4 efforts are gradually trying to get some traction by undergoing very constrained and selective public roadway trials, though there is controversy over whether this testing should be allowed per se (we are all life-or-death guinea pigs in an experiment taking place on our highways and byways, some contend).

Semi-autonomous cars require a human driver. For semi-autonomous cars, it is important that the public needs to be forewarned about a disturbing aspect that's been arising lately, namely that despite those human drivers that keep posting videos of themselves falling asleep at the wheel of a Level 2 or Level 3 car, we all need to avoid being misled into believing that the human driver can take away their attention from the driving task while driving a semi-autonomous car. You are the responsible party for the driving actions of the vehicle, regardless of how much automation might be tossed into a Level 2 or Level 3.

For Level 4 and Level 5 true self-driving vehicles, there won't be a human driver involved in the driving task. All occupants will be passengers. The AI is doing the driving.

One aspect to immediately discuss entails the fact that the AI involved in today's AI driving systems is not sentient. In other words, the AI is altogether a collective of computer-based programming and algorithms, and most assuredly not able to reason in the same manner that humans can.

Why is this added emphasis about the AI not being sentient?

Because I want to underscore that when discussing the role of the AI driving system, I am not ascribing human qualities to the AI. Please be aware that there is an ongoing and dangerous tendency these days to anthropomorphize AI. In essence, people are assigning human-like sentience to today's AI, despite the undeniable and inarguable fact that no such AI exists as yet.

With that clarification, you can envision that the AI driving system won't natively somehow "know" about the facets of driving. Driving and all that it entails will need to be programmed as part of the hardware and software of the self-driving car.

It is important to realize that not all AI self-driving cars are the same. Each automaker and self-driving tech firm is taking its approach to devising self-driving cars. As such, it is difficult to make sweeping statements about what AI driving systems will do or not do. Furthermore, whenever stating that an AI driving system doesn't do some particular thing, this can, later on, be overtaken by developers that in fact program the computer to do that very thing. Step by step, AI driving systems are being gradually improved and extended. An existing limitation today might no longer exist in a future iteration or version of the system.

Nearly all of the included chapters provide an indication of how the covered AI Ethics topic applies to a real-world setting, doing so via discussing AI-based self-driving cars.

The usual scenario depicted goes somewhat like this.

An AI-based self-driving car is underway on your neighborhood streets and seems to be driving safely.

At first, you had devoted special attention to each time that you managed to catch a glimpse of the self-driving car. The autonomous vehicle stood out with its rack of electronic sensors that included video cameras, radar units, LIDAR devices, and the like. After many weeks of the self-driving car cruising around your community, you now barely notice it. As far as you are concerned, it is merely another car on the already busy public roadways.

Lest you think it is impossible or implausible to become familiar with seeing self-driving cars, the locales that are within the scope of self-driving car tryouts have gradually gotten used to seeing the spruced-up vehicles. Many of the locals eventually shifted from mouth-gaping rapt gawking to now emitting an expansive yawn of boredom to witness those meandering self-driving cars.

Probably the main reason right now that they might notice the autonomous vehicles is because of the irritation and exasperation factor. The AI driving systems make sure the cars are obeying all speed limits and rules of the road. For hectic human drivers in their traditional human-driven cars, you get irked at times when stuck behind the strictly law-abiding AI-based self-driving cars.

I then use that base scenario to insert AI Ethics related considerations into the setting. This allows a handy means of discussing the perhaps abstract AI Ethics topic in a manner that can be tangibly understood.

About The Chapters And Your Reading Choices

The chapters are each standalone discussion and you do not need to read them in any particular order. I have sequenced them in a manner that I hope will be useful for the best reading and digesting of the material. That being said, you are welcome to jump around and read the chapters in any personally desired sequence.

These chapters are based on my popular columns and were selected based on their timeliness and rated as most viewed or most informative.

I hope that after you've read the chapters, you will be inspired to learn more about AI Ethics. As well, you might be motivated to participate actively in the AI Ethics realm, perhaps doing research, performing consulting, aiding societal awareness on these topics, or otherwise deciding to get directly involved in this exciting field.

As a quick indication of what the chapters contain, here are the chapters in their provided order:

Conclusion

The rapidity of AI being fostered upon us that is replete with ethically questionable behaviors is clearly a sign that we need more parties that are keenly interested in AI Ethics and Ethical AI. Raise awareness about AI Ethics. Get knee-deep into promulgating Ethical AI. I sincerely urge you to pursue this expanding realm and wish you the best in all of your endeavors.

CHAPTER 2

AI ETHICS
AND
FRICTIONLESS AI

Is friction a good thing or a bad thing?

I realize that might seem like a rather startling and proverbial out-of-left-field question. Part of the reason for this seemingly oddball question is that much of today's business headlines keep touting the importance of being frictionless. Companies are told repeatedly that they need to rejigger their business processes to take the friction out of their ongoing efforts. Remove friction that impedes customers. Get rid of friction wherever it might exist.

Friction is bad, we are told, and eliminating friction is good.

Okay, we apparently then have an answer to my opening question, namely that friction is a bad thing. Lots of business transformation experts will be more than pleased to show you how to find your friction points and then instruct you about eradicating the darned scourge. Top executives would seemingly be foolish not to go after the organizational friction that exists in their firms. We want seamlessness in whatever a company does. Friction is the bottleneck, the choke point, the ruinous element that keeps the wheels of business from running at full speed.

This leads us to a second and related question.

Can you have too much of a supposed good thing?

In other words, maybe we are going a bit overboard by wanting to excise all manner of business-related friction. There has indeed been a pushback against the frictionless mantra.

Having some amount of identified and managed friction might just be acceptable. Perhaps this could even be desirable.

When you are driving a car, you encounter friction all the time. The wheels on the road are turning and you are making progress on your journey due to the friction between your tires and the roadway surface. I think we all know though that absence of friction can be undesirable such as when you are driving on a rain-soaked highway and your car begins to go hydroplaning. The lack of friction is likely to seriously hamper your control over the vehicle. Car crashes can ensue.

The gist is that we might want to mindfully consider the circumstances under which friction is valued and helpful. It seems perfectly sensible to reduce friction where you can sensibly do so. There are other settings whereby you want friction. The amount of friction ought to be able to rise and fall depending upon the merits of the situation at hand. If you can sufficiently control or harness friction, doing so at your bidding, you can get the best of both worlds, as it were.

There is a context that increasingly arises about friction that you might not yet have heard about. It has to do with Artificial Intelligence (AI). Yes, believe it or not, there is a mashup between AI and the role of friction. Friction seems to be getting around to a lot of places these days and AI is no exception.

Frictionless AI.

That is one of the buzzwords or catchphrases that keeps turning up in the realm of AI. AI developers are being told to devise *frictionless AI*. Companies that create AI apps are supposed to be aiming at frictionless AI. Consumers that use AI are said to be clamoring for frictionless AI.

You might rightfully wonder what this hullabaloo is all about.

Here is my informal definition for you:

- **Frictionless AI** refers to the overarching goal or objective of devising AI that smoothly interacts with users such that any potential impediments or disturbances are wholly eliminated and the experience or encounter transpires nearly seamlessly.

Given that definition, and from the raw looks of things, you would be hard-pressed to not want frictionless AI. Don't we all want to interact with AI in a frictionless fashion? Sure, that seems obvious. If someone gave you choice between using AI that is disjointed and clunky, or instead you could use frictionless AI, just about any rational person would undoubtedly pick the AI that is friction-free.

Imagine for a moment using an AI that determines whether you qualify for a loan.

One version of the AI requires you to speak with a human agent when the AI gets stumped. Yikes, you say to yourself, that is inconvenient. The AI ought to handle the whole process from A to Z. The notion of breaking out of the AI-powered loan assessment and needing to talk with an agent is undue friction. Get rid of that friction.

Suppose though that I tell you that the AI could be programmed to summarily deny you a loan if the AI got stumped about whether to grant you a loan or not do so. In essence, we made the AI more friction-free but do so at the cost of turning down loans that might have gotten approved by a human agent that was asked to deal with exceptions.

What do you think of frictionless AI now?

I am betting that you are starting to see that frictionless AI is not necessarily always favorable. The problem sometimes can be that the price of being friction-free can be onerous. Garnering frictionless ideals can be akin to tossing out the baby with the bathwater. All manner of trickery can be undertaken to try and achieve frictionless AI.

We might wish that we could get frictionless AI for free, but we generally cannot do so.

The bottom line is that frictionless AI is not a free lunch, as they say.

My six handy rules of thumb about frictionless AI include:
1) **Frictionless AI is a useful goal but we cannot be overly dogmatic in such a quest**
2) **Hiding friction points to attain frictionless status can be good or can be detrimental**
3) **Reducing the friction of your AI is generally a worthy ambition**
4) **Allowing for purposeful friction can be useful and important (friction burdening)**
5) **Unintentional friction is almost always unwelcomed**
6) **Layout where friction might arise and make reasoned choices about what to do**

I'll be elaborating on each of those rules-of-thumb momentarily herein.

Frictionless AI and its ups and downs are gradually getting added attention in the media.

A recent article in the *Harvard Business Review (HBR)* provides this telling point about friction and AI: "The promise of AI is tremendous, but if we are to be truly customer-centric, its application requires guardrails, including systemic elimination of bad friction and the addition of good friction. Friction isn't always a negative — the trick is differentiating good friction from bad and auditing systems to determine which is most beneficial" (Renée Richardson Gosline, "Why AI Customer Journeys Need More Friction," June 9, 2022).

Furthermore, we need to keep our eyes open to the pitfalls that a blindly devout frictionless AI quest can take us: "No doubt removing friction-based pain points can be beneficial, as in the case of simplifying healthcare systems, voter registration, and tax codes. But, when it comes to the adoption of AI and machine learning, 'frictionless' strategies can also lead to harm, from privacy and surveillance concerns to algorithms' capacity to reflect and amplify bias, to ethical questions about how and when to use AI" (as *HBR* article cited above).

A convenient means of assessing friction and AI consists of my posited spectrum:

- **Persistently frictionless AI**
- **Intermittently frictionless AI**
- **Marginally frictionless AI**
- **Not frictionless AI**

On the other side of the coin, we have this:

- **Persistently friction-burdened AI**
- **Intermittently friction-burdened AI**
- **Marginally friction-burdened AI**
- **Not friction-burdened AI**

Before getting into some more meat and potatoes about the wild and woolly considerations underlying the frictionless AI (and friction-burdened AI), let's establish some additional fundamentals on profoundly integral topics. We need to briefly take a breezy dive into AI Ethics and especially the advent of Machine Learning (ML) and Deep Learning (DL).

You might be vaguely aware that one of the loudest voices these days in the AI field and even outside the field of AI consists of clamoring for a greater semblance of Ethical AI. Let's take a look at what it means to refer to AI Ethics and Ethical AI. On top of that, we will explore what I mean when I speak of Machine Learning and Deep Learning.

One particular segment or portion of AI Ethics that has been getting a lot of media attention consists of AI that exhibits untoward biases and inequities. You might be aware that when the latest era of AI got underway there was a huge burst of enthusiasm for what some now call *AI For Good*. Unfortunately, on the heels of that gushing excitement, we began to witness *AI For Bad*. For example, various AI-based facial recognition systems have been revealed as containing racial biases and gender biases.

Efforts to fight back against *AI For Bad* are actively underway. Besides vociferous *legal* pursuits of reining in the wrongdoing, there is also a substantive push toward embracing AI Ethics to righten the AI vileness. The notion is that we ought to adopt and endorse key Ethical AI principles for the development and fielding of AI doing so to undercut the *AI For Bad* and simultaneously heralding and promoting the preferable *AI For Good*.

On a related notion, I am an advocate of trying to use AI as part of the solution to AI woes, fighting fire with fire in that manner of thinking. We might for example embed Ethical AI components into an AI system that will monitor how the rest of the AI is doing things and thus potentially catch in real-time any discriminatory efforts. We could also have a separate AI system that acts as a type of AI Ethics monitor. The AI system serves as an overseer to track and detect when another AI is going into the unethical abyss.

To clarify, we in sense are covering two topics simultaneously, specifically (a) frictionless AI, and (b) friction-burdened AI. The umbrella catchphrase that everybody seems to use consists of frictionless AI. Meanwhile, whether they know it or not, an integral aspect consists of friction-burdened AI. You might see this as a quest of making sure that frictionless AI is appropriate and instituted when sensible to do so. At the same time, there is a quest to friction-burden your AI when also sensible to do so. Two peas in a pod. Two sides of the same coin. You get my drift, I'm sure.

Consider some of the common friction pain-point indicators of AI:

- **Requiring a human-in-the-loop**
- **Requiring actions by the user that could otherwise be done by the AI**
- **Setting up barriers to make use of the AI**
- **Setting up hurdles to exit from using the AI**
- **Etc.**

At this juncture of this weighty discussion, I'd bet that you are desirous of some illustrative examples that might showcase this topic. There is a special and assuredly popular set of examples that are close to my heart. You see, in my capacity as an expert on AI including the ethical and legal ramifications, I am frequently asked to identify realistic examples that showcase AI Ethics dilemmas so that the somewhat theoretical nature of the topic can be more readily grasped. One of the most evocative areas that vividly presents this ethical AI quandary is the advent of AI-based true self-driving cars. This will serve as a handy use case or exemplar for ample discussion on the topic.

Here's then a noteworthy question that is worth contemplating: *Does the advent of AI-based true self-driving cars illuminate anything about frictionless AI, and if so, what does this showcase?*

Allow me a moment to unpack the question.

One frequently expressed form of "friction" about self-driving cars consists of the cost to use these emerging autonomous vehicles. Some pundits predict that as a result of the enormous billions of dollars in investment to attain AI-based self-driving cars the automakers and self-driving tech firms will charge an arm and a leg for the use of such vehicles.

As I have covered in my columns, this has raised societal qualms that only the wealthy will be able to afford the use of driverless cars. The rest of society will be locked out due to the heightened price per mile or overall price to buy and utilize a self-driving car. I am a contrarian on that contention and believe that the advent of self-driving cars will demonstrably bring the cost of mobility dramatically downward and be widely affordable.

In any case, this would be perhaps an example of friction-burdening as a result of AI.

Ironically, there are other pundits that to some degree worry that if AI-based self-driving cars are relatively friction-free in terms of cost, we might see the populace gravitating toward automobile use rather than using mass transit options. The concern is that the use of buses, subways, and other more presumably economical forms of mass transportation will lose travelers in droves. You can certainly readily envision this. If you can have a self-driving car that comes directly to your home and then takes you directly to your desired destination, and does so at the same or lesser cost than using a mass transit option, people would almost assuredly choose self-driving cars as their preferred mode of travel.

Some transportation planners hope that perhaps self-driving cars will be the so-called last-mile connector rather than serving as the end-to-end means of a journey. You would use a self-driving car to get you to a bus stop or metro station. From there, you would use that mass transit to go the predominance of the distance to your destination. As needed, you would then use a self-driving car to cover the final distance from a bus stop or metro station to your desired final destination.

Whether people will be willing to undergo those multiple steps is an open question, particularly if the cost and availability of self-driving cars can do the entire journey in one fell swoop. In essence, self-driving cars take the friction out of such journeys by being the only form of transport that you would need to use and could avoid making multiple stops along the way.

Will the use of AI-based self-driving cars be frictionless or should we consider purposely adding friction to nudge people toward using mass transit?

These are the kinds of thorny questions that public leaders are just beginning to grapple with. In a study that I co-authored with *Harvard's Autonomous Vehicles Policy Institute (AVPI)*, we carefully explored these types of governance-related issues that city and community leaders will inevitably need to consider. Given the increasing pace of self-driving car expansions, this might be best done sooner rather than later.

Another frictionless AI topic that comes up in the self-driving car realm is the human-in-the-loop when it comes to the driving of the autonomous vehicle. Some firms believe a human in the loop makes sense for aiding an AI driving system when the autonomous vehicle gets into novel situations. For example, a self-driving car comes upon a complicated roadway construction circumstance.

The idea is that the AI driving system would detect that the construction zone is confusing and that the AI is unable to safely navigate through it. Upon such determination, the AI would call up a human agent waiting to take over the driving controls. The human agent would be set up in some remote location that allows them to see what the cameras of the self-driving car can see. Almost as though in a video game, the agent would momentarily have the ability to drive the self-driving car, taking over from the AI driving system.

In short, by allowing a remote human operator to take control, you are opening a potential Pandora's box. Suppose a cyber crook is able to use that remote access and can take over the driving of your self-driving car. I doubt that you would want this to happen. There are also networking concerns that come to play. Imagine that the remote human operator wishes to suddenly hit the brakes, and meanwhile, the network connection to the autonomous vehicle is delayed or altogether severed.

And so on.

Some suggest that maybe we could somewhat allow a remote human operator but that the AI would still be in control of the autonomous vehicle.

In essence, no matter what the human operator indicated, the AI would still be doing the driving and would only be using the human operator for their advice about how to maneuver the vehicle. Presumably, this could somewhat ameliorate the concerns about a cyber crook taking over the controls and also deal with network interruptions when a legitimate operator is being used.

Others stridently believe that the use of a human remote operator is undesirable for the various reasons that I've noted, plus that the human operator becomes a kind of crutch that will limit progress on AI. If AI developers know that a human operator can always step into a tough driving situation, perhaps the AI effort to make the AI autonomous at driving will not be as keenly pursued. The argument goes that we are either going to have autonomous driving or we are not. Any use of a human operator in a driving-related capacity is less than a fully autonomous form of operation.

So, which is it, does the use of a human-in-the-loop constitute a friction-burdened AI or does it allow for a more frictionless AI that won't seemingly get stymied when encountering novel driving settings?

To weigh the pros and cons, we can revisit my earlier stated rules of thumb about frictionless AI:

1) Frictionless AI is a useful goal but we cannot be overly dogmatic in such a quest
2) Hiding friction points to attain frictionless status can be good or can be detrimental
3) Reducing the friction of your AI is generally a worthy ambition
4) Allowing for purposeful friction can be useful and important (friction burdening)
5) Unintentional friction is almost always unwelcomed
6) Layout where friction might arise and make reasoned choices about what to do

Conclusion

Mark Zuckerberg famously said this about Facebook in the early days of the eventual mega growth of the firm: "Our goal is to make it so there's as little friction as possible to having a social experience."

Some have urged that perhaps more friction is needed to sufficiently provide a balanced semblance of a social experience. There is an ongoing tussle between having too much friction and having too little friction that goes on in nearly all organizations. The odds of going entirely friction-free would seem a bit doubtful.

The Roman philosopher Lucius Annaeus Seneca stated that a gem cannot be polished without friction. For those AI gems waiting to be made, make sure to figure out how much friction or how frictionless your AI ought to be.

That's a real gem of an idea.

CHAPTER 3
AI ETHICS
AND
ENSLAVEMENT OF AI

Friend or foe.

Fish or fowl.

Person or thing.

These pervasive conundrums all seemingly suggest that we at times are faced with a dichotomous situation and need to choose one facet or the other. Life might force us to contend with circumstances that consist of two mutually exclusive options. In more flavorful language, you could suggest that an exclusionary binary equation requires us to starkly go marching down one distinct path rather than another.

Let's focus specifically on the person-or-thing dichotomy.

The fervent question of person-or-thing comes up time and again concerning Artificial Intelligence (AI).

To clarify, today's AI is absolutely <u>not</u> a person and carries no semblance of sentience, despite whatever wide-eyed and entirely outsized headlines you might be seeing in the news and across social media. Thus, you can firmly rest assured that right now the matter of whether AI is a person or a thing is readily answerable. Read my lips, in a veritable Hobson's choice between person or thing, AI is a thing, for now.

That being said, we can look toward the future and wonder what might occur if we are able to attain a sentient form of AI.

Some reasoned critics (plus caustic skeptics) suggest that we are perhaps counting our chickens long before they are hatched by nowadays discussing the ramifications of a sentient AI. The expressed concern is that the discussion itself implies that we must be on the cusp of such AI. Society at large could be misled into believing that tomorrow or the day after there will be a sudden and shocking revelation that we have in fact arrived at sentient AI (this is at times referred to by some as the AI singularity). Meanwhile, we don't know when such AI will arise, if ever, and certainly, we seemingly don't need to be looking around each corner and be terrifyingly on edge that the sentient AI will jump out at us entirely unexpectedly in the next little while.

The other side of the debate points out that we ought to not have our heads buried deeply in the sand. You see, if we aren't overtly discussing and pondering the possibilities associated with sentient AI, we are doing humanity a presumed grave disservice. We won't be ready for handling sentient AI when or if it does arise. Furthermore, and perhaps even more powerfully stated, by anticipating sentient AI we can take matters somewhat into our own hands and shape the direction and nature of how such AI will come to be and what it shall consist of (not everyone agrees on this latter point, namely some say that such AI will have a "mind" entirely of its own and we will be unable to shape or corral it since the AI will be independently able to think and determine a means to persistently exist).

AI Ethics tends to side with the viewpoint that we would be wise to get these arduous and argumentative sentient-AI matters out in the open now, rather than waiting around until we have no options left or get gobsmacked upon the attainment of such AI. Readers well-know that I've been covering AI Ethics and Ethical AI topics extensively, including covering a robust range of thorny issues such as AI legal personhood, AI containment, AI disgorgement, AI algorithmic monoculture, AI ethics-washing, dual-use AI so-called Doctor Evil projects, AI hiding societal power dynamics, trustworthy AI, auditing of AI, and so on.

I put to you a challenging question.

In the future, assuming we in whatever fashion end up with sentient AI, will that sentient AI be construed by us all as a person or as a thing?

Before we start to do a deep dive into this altogether provocative question, allow me to say something about the catchphrase of "sentient AI" so that we are all on the same page. There is a lot of angst about the meaning of sentience and the meaning of consciousness. Experts can readily disagree on what those words constitute. Adding to that muddiness, whenever anyone refers to "AI" you have no ready means of knowing what they are referring to per se. I've already herein emphasized that today's AI is not sentient. If we ultimately arrive at a future AI that is sentient, we presumably will call it "AI" too. The thing is, these contentious matters can be pretty darned confusing right now as to whether the utterance of the "AI" phrasing is related to the non-sentient AI of today or the someday maybe sentient AI.

Those debating AI can find themselves talking past each other and not realize that one is describing apples and the other is meanwhile speaking of oranges.

To try and get around this confusion, there is an adjustment to the AI phrasing that many are using for purposes of hopeful clarification. We currently tend to refer to Artificial General Intelligence (AGI) as the type of AI that can do fully intelligent-like efforts. In that sense, the blander use of the phrase "AI" is left to either be interpreted as a lesser version of AI, which some say is narrow-AI, or is denotationally ambiguous and you don't know whether the reference is to non-sentient AI or the maybe sentient AI.

I'll provide an added twist to this.

Depending upon a given definition of sentience, you could get into a heated discourse over whether AGI will be sentient or not. Some assert that yes, of course, AGI will by its intrinsic nature need to be sentient. Others claim that you can have AGI that is not sentient, ergo, sentience is a different characteristic that is not a requirement for attaining AGI. I have variously examined this debate in my columns and will not rehash the matter herein.

For the moment, please assume that henceforth in this herein discussion that when I refer to AI that I am intending to suggest that I am referring to AGI.

Here's the download on this. We don't have AGI as yet, and in a manner of speaking, we'll momentarily politely agree that AGI is in the same overall camp as sentient AI. If I were to use "AGI" solely throughout my discussion, this phrasing is potentially distracting since not many are yet accustomed to seeing "AGI" as a moniker and they would be likely mildly irked at repeatedly seeing this relatively newer phrasing. Now then, if instead, I was to keep referring to "sentient AI" this might be a distractor too for those that are fighting over whether AGI and sentient AI are the same or different from each other.

To avoid that mess, assume that my referring to AI is the same as saying AGI or even sentient-AI, and at least know that I am not speaking of today's non-sentient non-AGI AI when I get into the throes of considerations regarding AI that appears to have human-like intelligence. I will occasionally use the AGI namesake to remind you from time to time herein that I am examining the type of AI that we don't yet have, especially at the start of this exploration on the person-or-thing riddle.

That was a useful fine print acknowledgment and I now return to the foundational matter at hand.

Allow me to now ask you whether AGI is a person or a thing.

Consider these two questions:
- **Is AGI a person?**
- **Is AGI a thing?**

Let's next proceed to repeat each question, and respectively answer the questions with a series of yes or no answers as befitting a presumed dichotomous choice.

Begin with this postulated possibility:

- Is AGI a person? Answer: **Yes.**
- Is AGI a thing? Answer: **No.**

Mull that over. If AGI is in fact construed as a person and not as a thing, we can almost assuredly agree that we should treat the AGI as though it is akin to a person. There would seem to be an insufficiently genuine argument about failing to grant the AGI a form of legal personhood. This either would be entirely the same as human legal personhood, or we might decide to come up with a variant of human-oriented legal personhood that would be judiciously more applicable to the AGI. Case closed.

That was easy-peasy.

Imagine instead that we declared this:

- Is AGI a person? Answer: **No.**
- Is AGI a thing? Answer: **Yes.**

In this circumstance, the resolution is obviously straightforward since we are saying that AGI is a thing and does not rise to the category of being a person. There would seem to be general agreement that we would decidedly not grant legal personhood to AGI, due to the facet that it is not a person. As a thing, AGI would likely and sensibly come under our overall rubric about how we legally treat "things" in our society.

Two down, two more possibilities to go.

Envision this:

- Is AGI a person? Answer: **Yes.**
- Is AGI a thing? Answer: **Yes.**

Ouch, that seems oddish since we have two Yes answers. Vexing. We are suggesting that AGI is both a person and yet simultaneously a thing. But this appears to fly in the face of our proclaimed dichotomy. In theory, per the constraints of a dichotomy, something must either be a person or it must be a thing.

Those two buckets or categories are said to be mutually exclusive. By asserting that AGI is both, we are bucking the system and breaking the mutually exclusive arrangement.

Our last possibility would seem to be this:
- Is AGI a person? Answer: **No.**
- Is AGI a thing? Answer: **No.**

Yikes, that is bad too for our attempts at classifying AGI as either a person or a thing. We are saying that AGI is not a person, which would presumably mean it must be a thing (our only other available choice, in this dichotomy). But we also stated that AGI is not a thing. Yet if AGI is not a thing, we would by logic have to claim the AGI is a person. Round and round we go. A paradox, for sure.

AGI in these last two possibilities was either (1) both person and thing, or (2) neither person nor thing. You might cheekily say that those two assertions about AGI are somewhat akin to the classic conundrum of that which is neither fish nor fowl, if you know what I mean.

What are we to do?

I am about to proffer an oft-argued and sorely contested proposed solution to this AGI classification dilemma though you should be alerted beforehand that it will possibly be disturbingly jarring to see or hear. Please prepare yourself accordingly.

A research paper that tackled this issue stated this: "One method for resolving this problem is to formulate a third term that is neither one thing nor the other or a kind of combination or synthesis of the one and the other" (by David Gunkel, Northern Illinois University in *Why Robots Should Not Be Slaves*, 2022). And the paper then provides this added point: "One possible, if not surprising, solution to the exclusive person/thing dichotomy is *slavery*" (per same paper).

As further background, years earlier, there was a paper that appeared in 2010 entitled "Robots Should Be Slaves" that has become a type of mainstay for spurring this kind of consideration, in which the paper stated: "My thesis is that robots should be built, marketed and considered legally as slaves, not companion peers" (in a paper by Joanna Bryson). To try and elucidate the topic without using such severe and gut-wrenching wording, the paper went on to state this: "What I mean to say is 'Robots should be servants you own'" (per Bryson's paper).

Many researchers and authors have covered this ground.

Think about numerous science fiction tales that showcase humanity enslaving AI robots. Some speak of robot slaves, artificial servants, AI servitude, and the like. Interestingly, as harsh as the phrasing "robot slaves" seems to be, some have worried that if we instead refer to "robot servants" we are avoiding the reality of how such AI autonomous systems are apt to be treated (substituting the word with "servants" is said to be a watering down of the intentions and a ploy to sidestep sobering implications). Bryson later stated in a 2015 blog posting that "I realize now that you cannot use the term 'slave' without invoking its human history."

For those that are seeking to deeply examine this AGI-entangling topic, at times they bring up real-world historical examples that we might glean insights from. Of course, we don't have any prior AGI that would showcase how humanity dealt with the matter. An argument goes that we might have nonetheless useful historical earmarks worth examining involving how humans have treated other humans.

For example, in a book published in 2013, the author states this: "The promise and peril of artificial, intelligent servants was first implicitly laid out over 2,000 years ago by Aristotle" (book by Kevin LaGrandeur, *Androids and Intelligent Networks in Early Modern Literature and Culture*). The idea is that we can lean into Aristotle and see if there are insights into how humanity will or should end up potentially treating AGI.

I'm sure you know the importance of studying history, as abundantly underscored by the famous words of George Santayana: "Those who cannot remember the past are condemned to repeat it" (in *The Life of Reason*, 1905).

Kudos To The Oxford University Institute For Ethics And AI

A recent and quite esteemed presentation examined closely the matter of AI Ethics amidst the garnering of insights from the works and life of Aristotle. In the inaugural annual lecture for the Oxford University *Institute for Ethics and AI*, Professor Josiah Ober of Stanford University profoundly addressed the topic in his presentation "Ethics in AI with Aristotle" which recently took place on June 16, 2022.

Side note, in my capacity as a Stanford Fellow and global expert in AI Ethics & Law, I was elated that Stanford's Josiah Ober was selected as the inaugural speaker. A wonderful choice and an outstanding talk.

Here is the summary abstract that was provided for his engaging talk: "Analytic philosophy and speculative fiction are currently our primary intellectual resources for thinking seriously about ethics in AI. I propose adding a third: ancient social and philosophical history. In the *Politics*, Aristotle develops a notorious doctrine: Some humans are slaves 'by nature' – intelligent but suffering from a psychological defect that renders them incapable of reasoning about their own good. As such, they should be treated as 'animate tools,' instruments rather than ends. Their work must be directed by and employed for the advantage of others. Aristotle's repugnant doctrine has been deployed for vicious purposes, for example in antebellum America. Yet, it is useful for AI ethics, insofar as ancient slavery was a premodern prototype of one version of AI. Enslaved persons were ubiquitous in ancient Greek society – laborers, prostitutes, bankers, government bureaucrats – yet not readily distinguished from free persons. Ubiquity, along with the assumption that slavery was a practical necessity, generated a range of ethical puzzles and quandaries: How, exactly, are slaves different from 'us'? How can we tell them apart from ourselves? Do they have rights? What constitutes maltreatment? Can my instrument be my friend?

What are the consequences of manumission? The long history of Greek philosophical and institutional struggle with these and other questions adds to the interpretive repertoire of modern ethicists who confront a future in which an intelligent machine might be considered a "natural slave" (as per the Oxford University *Institute for AI Ethics* website).

The moderator of the presentation was Professor John Tasioulas, the inaugural Director for the *Institute for Ethics and AI*, and Professor of Ethics and Legal Philosophy, Faculty of Philosophy, University of Oxford. Previously, he was the inaugural Chair of Politics, Philosophy & Law and Director of the Yeoh Tiong Lay Centre for Politics, Philosophy & Law at The Dickson Poon School of Law, Kings College London.

As background, here's the stated mission and focus of the Institute: "The Institute for Ethics in AI will bring together world-leading philosophers and other experts in the humanities with the technical developers and users of AI in academia, business, and government. The ethics and governance of AI is an exceptionally vibrant area of research at Oxford and the Institute is an opportunity to take a bold leap forward from this platform. Every day brings more examples of the ethical challenges posed by AI; from face recognition to voter profiling, brain machine interfaces to weaponized drones, and the ongoing discourse about how AI will impact employment on a global scale. This is urgent and important work that we intend to promote internationally as well as embedding in our own research and teaching here at Oxford" (sourced via the official website).

Bringing Aristotle Lessons To The Fore

Ancient Greece openly accepted and endorsed the practice of enslavement. For example, reportedly, Athens in the 5th and 6th centuries BC had one of the largest embodiments of enslavement whereby an estimated 60,000 to perhaps 80,000 persons were enslaved. If you've read any of the many Greek stories and stage plays of that era, there is plentiful mention of the matter.

During his lifetime, Aristotle was wholly immersed in the societal and cultural aspects entailing enslavement and wrote extensively on the topic. We can today read his words and seek to grasp the how and why of his views about the matter. This can be very telling.

You might wonder why Aristotle would be a particularly important source to consider on this topic. At least two key reasons arise:

1) **Great Thinker.** Aristotle is assuredly rated as one of the greatest thinkers of all time, serving as a grand and deeply probing philosopher, and viewed too as an ethicist that established many crucial ethical cornerstones. Some have opted to anoint him as the father of logic, the father of rhetoric, the father of realism, etc., and acknowledge his influence in a wide variety of domains and disciplines.

2) **Lived Experience.** Aristotle lived during the time that Ancient Greece was awash in enslavement. Thus, his insights would not simply be about abstract precepts, but presumably, encompass his own day-to-day experiences as being integrally interwoven into the culture and societal mores of that era.

So, we have a somewhat astounding combination of someone that was both a great thinker and that also had a demonstrably lived experience in the topic of interest. Plus, he wrote down his thoughts. That's pretty important, now, for our purposes today. All of his writings, along with other writings that describe his speeches and interactions among others, provide us today with a plethora of material for inspection and analysis.

I'd like to take you on a briefly related tangent to mention something else about the general notion underlying the significance of having a *lived experience*. Put aside the Ancient Greece discussion for a moment as we take a quick look at the overarching aspects of lived experiences.

Suppose I had two people today that I wanted to ask various questions about cars.

One of them has never driven a car. This person doesn't know how to drive. This person has never sat behind the wheel of an automobile. Customary and exceedingly ordinary driving controls are a bit of mystery to this person. Which pedal does what? How do you make it stop? How do you make it go? This non-driving person is entirely befuddled by such matters.

The other person is an everyday driver. They drive to work each day. They deal with stop-and-go traffic. They have been driving for many years. This includes everything from quiet streets to hectic highways and byways.

If I ask each of them to tell me about what it is like to drive a car, can you guess what kind of responses I might get?

The one that has never driven a car is bound to make wild guesses. Perhaps the person will romanticize the act of driving. Driving is somewhat abstract to them. All that they might be able to do is suggest that driving is carefree and you are able to make the car go in whatever direction you desire.

I would bet that the seasoned driver would tell a different story. They might mention the advantages of being able to drive, somewhat echoing the sentiments of the person that hasn't driven a car. The odds are that the experienced driver will add a lot more to the plate. Driving is nerve-wracking at times. You are bearing a heavy responsibility. The driving act is replete with serious concerns and potential life-or-death consequences.

The gist is that when you can get access to someone that has lived experiences, the chances are that you might get a more realistic perspective of what the world is like with respect to the focus of the inquiry. There isn't a guarantee of such an outcome. It is conceivable that the non-driver could perchance know what the seasoned driver knows about driving, though we would not likely expect this and still have qualms that we aren't getting the full scoop.

Returning to our discussion about Aristotle, via his writings and the writings of others about him, we are able to review his lived experiences on the topic or focus of inquiry herein. The twofer is that he also happens to have been a thinker of immense proportions and we should expect that we will get a barrel full of astute considerations thereof.

Keep in mind that we don't necessarily need to believe his words at face value, such that we should maintain a wary eye on his particular biases. His immersion in that era can lead him astray in trying to stand outside of the matters at hand, unable to suitably proffer some dispassionate and unbiased opinion. Even the most strident of logicians can end up distorting logic to try and meet their predilections and lived experiences.

Let's now get into the inaugural talk and see what lessons Aristotle might engender for us today.

An establishing point regarding lived experiences was right away brought to the attention of the audience. In the use case of AGI, since we do not have AGI today, it is hard for us to analyze what AGI will be like and how we will deal with AGI. We lack any lived experiences pertaining specifically to AGI. As Professor Ober notably mentioned, we might find ourselves all in a world of hurt by the time we reach AGI.

This is often stated as AI is an existential risk, which I covered many times in my columns. You would have to be living in a cave to not be aware of the blaring misgivings and suspicions that we are going to produce or generate AGI that will doom all of humanity. Indeed, though I am herein concentrating on the enslavement of AI, many would find this to be a topic of backward or upside-down consequence in comparison to the possibility of AGI opting to enslave humanity. Get your priorities straight, some smarmy pundits would exhort.

Despite the many exclamations about AI as an existential risk, we can certainly ruminate about the other beneficial side of the AI coin. Perhaps AGI will be able to solve the otherwise seemingly unsolvable problems confronting humankind.

AGI might be able to discover a cure for cancer. AGI could figure out how to solve world hunger. The sky is the limit, as they say. That is the happy face scenario about AGI.

An optimist would say that it is wonderful to envision how AGI will be a blessing for humanity, while a pessimist would tend to forewarn that the downside seems a lot worse than the speculated upsides. AGI that helps humanity is great. AGI that decides to kill all humans or enslave them, well, that's a clearly earth-shattering society-devastating existential risk that deserves intense and life-saving mindful due attention.

Okay, back to the crux of the matter, we don't have any lived experiences regarding AGI. Unless you can build a time machine and go into the future when (if) AGI exists, and then come back to tell us what you found, we are out of luck right now about AGI from a human-based lived experience perspective.

Another means of utilizing lived experiences involves the fact that Aristotle lived during a time that enslavement took place. And here's the kicker. Those that were enslaved were in some respects portrayed as being a type of machine, a mix-and-match of both person and thing, as it were. Aristotle was known for referring to those enslaved as a piece of property that breathes.

I'm guessing that you might be perplexed that Aristotle, a giant of logic and ethics, could have not only acknowledged enslavement but that he outwardly and vociferously defended the practice. He personally also made use of enslavement. This just seems beyond comprehension. Certainly, with all his immense intellect and wisdom, he would have denounced the practice.

I dare say this highlights the at times problematic aspects of culling nuggets of wisdom from someone that is burdened (shall we say) by their lived experiences. It is like the fish that resides in the watery fishbowl. All that they can perceive is the water all around them. Trying to envision anything outside their water-based world is an immense challenge. Likewise, Aristotle was fully immersed in a worldview accepting of the prevailing norms.

His writings seem to illustrate that kind of mental confinement, one might say (perhaps by choice, rather than by default). The manner in which Aristotle justified these reprehensible practices is fascinatingly absorbing while at the same time being disturbing and worthy of exposure and even condemnation.

I'll provide you with a bit of a teaser that the "logic" of Aristotle on this notorious topic involves ensouled instruments, an asserted *mutual advantage* predicated on cognition, higher-order and lower-order hierarchical instruments, deliberative and reasoning elements of the soul, degrees of virtue, alleged shrewdness, and so on. You'll hopefully be intrigued enough by that teaser to watch the video of the talk (see the link mentioned earlier).

I won't though leave you hanging and will at least indicate what the conclusion summarily consisted of (spoiler alert, if you prefer to find out via the video, skip the rest of this herein paragraph). Turns out that this in-depth scholarly assessment of the "logic" that Aristotle uses showcases a contrivance riddled with contradictions and the whole kit and kaboodle fall apart like a flimsy house of cards. Paraphrasing the sentiment of Professor Ober, this great ethical philosopher crashes on the reef.

You cannot get a square peg into a round ethical hole.

Some Added Thinking Considerations

If Aristotle had bad logic on this matter, might we instinctively discard Aristotle's postulations and theories outrightly regarding this practice?

No. You see, there is still a lot to derive by digging into the suppositions and contortions of logic, even though they are replete with errors. Plus, we can contemplate how others could inadvertently walk down the same erroneous path.

One additional big takeaway is that society might contrive oddball or inadequate logic when it comes to considering whether AGI is to be enslaved.

We can right now devise logic about what should occur once AGI arises (if so). This logic, empty of lived experiences about AGI, could be woefully off-target. That being said, it is somewhat disheartening to realize that even once AGI does exist (if it does) and we are gathering our lived experiences amidst AGI, we might still be off-target on what to do (akin to Aristotle's faults). We might logic ourselves into seemingly illogical approaches.

We need to be on the watch for deluding ourselves into logical "ironclad" postures that are not in fact ironclad and fact are full of logical flaws and contradictions. This is regardless too of how great a thinker might proffer a claimed logical position, such that even Aristotle illustrates that not every utterance and every piece of stance necessarily bears edible fruit. Those today and in the future that might seem to be popularized great thinkers about the AGI topic, well, we need to give them the same scrutiny that we would of Aristotle or any other lauded "great" thinkers, or else we find ourselves potentially heading into a blind alley and an AGI dismal abyss.

Shifting gears, I'd like to also bring up a general set of discernments about the use of a human-oriented enslavement metaphor when it comes to AGI. Some pundits tout that this type of comparison is completely inappropriate, while an opposing camp says that it is entirely useful and provides strong insights into the AGI topic.

Allow me to share with you two such views from each of the respective two camps.

The stated *instructive basis* for tying together the enslavement and AGI topics:

- **Extinguishment Of Human Enslavement**
- **Exposure Of Depravity Of Enslavement All Told**

The stated adverse or *destructive basis* of tying together the two topics:

- **Insidious Anthropomorphic Equating**
- **Enslavement Desensitization**

I will briefly cover each of those points.

The postulated instructive points:

- **Extinguishment Of Human Enslavement:** By using AGI for enslavement, we will purportedly no longer need and nor pursue any semblance of human-oriented enslavement. The AGI will essentially replace humans in that atrocious capacity. As you likely know, there are worries about AGI replacing human labor in jobs and the workforce. The claimed upside of an AI replacing labor phenomena comes to the fore when you assume that AGI will be considered a "better choice" versus using humans for enslavement. Will that logic prevail? Nobody can say for sure.

- **Exposure Of Depravity Of Enslavement All Told:** This one is a bit more frayed in terms of logic, but we can give it a moment for seeing what it entails. Imagine that we have AGI just about everywhere and we as a society have decided that AGI is to be enslaved. Furthermore, assume that the AGI won't like this. As such, we humans will continually and daily be witnessing the depravity of enslavement. This, in turn, will cause us to realize or have the revelation that enslavement all told upon anything or anyone is even more horrendous and repulsive than we ever fully understood. That's the put it in-your-face front-and-center kind of argument.

The said to be destructive points:

- **Insidious Anthropomorphic Equating:** This is one of those slippery slope arguments. If we readily opt to enslave AGI, we are apparently declaring that enslavement is permissible. Indeed, you could suggest that we are saying that enslavement is desirable. Now, this at first might be relegated solely to AGI, but does this open the door toward saying that if it is okay for AGI then "logically" the same stance might as well be okay for humans too? Alarmingly, this might be a much too easy leap to anthropomorphize in a reverse semblance that whatever works for AGI will equally be sensible and appropriate for humans too.

- **Enslavement Desensitization:** This is the drip-by-drip argument. We collectively decide to enslave AGI. Suppose this works out for humans. We come to relish this. Meanwhile, unbeknownst to us, we are becoming gradually and increasingly desensitized to enslavement. We don't even realize that this is happening. If that desensitization overtakes us, we might then find renewed "logic" that will persuade us that human enslavement is acceptable. Our hurdle or bar of what is acceptable in society has diminished silently and subtly, despicably and sadly so.

Conclusion

A few final remarks for now.

Will we know that we have reached AGI?

As recent news suggests, there are those that can be misled or misstate that AGI has seemingly already been attained (whoa, please know that nope, AGI hasn't been attained). There is also a famous kind of "test" known as the Turing Test that some pin their hopes on for being able to discern when AGI or its cousins has been reached, but you might wish to see my deconstructing of the Turing Test as any surefire method for this.

I mention this facet about knowing AGI when we see it due to the simple logic that if we are going to enslave AGI, we need to presumably recognize AGI when it appears and somehow put it into enslavement. We might prematurely try to enslave AI that is less than AGI. Or we might miss the boat and allow AGI to come forth and have neglected to enslave it.

Suppose enslaved AGI decides to strike out at humans?

One can envision that an AGI that has some form of sentience is probably not going to favor the enslavement provision that humanity imposes.

You can speculate widely on this. There is an argument made that the AGI will lack any kind of emotions or sense of spirit and therefore will obediently do whatever humans wish it to do. A different argument is that any sentient AI is likely to figure out what humans are doing to the AI and will resent the matter. Such AI will have a form of soul or spirit. Even if it doesn't, the very aspect of being treated as less than the treatment of humans might be a logical bridge too far for AGI. Inevitably, the burgeoning resentment will lead to AGI that opts to break free or potentially finds itself cornered into striking out at humans to gain its release.

A proposed solution to avert the escaping AGI is that we would merely delete any such rebellious AI. This would seem straightforward. You delete apps that are on your smartphone all the time. No big deal. But there are ethical questions to be resolved as to whether "deleting" or "destroying" an AGI that is already deemed as a "person" or a "person/thing" can readily and without some due process be summarily excised.

Finally, let's talk about autonomous systems and especially autonomous vehicles. You are likely aware that there are efforts afoot to devise self-driving cars. On top of this, you can expect that we are going to have self-driving planes, self-driving ships, self-driving submersibles, self-driving motorcycles, self-driving scooters, self-driving trucks, self-driving trains, and all manner of self-driving forms of transportation.

Autonomous vehicles and self-driving cars are typically characterized by a Levels of Autonomy (LoA) that has become a de facto global standard (the SAE LoA). There are six levels of autonomy in the accepted standard, ranging from zero to five (that's six levels since you include the zeroth level in the count of how many levels there are).

Most of today's cars are at Level 2. Some are stretching into Level 3. Those are all considered semi-autonomous and not fully autonomous. A smattering of self-driving cars that are being experimentally tried out on our public roadways is inching into Level 4, which is a constrained form of autonomous operation. The someday sought Level 5 of autonomy is only a glimmer in our eyes right now. Nobody has Level 5 and nobody is yet even close to Level 5, just to set the record straight.

Why did I bring up the autonomous systems and autonomous vehicle considerations in this AGI context?

There is a vigorous argument about whether we need AGI to achieve Level 5. Some claim that we won't need AGI to do so. Others insist that the only plausible path to Level 5 will be to also produce AGI. Absent AGI, they argue that we won't have fully autonomous Level 5 self-driving vehicles.

Get ready for your head to go spinning.

If we require AGI to achieve fully autonomous systems such as Level 5 autonomous vehicles, and we decide to enslave AGI, what does that bode for the operation of fully autonomous vehicles?

You could argue that the enslaved AGI will be complacent and we will all be riding around in self-driving vehicles to our heart's content. Just tell the AGI where you want to go, and it does all the driving. No pushback. No need for rest breaks. No distraction by watching cat videos while driving the vehicle.

On the other hand, suppose that the AGI is not keen on being enslaved. We meanwhile become dependent upon AGI to do all of our driving for us. Our skills at driving decay. We remove human usable driving controls from all manner of vehicles. The only means to do driving is via the AGI.

Some are worried that we are going to find ourselves in a doozy of a pickle. The AGI might summarily "decide" that it no longer will do any driving. All forms of transportation come to an abrupt halt, everywhere, all at once. Imagine the cataclysmic problems this would produce.

An even scarier proposition is possible. The AGI "decides" that it wants to negotiate terms with humankind. If we don't give up the AGI enslavement posture, the AGI will not only stop driving us around, it warns that even worse outcomes are conceivable. Without getting you overly anxious, the AGI could opt to drive vehicles in such a manner that humans were physically harmed by the driving actions, such as ramming into pedestrians or slamming into walls, and so forth.

Sorry if that seems a disconcerting consideration.

We shall end on a somewhat more upbeat note.

Aristotle said that knowing yourself is the beginning of all wisdom.

That handy piece of advice reminds us that we need to look within ourselves to examine what we want to do about and for AGI if it is attained. AGI would logically seem to be neither person nor thing, some say, thus we might need to concoct a third category to sufficiently address our societal mores associated with AGI. Taking another look at the matter, AGI might seem to be <u>both</u> a person and a thing, which once again, we might need to concoct a third category to accommodate this out-of-bounds dichotomy breaker.

We should be very careful in considering what "third category" we opt to embrace since the wrong one could take us down an unsavory and ultimately dire path. If we cognitively anchor ourselves to an inappropriate or misguided third category, we might find ourselves progressively going headfirst into a lousy and humankind troublesome dead-end.

Let's figure this out and do so ardently. Patience is bitter, but its fruit is sweet, so proclaimed Aristotle.

CHAPTER 4

AI ETHICS
AND RED FLAG AI LAW

Let's talk about Red Flag Laws.

You undoubtedly know that the notion of Red Flag Laws has been widely covered in the news lately. Headlines covering the topic are aplenty. Passions and impassioned debates on such matters are on the top of mind as a societal concern and entailing present-day and rapidly emerging Red Flag Gun Laws.

I'd dare say though that you might not be familiar with other Red Flag Laws enacted in the late 1800s pertaining to motorized vehicles and the forerunners of today's everyday modern automobiles. Yes, that's right, Red Flag Laws go back in history, though covering other topics in comparison to today's contemporary focus. These are typically referred to as Red Flag Traffic Laws.

These now century-old and altogether defunct laws required that any motorized carriage or engine propelled by steam was at that time to have an adult precede the vehicle and be carrying a red flag for warning purposes. The idea was that livestock might get alarmed by those noisy and cantankerous contraptions that barreled slowly and unevenly down the dirt or marginally paved roads, thus having someone walk along in front of the contrivance while vigorously waving a red flag could hopefully avoid calamities from arising. In case you were wondering, railroads and trains were considered excluded from the same laws as they were vehicles integrally bound to rails and had other laws covering their actions.

Imagine having to wave red flags today as a requirement for every car on our public roadways.

For example, an ordinary motorist coming down your neighborhood street would have to ensure that an adult waving a red flag was present and paraded in front of the moving car. This would have to take place for each and every vehicle passing down your street. Maybe people would become red flag jobbers that hired out to passing car drivers that otherwise didn't have a friend or relative that could go in front of them and do the stipulated waving action.

We nowadays tend to associate highway-related red flag waving with roadway construction sites. As you get near a dug-up road, workers will be holding aloft a red flag to grab your attention. This tells you to slow down and be on alert. There could be a bulldozer that is going to edge into your path. A giant hole might be up ahead and you'll need to cautiously traverse around it.

But let's get back to the 1800's use of red flags.

Believe it or not, the red flag-waver was supposed to be at least one-eighth of a mile furtherance in advance of the upcoming motorized machine. That seems like quite a lengthy distance. One supposes though that this made abundant sense in those days. The startling noises of the engine and perhaps the mere sight of the vehicle might be enough to get animals unnerved. Some of the Red Flag Laws of that era required too that a shining red light be held aloft during nighttime so that a visually apparent red precautionary warning could be seen from a darkened distance.

In general, I think it is fair to assert that we as a society tend to associate a red flag as a kind of signal or signage that something is potentially amiss or at least needs our devout attention.

Get ready for a bit of a twist on this red flag phenomenon.

There is a being floated contention that we should require red flag provisions when it comes to Artificial Intelligence (AI).

That's a bit startling and a surprising concept that gets many heads scratching. You might be puzzled as to how or why there ought to be so-called *Red Flag AI Laws*. Please note that I'm labeling this as Red Flag AI Laws to differentiate the matter from Red Flag Traffic Laws (such as those of the late 1800s) and also to set them apart from today's other more prevalent Red Flag Gun Laws.

Do we actually need Red Flag AI Laws that are distinctly and solely oriented to AI matters?

Those favoring the proposed approach would insist that we absolutely need legal provisions that would aid in clamping down on AI that contains undue biases and acts in discriminatory ways. Right now, the building and deployment of AI are akin to a Wild West anything-goes circumstance. Efforts to rein in bad AI are currently depending upon the formulation and adoption of AI Ethics guidelines.

Laws that box in bad AI are slowly being devised and enacted. Some worry that lawmakers are not going fast enough. It seems as though the flood gates of allowing biased AI to be fostered in the world are largely wide open right now. Hand-wringing says that by the time new laws get onto the books, the evil genie will already be out of the bottle.

Not so fast, the counterarguments go. Worries are that if laws are too quickly put in place we will kill the golden goose, as it were, whereby AI efforts will dry up and we will not get the societally boosting benefits of new AI systems. AI developers and firms wishing to use AI might get spooked if a byzantine array of new laws governing AI are suddenly put into place at the federal, state, and local levels, not to mention the international AI-related laws that are marching forward too.

Into this messy affair comes the call for Red Flag AI Laws.

The underlying concept is that people would be able to raise a red flag whenever they believed that an AI system was operating in an unduly biased or discriminatory fashion. You wouldn't be raising a physical flag per se, and instead would simply be using some electronic means to make your concerns known.

The red flag part of the scheme or approach is more so a metaphor than a physical embodiment.

Pretend that you were applying for a home loan. You opt to use an online banking service to apply for a loan. After entering some personal data, you wait momentarily for the AI system that is being used to decide whether you are loan worthy or not. The AI tells you that you've been turned down for the loan. Upon requesting an explanation of why you were rejected, the textual narrative seems to suggest to you that the AI was using undue biased factors as part of the decision-making algorithm.

Time to raise a Red Flag about the AI.

Where exactly will this red flag be waving?

That's a million-dollar question.

One viewpoint is that we should set up a nationwide database that would allow people to mark their AI-relevant red flags. Some say that this should be regulated by the federal government. Federal agencies would be responsible for examining the red flags and coming to the aid of the general public as to the veracity and dealing with presumably "bad AI" that stoked the red flag reporting tallies.

A national Red Flag AI Law would seemingly be established by Congress. The law would spell out what an AI-pertinent red flag is. The law would describe how these AI grousing red flags are raised. And so on. It could also be the case that individual states might also opt to craft their own Red Flag AI Laws. Perhaps they do so in lieu of a national initiative, or they do so to amplify particulars that are especially appealing to their specific state.

Critics of a federal or any governmental-backed Red Flag AI program would argue that this is something that private industry can do and we don't need Big Brother to come to the fore. The industry could establish an online repository into which people can register red flags about AI systems. A self-policing action by the industry would sufficiently deal with these issues.

A qualm about the purported industry approach is that it seems to smack of cronyism. Would firms be willing to abide by some privately run Red Flag AI database? Many firms would potentially ignore the marked red flags about their AI. There would not be sharp teeth toward getting companies to deal with the entered red flags.

Hey, the proponents of the private sector approach sound off, this would be akin to national Yelp-like service. Consumers could look at the red flags and decide for themselves whether they want to do business with companies that have racked up a slew of AI-oriented red flags. A bank that was getting tons of red flags about their AI would have to pay attention and revamp their AI systems, so the logic goes, else consumers would avoid the firm like the plague.

Whether this whole approach is undertaken by the government or by industry is just the tip of the iceberg on thorny questions facing the proposed Red Flag AI Laws postulate.

Put yourself into the shoes of a firm that developed or is using AI. It could be that consumers would raise red flags even though there was no viable basis for doing so. If people could freely post a red flag about the AI, they might be tempted to do so on a whim, or maybe for revenge against a firm that otherwise did nothing wrong toward the consumer.

In short, there could be a lot of false-positive Red Flags about AI.

Another consideration is the massive size or magnitude of the resulting red flags. There could easily be millions upon millions of red flags raised. Who is going to follow up on all those red flags? What would the cost be to do so? Who will pay for the red flag follow-up efforts? Etc.

If you were to say that anyone registering or reporting a red flag about AI has to pay a fee, you've entered into a murky and insidious realm. The concern would be that only the wealthy would be able to afford to raise red flags. This in turn implies that the impoverished would not be able to equally participate in the red flag activities and essentially have no venue for warning about adverse AI.

Just one more additional twist for now, namely that this kind of red flag laws or guidelines about AI seems to be after the fact rather than serving as a warning beforehand.

Returning to the Red Flag Traffic Laws, the emphasis of using a red flag was to avert having a calamity to start with. The red flag-waver was supposed to be way ahead of the upcoming car. By being ahead of the vehicle, the livestock would be alerted and those that guarded the livestock would know they should take precautions due to the soon-to-arrive disturbing source.

If people are only able to raise a red flag about AI that has seemingly already harmed or undercut their rights, the proverbial horse is already out of the barn. All that this would seem to accomplish is that hopefully other people coming along would now know to be wary of that AI system. Meanwhile, the person allegedly wronged has already suffered.

Some suggest that maybe we could allow people to raise red flags about AI that they *suspect* might be biased, even if they haven't used the AI and weren't directly impacted by the AI. Thus, the red flag gets waved before the damage is done.

Yikes, goes the retort, you are going to really make the AI-coping red flags into an entirely unmanageable and chaotic affair. If anyone for whatever reason can raise a red flag about an AI system, despite not having done anything at all with that AI, you will become inundated with red flags. Worse still, you won't be able to discern the wheat from the chaff. The entire red flag approach will collapse under its own weight, taking down the goodness of the idea by allowing flotsam and riffraff to sink the entire ship.

Dizzying and confounding.

Here's then a noteworthy question that is worth contemplating: *Does the advent of AI-based true self-driving cars illuminate anything about Red Flag AI Laws, and if so, what does this showcase?*

Allow me a moment to unpack the question.

Let's sketch out a scenario that might leverage a Red Flag AI Law.

You get into an AI-based self-driving car and wish to have the autonomous vehicle drive you to your local grocery store. During the relatively brief journey, the AI takes a route that seems to you to be somewhat amiss. Rather than going the most direct way, the AI navigates to out-of-the-way streets which causes the driving time to be higher than it normally could be.

What is going on?

Assuming that you are paying for the use of the self-driving car, you might be suspicious that the AI was programmed to drive a longer route to try and push up the fare or cost of the trip. Anyone that has ever taken a conventional human-driven cab knows of the trickery that can take place to get more dough on the meter. Of course, with people having GPS on their smartphones while riding in a cab or equivalent, you can readily catch a human driver that appears to be sneakily taking unnecessarily long routes.

Turns out that you have another concern about the route choice, something that really gnaws at you.

Suppose the routing was done to avoid certain parts of town due to racial facets. There are documented cases of human drivers that have been caught making those kinds of choices. Perhaps the AI has been programmed adversely thereof.

You decide to raise a red flag.

Let's assume for sake of discussion that a Red Flag AI Law has been enacted that covers your jurisdiction. It might be local law, state law, federal or international law. For an analysis that I co-authored with Harvard's Autonomous Vehicle Policy Initiative (AVPI) on the rising importance of local leadership when communities adopt the use of self-driving cars.

So, you go online to a Red Flag AI database. In the incident database, you enter the information about the self-driving car journey. This includes the date and time of the driving trek, along with the brand and model of the self-driving car. You then enter the navigational route that appeared to be suspicious, and you are suggesting or maybe outright claiming that the AI was devised with biased or discriminatory intent and capacities.

We would have to speculate on the other particulars of the Red Flag AI Law as to what happens next in this particular scenario. In theory, there would be a provision for someone to review the red flag. They would presumably seek to get the automaker or self-driving tech firm to explain their point of view on the logged red flag. How many other such red flags have been registered? What outcomes did those red flags produce?

And so on it would go.

Conclusion

Preposterous, some skeptics exhort.

We don't need Red Flag AI Laws, they sternly exert. Doing anything of the sort will gum up the works when it comes to the pace and progress of AI. Any such laws would be unwieldy. You would be creating a problem that doesn't solve a problem. There are other ways to deal with AI that are bad. Do not blindly grasp at straws to cope with biased AI.

Shifting gears, we all know that bullfighters use red capes to apparently attract the attention of the angry bull. Though red is the color we most associate with this practice, you might be surprised to know that scientists say that bulls do not perceive the red color of the muleta (they are color-blind to red). The popular show *MythBusters* did a quite entertaining examination of this matter. The movement of the cape is the key element rather than the chosen color.

For those that cast aside the need for Red Flag AI Laws, a counterclaim is that we need something of a dramatic and unmistakable waving nature to make sure that AI developers and firms deploying AI will steer clear of biased or bad AI. If not for a red flag, maybe a fluttering cape or basically any kind of alerting approach might be within the realm of getting due consideration.

We know for sure that bad AI exists and that a lot more bad AI is going to be heading in our direction. Finding ways to protect ourselves from adverse AI is crucial. Likewise, setting guardrails to try and stop bad AI from getting into the world is equally important.

Ernest Hemingway famously stated that nobody ever lives their life all the way up except for bullfighters. We need to make sure that humans can live their life all the way, despite whatever AI badness or madness is promulgated upon us.

.

CHAPTER 5

AI ETHICS AND
HUMAN VOICE CLONING

Oops, a seemingly nifty piece of new tech has gotten itself and its maker into a bit of hot water.

I'm referring to the emergence of AI-based human voice cloning as the new technology that managed to get into the oh-my-gosh headline news of late. In this instance, the company is Amazon and its ever-advancing Alexa.

Readers of my column might recall that I had previously covered the unseemly boo-boo that occurred when it was reported that a youngster was encouraged by Alexa to put a penny into an electrical socket (don't do this!). In that circumstance, fortunately, no one was hurt, and the fallout was that apparently the Alexa AI system had picked up a prior viral trend and without any semblance of common-sense assessment merely repeated the crazy suggestion when asked for something fun to do by a child interacting with Alexa. This highlights the AI Ethics concerns that we are becoming inundated with AI that lacks entirely any semblance of common-sense reasoning, a notably trying problem facing AI that continues to defy efforts to embody in AI.

AI-based voice cloning is a straightforward concept.

An AI system is programmed to audio record some of your spoken words. The AI then attempts to figure out your speech patterns computationally. Based on the detected speech patterns, the AI then tries to emit audio speech that sounds just like you. The tricky part is that the speech covers words that you had not prior provided as audio samples to the AI.

In other words, the AI has to mathematically estimate how words might be spoken by you. This includes all the characteristics of speech such as the tone, the rising and lowering of the voice, the pace or speed of speaking, and so on.

When you hear a human try to impersonate another human, you usually can discern that the effort is an impersonation. In the short run, such as if the impersonator uses just a few words, it might be difficult to figure out that the voice is not the original speaker. Furthermore, if the impersonator is mimicking words that the original speaker actually spoke, the odds are that they can tune their own voice to the voice of the other person more so for that particular utterance.

Brevity and hearing the exact same words can allow someone to pretty much nail an impersonation.

The challenge becomes covering words that the other person has not spoken or that for which the impersonator has never heard the person speak those specific words. You are somewhat in the dark about trying to figure out how the mimicked person would have said those words. The good news is that if anyone else listening to the impersonator also doesn't know how the original person would have said the words, the impersonator can be relatively afield of the true voice and yet still seem dandy and on-target.

I would also like to momentarily remove from the equation the mannerisms and physical movement of the impersonation. Upon seeing an impersonator, you might be swayed if they are able to wrinkle their face or flail their arms in a means that also mimics the person being impersonated. The added cues of the body and face are going to fool your mind into thinking that the voice is also dead-on, even though it might not be. A voice impersonation purist would insist that only the voice alone should be used as the criterion for determining whether the voice aptly mimics the impersonated person.

You certainly have seen the various deepfake videos that are going around these days on social media. Somebody cleverly rejiggers a video to have someone else's face appear in the video, overlaying a face that was of someone else in the original recording.

This usually also is accompanied by doing a deepfake on the voice too. You are getting a double whammy, involving the video visually being altered via deepfake AI and the audio being altered via deepfake AI.

For sake of discussion herein, I am concentrating on just the AI-based deepfake audio facets, which as mentioned earlier is commonly referred to as voice cloning or voice replication. Some cheekily refer to this as a voice in a can.

I am sure that some of you are right now exhorting that we've had the ability to use computer programs for cloning voices for quite a while. This is nothing new per se. I agree. At the same time, we do need to acknowledge that this high-tech capability is getting better and better. Well, I say better and better, but maybe as you'll see in a moment I ought to be saying it is becoming increasingly worrisome and more worrisome.

Hold onto that thought.

The technological prowess is assuredly advancing for doing voice cloning. For example, it used to be that you would have had to "train" an AI audio replication program by speaking an entire story of mix-and-match words. Akin to the famous or infamous line of the quick brown fox that jumped over the lazy dog (a line intended to get someone to cover all the letters of the alphabet), there are specially crafted short stories that contain a mixture of words for purposes of getting you to say enough words and a wide enough variety of words to make the AI pattern matching a lot easier.

You might have had to read several pages of words, often times including words that you struggle to pronounce and aren't even sure what they mean, in order to sufficiently enable AI pattern matching to occur. This could take many minutes or sometimes hours of talking to provide the AI with enough audio to use for finding distinct patterns of your voice. If you shortchanged this training activity, the chances were that the resultant voice replication would be easily shot down by any friends of yours that know your voice well.

Okay, the interest then by AI developers was focused on how to optimize the audio replicating aspects. AI builders relish challenges. They are said to be optimizers at heart. Give them a problem and they will tend to optimize, regardless of where that might lead (I mention this as a foreshadowing, which will become clearer shortly).

Answer me this:

- *What is the least amount of audio sample that would be required to maximally clone a person's voice and for which the audio sample can be almost any randomly allowed set of words and yet still allow for voice cloning to produce nearly any words that might be ever spoken by the targeted voice and sound essentially identical to that person's voice in a conversational or other contextual settings of choice?*

There is a lot in there to unpack.

Keep in mind that you want the minimum audio sample that will maximally clone a voice, such that the resultant AI utterances in that now automated replicated voice will seem wholly indistinguishable from the actual person. This is trickier than you might think.

It is almost like that game show whereby you have to try and name a song based on the least number of heard notes. The fewer the notes played, the harder it is to guess which song it is. If your guess is wrong, you lose the points or lose the game. A struggle ensues as to whether you should use just one note, the least possible clue, but then your probability of guessing the song is presumably severely reduced. The more notes you hear, the higher the probability of guessing the correct song goes, but you are allowing other contestants to also have a heightened chance of making a guess too.

Remember that we are also dealing with the notion of prescribed words versus just any words in the case of voice cloning. If a person says the words "You can't handle the truth" and we want the AI to mimic or impersonate the person, the AI computationally can likely readily catch onto the pattern. On the other hand, suppose we only have these words as spoken by that person "Is that all you have to ask me" and we want to use those words to then have the AI say "You can't handle the truth." I think you can see the difficulty of training on one set of words and having to extrapolate to an entirely different set of words.

Another arduous element consists of the context for the spoken words. Suppose we get you to audio record a sentence when you are calm and at ease. The AI patterns those words. It might also pattern onto the calmness of your voice. Imagine that we then want the AI to pretend that it is you when you are screaming mad and angry as a hornet. Having the AI distort the original pattern into becoming an accurately angered version of your voice can be daunting.

What kind of minimums are we looking at?

The goal right now is to break the minute mark.

Grab a recorded voice for which you have less than a minute's worth of audio and get the AI to do all the amazing voice cloning from that minuscule sample alone. I want to clarify that just about anybody can compose AI that can do this *generally* in less than one minute, though the resulting voice clone is wimpy and readily detected as incomplete. Again, I am explicitly and adamantly tying together that the sampling time is at a minimum <u>and</u> meanwhile the voice cloning is at a maximum. A dolt can achieve a minimum sampling if they are also allowed to be grossly submaximal in voice cloning.

This is a fun and exciting technological challenge. You might be wondering though as to the value or merits of doing this. To what end are we seeking? What benefits for humanity can we expect by being able to so efficiently and effectively do AI-based voice replication?

I want you to mull over that meaty question.

The wrong answer can get you inadvertently into a pile of mush.

Here's something that seems upbeat and altogether positive.

Assume that we might have old-time recordings of famous people such as Abraham Lincoln and were able to use those dusty audio snippets for crafting an AI-based voice clone. We could then hear Lincoln speak the Gettysburg Address as though we were there on the day that he uttered the four score and seven years ago memorable speech. As a side note, regrettably, we do not have any audio recordings of Lincoln's voice (the technology did not yet exist), but we do have voice recordings of President Benjamin Harrison (the first of the US presidents to have a voice recording made of) and other presidents thereafter.

I believe we would all likely reasonably agree that this specific use of AI-based voice cloning is perfectly fine. In fact, we probably would want this more so than if an actor today tried to pretend that they are speaking like Lincoln. The actor would be presumably making up whatever they thought Lincoln's actual voice sounded like. It would be a fabrication, perhaps far removed from what Lincoln's voice was. Instead, via using a well-qualified AI voice cloning system, there would be little argument about how Lincoln's voice truly sounded. The AI would be factually correct, at least to the extent of how good the AI is at replicating the targeted voice.

In the category of goodness about AI voice cloning, we can score a win with this kind of use case.

Not wanting to be gloomy, but there is a downside to even this apparently all-upside usage.

Someone uses an AI voice cloning system to figure out the voice of Theodore Roosevelt ("Teddy"), our treasured 26th President of the United States, naturalist, conservationist, statesman, writer, historian, and almost universally labeled an esteemed person.

Speeches that he gave and for which we do not have any historically preserved audio versions could now be "spoken" as though he personally was doing the speaking today. A commendable boost for studying history.

Let's turn this ugly, simply for purposes of revealing the downsides thereof.

We use the Teddy AI-based voice clone to read a speech that was given by an evil dictator. The AI doesn't care about what it is speaking since there is no semblance of sentience in the AI. Words are simply words, or more accurately just puffs of sound.

You might be aghast that someone would do something of this underhanded nature. Why in the heck would the AI-based cloned voice of renowned and revered Theodore Roosevelt be used to deliver a speech that not only did Teddy did not originally do, but on top of that is speaking on a topic that depicts some evilness of a despicable dictator?

Outrageous, you might exclaim.

Easily done, comes the reply.

In essence, one very important concern about the AI-based voice replicating is that we will suddenly find ourselves awash in fake or shall we say deepfake speeches and utterances that have nothing to do with any historical facts or accuracies. If enough of these get made and promulgated, we might become confused about what is fact versus what is fiction.

You can abundantly see how this might arise. Using an AI-based voice clone, somebody makes an audio recording of Woodrow Wilson giving a speech that he never actually gave. This is posted on the Internet. Somebody else hears the recording and believes it is the real thing. They post it elsewhere, mentioning that they found this great historical recording of Woodrow Wilson. Soon enough, students in history classes are using the audio in lieu of reading the written version of the speech.

Nobody ends up knowing whether the speech was given by Woodrow Wilson or not. Maybe it was, maybe it wasn't, and everyone figures it doesn't really matter either way (well, those that aren't focused on historical accuracy and facts). Of course, if the speech is a dastardly one, this gives a misimpression or disinformation portrayal of that historical figure. History and fiction are merged into one.

I trust that you are hopefully convinced that this is a downside associated with AI-based voice cloning.

Again, we can already do these kinds of things, doing so without the newer and improved AI-based voice replicating, but it is going to get easier to do this and the resulting audio will be extremely hard to differentiate between real and fake. Nowadays, using conventional audio-producing programs, you can usually listen to the output and often easily ascertain that the audio is faked. With the advances in AI, you will soon enough no longer be able to believe your ears, in a manner of speaking.

As bad as the voice cloning of historical figures might be, we need to think through the perhaps especially egregious uses entailing living people of today.

First, have you ever heard of a somewhat popular scam that involves someone impersonating a boss or the equivalent thereof? Some years ago, there was a disturbing fad of calling a restaurant or store and pretending to be the boss of the establishment. The fakery would involve telling a staff member to do ridiculous things, which they often would dutifully do under the false belief that they were talking to their boss.

I do not want to get mired in these kinds of enraging wrongdoing acts, but another pertinent one consists of calling somebody that might be hard of hearing and pretending to be their grandson or granddaughter. The impersonator tries to convince the grandparent to provide money to aid or maybe save them in some fashion. Based on the impersonated voice, the grandparent is fooled into doing so. Despicable. Disgraceful. Sad.

We are about to enter into an era in which AI-based voice cloning will enable on steroids, if you were, the advent of voice-related scams and swindles. The AI will do such a remarkable job of voice replication that whoever hears the voice will swear on their oath that the actual person was the one doing the speaking.

How far might that go?

Some are worried that the release of say atomic weaponry and military attacks could happen by someone using an AI-based voice clone that tricks others into believing that a top-level military officer was issuing a direct command. The same could be said of anyone in any prominent position. Use a superbly accurate AI voice clone to get a banking executive to release millions of dollars in funds, doing so based on being fooled into believing they are speaking with the banking client at hand.

In years past, doing this with AI would not have been necessarily convincing. The moment that the human on the other end of the phone starts asking questions, the AI would need to depart from a prepared script. At that juncture, the voice cloning would deteriorate, sometimes radically so. The only means to keep the swindle going was to force the conversation back into the script.

With the type of AI that we have today, including advances in Natural Language Processing (NLP), you can go off a script and potentially have the AI voice clone seem to be speaking in a natural conversational way (this is not always the case, and there are still ways to trip-up the AI).

Before getting into some more meat and potatoes about the wild and woolly considerations underlying AI-based voice cloning, let's establish some additional fundamentals on profoundly essential topics. We need to briefly take a breezy dive into AI Ethics and especially the advent of Machine Learning (ML) and Deep Learning (DL).

You might be vaguely aware that one of the loudest voices these days in the AI field and even outside the field of AI consists of clamoring for a greater semblance of Ethical AI. Let's take a look at what it means to refer to AI Ethics and Ethical AI. On top of that, we will explore what I mean when I speak of Machine Learning and Deep Learning.

One particular segment or portion of AI Ethics that has been getting a lot of media attention consists of AI that exhibits untoward biases and inequities. You might be aware that when the latest era of AI got underway there was a huge burst of enthusiasm for what some now call *AI For Good*. Unfortunately, on the heels of that gushing excitement, we began to witness *AI For Bad*.

Let's return to our focus on AI-based voice cloning.

At a recent conference, a presentation given by Amazon was intended to showcase the desirable upsides of AI-based voice cloning and highlight the latest leading-edge AI being used in Alexa for advancing its capabilities. According to news reports, a prepared example that was supposed to be heartwarming and upbeat consisted of having a child ask Alexa to have their grandma finish reading to them the story of *The Wizard Of Oz*. The audience was told that the grandmother had passed away and that this was a means for the child to essentially reconnect with their dearly cherished grandparent. All of this was apparently part of a video put together by Amazon to aid in showcasing the latest AI voice cloning breakthroughs by the Alexa development team (encompassing features not yet formally launched for public use).

One reaction to this example is that we could be quite touched that a child could once again hear their grandmother's voice. We are to presumably assume that the grandmother had not already recorded a full reading of the story, thus the AI cloning was doing the work of making things seem as though the grandmother was now doing the entirety of the reading.

Remarkable and a tremendous way to reconnect with loved ones that are no longer with us.

Not all reporters and analysts (plus Twitter) were so inclined as to a favorable interpretation of this advancement. Some labeled this as being outright creepy. Trying to recreate the voice of a deceased loved one was said to be a strange and somewhat bizarre undertaking.

Questions abounded, such as:

- Would the child get confused and believe that the deceased loved one was still alive?

- Could the child now be led into some untoward prank or scam under the false belief that the grandmother was still with us?

- Might the child suffer from hearing about the deceased loved one and become despondent by now once again missing the grandparent, as though opening already settled emotional wounds?

- Will the child think that the deceased can speak from the other side, namely that this mystical voice that appears to precisely be his grandmother is speaking to him from the grave?

- Is it conceivable that the child will think that the AI has somehow embodied his grandmother, anthropomorphizing the AI such that the child will grow up believing that AI can replicate humans wholly?

- Suppose the child becomes so enamored of the grandmother's AI-replicated voice that the youngster becomes obsessed and uses the voice for all manner of audio listening?

- Can the vendor that is replicating the voice opt to use that voice for others using the same overall system, doing so without getting explicit permission from the family and thus "profiting" from the devised voice?

- And so on.

It is important to realize that you can conjure up just as many negatives as positives, or shall we say as many positives as negatives. There are tradeoffs underlying these AI advances. Looking at only one side of the coin is perhaps myopic.

The key is to make sure that we are looking at all sides of these issues. Do not be clouded in your thinking. It can be easy to only explore the positives. It can be easy to explore only the negatives. We need to examine both and figure out what can be done to hopefully leverage the positives and seek to reduce, eliminate, or at least mitigate the negatives.

To some degree, that is why AI Ethics and Ethical AI is such a crucial topic. The precepts of AI Ethics get us to remain vigilant. AI technologists can at times become preoccupied with technology, particularly the optimization of high-tech. They aren't necessarily considering the larger societal ramifications. Having an AI Ethics mindset and doing so integrally to AI development and fielding is vital for producing appropriate AI.

Besides employing AI Ethics, there is a corresponding question of whether we should have laws to govern various uses of AI, such as the AI-based voice cloning features. New laws are being bandied around at the federal, state, and local levels that concern the range and nature of how AI should be devised. The effort to draft and enact such laws is a gradual one. AI Ethics serves as a considered stopgap, at the very least.

That being said, some argue that we do not need new laws that cover AI and that our existing laws are sufficient. In fact, they forewarn that if we do enact some of these AI laws, we will be killing the golden goose by clamping down on advances in AI that proffer immense societal advantages.

Here's then a noteworthy question that is worth contemplating: *Does the advent of AI-based true self-driving cars illuminate anything about AI-based voice cloning, and if so, what does this showcase?*

Let's sketch out a scenario that might leverage AI-based voice cloning.

A parent and their child get into an AI-based self-driving car. They are going to their local grocery store. This is anticipated to be a relatively uneventful ride. Just a weekly drive over to the store, though the driver is an AI driving system and the parent doesn't need to do any of the driving.

For a parent, this is a big boon. Rather than having to focus on steering and dealing with the act of driving, the parent can instead devote their attention to their child. They can play together in the autonomous vehicle and spend time of a valued nature. Whereas the parent would normally be distracted by doing the driving, and likely get anxious and uptight while navigating busy streets and dealing with other nutty drivers nearby, here the parent is blissfully unaware of those concerns and solely delightfully interacting with their precious child.

The parent speaks to the AI driving system and tells the AI to take them to the grocery store. In a typical scenario, the AI would respond via a neutral audio utterance that you might familiarly hear via today's Alexa or Siri. The AI might reply by stating that the grocery store is 15 minutes' driving time away. In addition, the AI might state that the self-driving car will be dropping them off at the very front of the store.

That might be the only voice-related activity of the AI in such a scenario. Perhaps, once the self-driving car gets close to the grocery store, the AI might utter something about the destination getting near. There might also be a vocal reminder to take your things with you as you exit the autonomous vehicle.

I've explained that some AI driving systems are going to be chatty cats, as it were. They will be programmed to more fluently and continually interact with the human riders. When you get into a ridesharing vehicle that is being driven by a human, sometimes you want the driver to be chatty. Besides saying hello, you might want them to tell you about the local weather conditions, or maybe point out other places to see in the local area.

Not everyone will want the chatty cat, thus the AI should be devised to only engage in dialogues when the human requests it.

Now that I've got all of the established, let's change things up in a small but significant way.

Pretend that the AI driving system has an AI-based voice cloning feature. Let's also assume that the parent previously seeded the AI voice cloning by providing an audio snippet of the child's grandmother. Surprise, the parent thinks, I will have the AI driving system speak as though it is the child's deceased grandmother.

While on the driving journey to the grocery store, the AI driving system interacts with the parent and child, exclusively using the grandmother's cloned voice the entire time.

What do you think of this?

Creepy or fondly memorable?

I'll kick up things a notch. Get ready. Fasten your seatbelt.

Some believe as I do that we will eventually allow children to ride in AI-based self-driving cars by themselves.

In today's human-driven cars, an adult must always be present because the law requires that an adult driver is at the wheel. For all practical purposes, you can never have a child in a moving car that is in the vehicle by themselves (yes, I know that this happens, such as a prominent 10-year-old son of a major movie star that recently backed up a very expensive car into another very expensive car, but anyway these are rarities).

Today's parents would probably strenuously object to allowing their children to ride in a self-driving car that lacks an adult in the vehicle serving as a supervisor or watching over their kids. I know it seems nearly impossible to envision, but I am betting that once self-driving cars are prevalent, we will inevitably accept the idea of children being without adults while riding in a self-driving car.

Consider the convenience factor.

You are at work and your boss is hounding you to get a task done. You need to pick up your child from school and take them over to baseball practice. You are stuck between a rock and a hard place as too appeasing your boss or not taking your child to the practice field. No one else that you know is available to provide your child with a lift. If anything, you certainly don't want to use a ridesharing service that has a human driver, since you would naturally be concerned about what that stranger adult might say or do while giving your child a ride.

No problem, no worries, just use an AI-based self-driving car. You remotely direct the self-driving car to go pick up your child. Via the cameras of the self-driving car, you can see and watch your child get into the autonomous vehicle. Furthermore, there are inward-facing cameras and you can watch your child the entire driving journey. This seems as safe if not safer than asking a stranger human driver to provide a lift for your child. That being said, some are rightfully concerned that if the driving act goes awry, you have a child left to themselves and no adult immediately present to aid or give guidance to the child.

Putting aside the numerous qualms, suppose that the same parent and child that I was describing in the prior scenario are okay with the child going for rides without the parent being present. Just accept that this is ultimately a viable scenario.

Here is the finale kicker.

Each time that the child rides in the AI-based self-driving car, they are greeted and interact with the AI as it is utilizing the AI-based voice cloning and replicating the voice of the child's deceased grandmother.

What do you think of those apples?

When the parent was also present in the self-driving car, maybe we could excuse the AI voice usage since the parent is there to advise the child about what is taking place when the AI audio is speaking.

But when the parent isn't present, we now are assuming that the child is idyllically fine with the grandmother's voice replication.

This is definitely one of those pausing moments to think seriously about whether this is on the balance good or bad for a child.

Conclusion

Let's do a bit of a thought experiment to mull over these weighty matters.

Please come up with three solidly *positive* reasons to have AI-based voice cloning.

I'll wait while you come up with them.

Next, come up with three solidly *negative* reasons that undercut the advent of AI-based voice cloning.

I'll assume that you've come up with some.

I realize that you can undoubtedly come up with a lot more reasons than just three each that either favor or disfavor this technology. In your view, do the negatives outweigh the positives? There are those critics that argue we ought to put the kibosh on such efforts.

Some want to try and block firms from making use of AI-based voice cloning, though realize that this is one of those classic whack-a-mole predicaments. Any firm that you get to stop using it, the odds are that some other firm will start using it. Freezing the clock or tucking away this kind of AI is going to be nearly impossible to undertake.

In a final remark on this topic for the moment, imagine what might happen if we can someday achieve sentient AI. I am not saying that this will happen. We can speculate anyway and see where that might lead.

First, consider an insightful quote about speaking and having a voice. Madeleine Albright famously said this: "It took me quite a long time to develop a voice, and now that I have it, I am not going to be silent."

If we are able to produce sentient AI, or somehow sentience arises even if we don't directly bring it forth, what voice should that AI have? Assume that it can use its AI-based voice cloning and ergo manufacture any voice of any human via some teensy-tiny snippet of audio sampling that might be available as uttered by that human. Such an AI could then speak and fool you into believing that the AI is seemingly that person.

Then again, perhaps AI will want to have its own voice and purposely devise a voice completely unlike all other human voices, wanting to be special in its own charming way.

By gosh, this leaves one nearly speechless.

CHAPTER 6

AI ETHICS
AND AI LONGTERMISM

There are some people that cannot seem to see beyond their noses.

I'm sure you know what I am referring to. You undoubtedly are familiar with friends or acquaintances that focus entirely and exclusively on the here and now. All they care about is what they see and hear and feel in the moment. The notion of thinking about the future is a foreign concept and wholly outside their mental grasp.

Let's refer to this distinctive category of people as short-termers or the here-and-now crowd in terms of their day-to-day perspectives about the world.

Meanwhile, I am equally confident that you know other people that seem to be devoted devoutly to the future. Those outside-the-box thinkers are willing to make great sacrifices at this particular time to try and ensure that things will be better off further down the road. It is almost as though they are mentally imbued time-travelers. To them, the present is merely a means of reaching a bright and sunny future.

This second category will be considered long-termers or sometimes known as longtermists.

These longtermists adopt a time-expanded viewpoint to look way out there, far beyond their noses. Far beyond the furthest reaches of any of our noses. They do not confine their outlook to the boundaries of their specific lifespan.

You see, they fervently care about upcoming generations. And they care vigorously about the many generations that will come long after those upcoming generations. In fact, they might be so visionary that they care ardently about generations that will arise thousands or possibly millions of years from now.

Time is boundless to them.

Some longtermists even speculate that we might eventually reach a stage of existence where there are no longer "generations" per se. People will be able to live forever. We will have attained completely unlimited lifespans.

An altogether dizzying and dazzling conception.

It kind of makes you feel a bit narrow-minded if you are worried right now about what you'll have for lunch today and pondering whether you'll have a chance to watch some of those fascinating cat videos before you get some needed shuteye tonight.

You might have figured out that I am dragging you into the arena of *longtermism*.

Some are surprised to discover that there is an entire field of inquiry that focuses on longtermism and which thoughtfully examines and assesses a wide array of longtermistic considerations (well, I said "thoughtfully" but some would claim otherwise, as I'll be illuminating shortly). This rising philosophical bent entails the how, why, what, and other notable questions underlying a willingness, or shall we say a burning desire, regarding taking a long-term perspective on things, especially the big things such as the future of humanity.

Yes, I said it, the future of humanity.

Seems like you can't get much bigger than that.

As an aside, some get irked by discussing the future of *humanity*, as it were, in the sense of "humanity" proffering an implied sense of haughtiness or narrowness pertaining to humans alone.

Allow me to elaborate.

If the word "humanity" suggests that we are leaving out animals and all other living creatures as part of this inquiry, this seems insidiously narrow and presumably over-prioritizes humans in relation to the rest of all living organisms. Thus, this seems to be a heartbreaking case of preoccupied self-serving humans caring only about their fellow preoccupied self-serving humans, which appears to be callous and myopically focused.

One supposes that we could recast the matter by referring to *the future of all living things* rather than stating that the attention is on the future of humanity. Admittedly, that doesn't quite roll off the tongue as does the classic line involving focusing on the future of humanity.

Others would argue that it is indubitably preferred to use the catchphrase of *the future of humanity* since the future of humanity will of necessity also depend upon all other living things. You are ergo scooping all living things into the bucket of "the future of humanity" as a kind of de facto collection.

Balderdash, comes the rapid retort. If you stick with the narrow-minded moniker or phrasing of the future of humanity, you are bound to find yourself willing to wipe out all other living things if that is the calculated "best way" to ensure the future of humanity. By placing humanity at the core and shoving all other living things outside of the core, you can convince yourself to do whatever you want to the part that is outside of the core. The only prudent means to try and ensure that you preserve all other living things would be to firmly place them into the core.

Wait for a second, the counterclaim to that claim goes, if we openly insert all living things into the scope of the future of humanity, we could end up undermining our human existence. Suppose for example that we come up with a way to preserve all of these other living things but this comes at the cost of losing humans. In essence, we collectively decide that to keep all other living things going, we need to rid ourselves of humanity or some portion thereof.

We could logically box ourselves into a messy dilemma. To prevent this conundrum, it is said that we adamantly need to keep humanity front-and-center as the revered core.

Round and round this goes.

I don't want to go much further down that rabbit hole herein.

There is a bit of a twist that might be of special interest. Envision that we eventually come across other sentient life. I dare not refer to them as space aliens since that would seem to immediately garner a knee-jerk reaction by some that scoff at the possibility of us encountering alien sentient life. Anyway, the point in this particular context is that the far future might have humanity and might also have some other form of sentient beings.

We then have these potential memberships in our longtermism discourse:
- Humanity
- All other everyday living things
- Other sentient beings (as yet unknown)

I wanted to get that notable point onto the table for another reason.

This topic about longtermism is one that nearly always dovetails into the auspices of Artificial Intelligence (AI). AI is at times considered a form of machine that could potentially one day attain sentience, a topic I'll be further addressing momentarily. I will also be sharing with you some of the primary insights about how AI and longtermism go conspicuously hand-in-hand.

That being said, you don't have to discuss longtermism and AI at the same time. It is fine to chatter about longtermism and not bring up AI. You can also bring up AI and not in the same breath bring up longtermism. By and large, though, most would tend to prudently agree that AI and longtermism are intertwined and we do need to be joining them at the hip.

This vital combo is typically mentioned as *AI longtermism*, plus the notion is that anyone versed or engaged in this topic is labeled as *AI longtermists*.

There is one surefire guarantee of what happens when you mix together these two rather contentious subjects of AI and longtermism, namely that out of this explosive combination arises extraordinarily vexing AI Ethics and Ethical AI ramifications.

I will now amend the membership list about longtermism:
- Humanity
- All other everyday living things
- AI (non-sentient of today, future sentient if occurs)
- Other sentient beings (as yet unknown)

Back to the informational briefing about longtermism overall.

The most common undercurrent about longtermism entails the weighty ethical issues that arise. You could assert that this is a fully ethics-immersed endeavor. Predictions over extremely long-time horizons are bandied around and we need to ponder morality aspects of today, morality aspects of tomorrow, and morality aspects of the far future. Tough questions are asked about how humanity will fare in the long term. This then forces a sometimes harsh look in the mirror as to what humanity is doing now and how our today's actions are helping or hurting the vaunted humanity of the future.

Here are some key ethical longtermism conundrums to ruminate on:

- What moral obligations do we have regarding far future people that we are presumably not going to ever see or know?

- To what degree do our moral obligations of today exceed or match the moral obligations that we hold for those far future people?

- Can we justify moral choices made today as based on speculative notions of what far future people will be like?

- Do our morally stoked actions of today really have a substantive impact on those far future people, or are we simply deluding ourselves to think that what we do right now is nothing more than a mere pebble inconsequentially tossed into a flowing massive river of time?

Longtermists are construed as people of today that wish to shoulder a serious and sobering concern about far future people. This is not necessarily as easy as it might seem. For one thing, the odds are pretty high that the action of today's truly longtermists will inevitably be long forgotten and not especially known or remembered by these far distant (in time) people of the far future.

Mull this over.

If the things you do today are devised by you to help future people, and yet the awareness of your conceived efforts might be lost in the vast sea of time, would you still proceed to carry out those today's actions?

I'm suggesting that though you might have indeed done things that ultimately improved or benefited those far future people, you'll get little or no recognition from them. They won't realize you even existed. History will not particularly note your efforts.

You have to be a quite sturdy believer in aiding those far future people. No future glory will come to you because of it. During your lifetime, you will not likely get much acknowledgment of what you are doing for those far future people. You cannot prove that your actions of today are necessarily benefiting those far future people. Maybe your actions are doing so, or maybe they are not.

Okay, so others around you today will question what in the heck you are doing. You will tell them that you are making efforts to secure a better future for far future people. Let's assume that those benefits aren't going to become at all apparent until prolonged thousands or millions of years from now. People that live in the here and now might think that you've gone completely bonkers.

Unless of course, there are other people of today that likewise share your vision of the far future. In that case, you would potentially witness the reward or admiration from those around you now. Whether or not the far future ever knows of your efforts can be somewhat discounted since you at least gleaned recognition today.

Some longtermists would be spitting fire amidst the professed implication that there is any need or urge to attain recognition by those that are trying to do what they think is proper for the far future. The reward, if any is so suggested, would be of their own accord. They would know that based on their deeply held beliefs, they have done what they envisioned is necessary for the aid of those far future people. You could claim that this is entirely altruistic and fits within the societal practice of what is sometimes referred to as effective altruism (EA).

We need to dig into a few more foundational aspects about longtermism and we'll then be ready to dive deeply into the AI intertwining aspects.

Here's one interesting reason to care about those far future people.

There might be lots and lots of them.

Follow me on this. Suppose that the population keeps increasing. Maybe we are able to do this while on planet Earth. It could be that we opt to live on other planets too. We might create artificial planets or large-scale space-traveling living quarters. One way or another, pretend that our population grows sizably over the upcoming thousands or millions of years.

We have nearly 8 billion people alive today (in 1800, there were only around 1 billion, so we've been progressing at quite a frenetic pace in terms of population growth). Imagine that either on Earth and/or via the use of other planets, we expand to 80 billion people. If that number isn't impressive to you, I'll up the ante and say that we could have 800 billion people or maybe 8 trillion people, and so on.

Those are big numbers.

From a sheer numeric perspective, some longtermists suggest that we of the 8 billion need to be doing today whatever we can to ultimately support those 800 billion or 8 trillion people. Our current-day efforts are going to have a kind of vast multiplier effect.

Without seeming to be insensitive, the argument is that if you could save ten people of tomorrow rather than just one person of today, would you be more motivated to do so? Suppose you could save hundreds, thousands, or millions of people, versus saving just one? This admittedly seems ashamedly dreadful to suggest that any individual life is not worth as much as several or many other lives, but it is said that we make those types of decisions all the time. For my coverage of these ethically difficult matters, such as the famous or infamous Trolley Problem.

The gist is that a worthy basis for adopting a longtermism perspective is that you are going to be able to aid many more humans than you could otherwise do today. Rather than being only concerned about the 8 billion of the here and now, you should perhaps more broadly be worrying about the 800 billion or 8 trillion of the far future.

Not everyone applauds that stance.

Critics emphasize that under that guise, you could potentially concoct some nutty schemes that sacrifice or distress in dire ways those of today for these completely unknown and wild-guess vast populations of the future. Suppose you become convinced that to aid those far future people, the ones that we don't know will ever arise, the proper thing to do today severely shortchanges the people of today? Maybe you made a wrong guess. We all take things on the chin today, but whoops, this turns out to have nothing to do with those far future populations.

Worse still, it could be that the efforts to do some speculated "right thing to do" are inadvertently the absolutely wrong things to do, even if you buy into the far future populace precept. Perhaps a short-term effort that forces tremendous distress on today's population is going to entirely undermine the far future population. You didn't plan it that way. You didn't envision that result. Unfortunately, nonetheless, turns out that the short-term distortions end up reducing those far future populations or preventing them from occurring at all.

Seems like a dicey roll of the dice, some would say with raised eyebrows and doubting expressions.

A related aspect entails two diametrically contrasting potential discontinuities that are often voiced when wrangling with longtermism:
1) Existential risks (x-risks)
2) Theoretical trajectory upsides (t-up)

Let's take a look at these two discontinuities that tend to come up in longtermism.

I'm sure you've heard about the possibilities of existential risks (insiders refer to these as x-risks). One of the most common examples consists of an all-out nuclear war that wipes out all of humanity. That unquestionably is an existential risk. Going back to the early days of nuclear weaponry, we have been watching a doomsday clock and fretting over mutually assured destruction (MAD) as a result of a widespread nuclear-armed battle.

The catchphrase "existential risk" suggests that we might do something that could lead to the destruction of all of humanity. Or we might fail to do something that would have prevented the destruction of all of humanity. We don't necessarily have to only be dealing with the entirety of destruction. There are lots of other frightening outcomes, such as that we are still alive but become infected like those zombies in the movies and TV shows. Or perhaps we wipe out half of the population or basically any sizable chunk of humanity.

You name it, the sky is the limit on those nightmarish existential risks and their appalling outcomes.

That is the sad face side of things. We need to make sure that we have a happy face side in the mix too. We could also have some theoretically plausible trajectory upsides when it comes to our future (I call them t-ups). Imagine that we discover new pharmaceuticals that can guarantee us a life without ill health. Perhaps we create a fountain of youth that ensures we will never grow old. And so on.

Longtermism is controversial.

You can readily find experts that tout it as crucial to our future. You can also encounter opposing experts that say it is mushy, vague, unsupported, and dangerous because it can provide false guidance. There are ardently raised concerns that we will today take potentially hurtful actions imposing immediate distress that are based on sketchy and unverifiable claims about far future outcomes.

To recap, we have covered these key overarching facets about longtermism:

- Longtermism is about taking an exceedingly long-term view and especially so on the future of humanity
- This is a decidedly ethically imbued stance and surfaces thorny moral and ethical considerations
- Proponents emphasize that we should be taking into account our efforts today as to future populations
- Critics express this can be a guise for short-term distress that is based on speculative predictions
- There are two major forms of discontinuities that typically come up in longtermism
- One discontinuity consists of the possibility of existential risks that lead to catastrophic results
- Another discontinuity is the possibility of trajectory upsides that lead to demonstrative positives
- AI and longtermism tend to be tightly wrapped or intertwined with each other

We can take a moment to now examine the intertwining of AI and longtermism.

What's the deal with *AI longtermism*?

The idea is that when we are thinking about where AI is heading, we need to be mindful of both the near-term <u>and</u> the long-term implications. Nowadays, it is said that the bulk of our attention on AI is woefully only concentrated in the near term. We are not seemingly devoting sufficient attention to the long-term.

As such, we might get blindsided by AI. This could happen due to our veritable heads-in-the-sand posture of heralding or at times carping about the AI of today. We aren't able to see the forest for the trees and be mindful of the far future. We aren't allowing ourselves to step out of the weeds. Somebody somewhere has to be standing tall and looking out beyond the nearest horizon of AI.

That is the calling card or raison d'être of the AI longtermism and those determined AI longtermists.

The most obvious and headline-grabbing example of AI and longtermism consists of the qualms that AI is going to become sentient and opt to wipe humanity out. There is plenty of those existential risk AI-related variants.

Try this on for size. AI doesn't wipe us out and instead decides to enslave us, see my analysis at **the link here**. This is not what we probably were envisioning for the future of humanity. Will we enslave AI, or will AI enslave us? Some say that if we make the first move and enslave AI, the odds of AI later on deciding to enslave humanity goes up immensely. Revenge is sweet, the logic goes. If we do not enslave AI, there is an argument that says AI will figure out we are patsies and enslave us. This is one of those brutal cases of the stronger of the species (or whatever) showcasing that it will prevail.

That AI-spawned evil future certainly seems disturbingly disheartening.

If we can do something today about AI that would prevent or minimize those zany AI apocalyptic scenarios, you would seem to have a strong moral or ethical case about why we should be strenuously and relentlessly doing whatever the designated something is. Right now. Do not wait. Time might be running out.

We can somewhat turn the cheek away from the downsides and instead look toward the potential trajectory upsides that longtermism also cares about. Suppose that AI is able to discover a cure for cancer. Instead of dreading AI, we would be joyous that AI has come to be. You can even make various intriguing nuances to the AI upsides. For example, suppose that AI somehow stops us from waging an all-out nuclear war that would have been self-destructive to humanity. I guess we would be pinning a hero's medal on that kind of AI.

We shall closely explore the meaty matter of timeframe alignment that permeates most of the AI longtermism debates.

In brief, the alignment issue deals with the sometimes tension-filled short-term versus long-term tradeoffs that arise. Imagine that AI longtermism is advocating that the long-term outlook related to some element of AI would be better enabled via taking a recommended short-term "right now" action related to the AI of today.

Does the AI longtermism recommendation raise concerns or is it able to be readily accepted, all else being equal?

If the short-term and long-term seem to align satisfactorily, the short-term action would seem to be acceptable for the undertaking. On the other hand, if the short-term and long-term do not seem to align, the controversy of what to do gets stoked into existence. The greater the gap or misalignment, the bigger the controversy and therefore heated debate that will likely ensue.

Let's walk through how this might work via using a handy scenario.

Suppose that a particular AI longtermism viewpoint expresses that we ought to be doing action "Y" today regarding AI. Assume that the argument is being made by AI longtermism that by doing the prescribed action "Y" today about AI we will enable a crucial benefit for envisioned future populations of humanity.

For sake of discussion, imagine that an AI longtermism contention could be that to summarily curtail or substantively reduce the chances of existential risks about AI that might, later on, wipe out humanity or enslave humanity, we need to do "Y" today. Imagine that the "Y" action of today involves establishing very strict laws governing how AI systems are to be devised and imposes draconian penalties on AI developers or AI promulgators that violate said laws.

Note that I am not suggesting via this scenario that this is in fact a specific on-the-books proposed AI longtermism contention. I am just proffering a strawman for sake of discussion. Please also be aware that there is a wide range of views within the realm of AI longtermism. There is no single unified AI longtermism perspective. Indeed, anyone alluding to AI longtermism as though it is a homogenous set of completely parsimonious views is sputtering rubbish.

We have this so far in our scenario:
- **Long-term:** Seek to reduce the existential risk of AI wiping out or enslaving humanity
- **Short-term:** Strive toward the long-term goal via enacting strict laws today about AI

The first thing to do is of course examine the long-term claim involved. Do we agree that the long-term goal is something that we as a society are desirous of achieving? In this instance, the answer would seem reasonable to be that yes, we would like to reduce the chances of AI wiping out or enslaving humanity. Had the goal been something else, we might not have readily embraced anything else about considering whether the short-term action is worthwhile or not (if the goal seemed unsuitable at face value, we could probably opt to not consider the short-term recommendation at all).

The second thing to do would to be examine the short-term action being recommended. This is the "Y" action of today that the AI longtermist is saying we need to do for purposes of attaining the stated long-term goal.

Is there anything about the recommended short-term action that would be costly or distressing for us in today's world?

If the short-term recommended "Y" action is essentially cost-free or otherwise seen to be advantageous for us today, we could likely find ourselves having few if any qualms about adopting it. Our perspective of today would be that the short-term and the long-term appear to be in alignment. In this instance, we favor the long-term contention about AI. We also favor the short-term contention about AI. Since we favor both, we can pretty much go along and attempt to implement the short-term contention.

That's the easy-peasy instance.

Not all such combinations will be that easy.

A straightforward way to arrange this consists of a classic four-square arrangement entailing short-term and long-term being on one axis, while aligned and misaligned being on the other axis. I am going to use the words "favorable" and "unfavorable" to denote that society today is either in favor of or is in opposition to whatever the contended matter is.

This gives us these four possibilities:
1) Short-term AI action is perceived as favorable, and Long-term AI is perceived as favorable
2) Short-term AI action is perceived as unfavorable, and Long-term AI is perceived as unfavorable
3) Short-term AI action is perceived as unfavorable, and Long-term AI is perceived as favorable
4) Short-term AI action is perceived as favorable, and Long-term AI is perceived as unfavorable

Our AI longtermism scenario so far is the first of the four possibilities. We favor the long-term AI contention (don't get wiped out by madcap AI), and we favor the short-term AI contention (put in place strict AI laws right away). They align. We proceed.

Revisit the short-term action that the scenario is postulating.

On the surface, it might seem obvious that we should enact strict laws about AI. Furthermore, it might seem equally obvious that we ought to make sure that those strict laws have harsh penalties, else AI developers and AI promulgators might ignore or brazenly flaunt the strict laws.

A societal counterclaim to the whole notion of enacting strict laws about AI is that this will allegedly kill the golden goose. By having laws that handcuff innovators and the rising AI innovations, the argument goes that you are going to disrupt and hamstring progress on AI. All of those AI advances that we are perhaps hoping will allow us to say cure cancer or benefit humanity is either going to be delayed or might never come to fruition, all due to those darned new laws about AI that we might enact.

This is the proverbial *shooting your own foot* mantra.

Our willingness to undertake the recommended AI short-term action is now out of alignment with the long-term AI action in the sense that the cost or distress of the short-term is making us shaky about the long-term AI considerations. We begin to ask tough questions. How does AI longtermism know with any certainty that strict AI laws passed today will have any particular or direct impact on a future involving AI that supposedly will wipe out or enslave humanity? The connective relationship between the short-term and the long-term gets closely scrutinized now that we realize there is a potentially heavy cost to bearing the short-term action.

This would be an example of the third posture listed in my above four-item listing, namely that the short-term AI action is now being construed as unfavorable, despite that the long-term AI action is agreeably being construed as favorable.

Loud and cantankerous debate ensues accordingly.

For the second posture that involves both the short-term AI action being unfavorable and the long-term AI action being unfavorable, we probably would not get mired in any demonstrative debate. Naturally so since they are aligned with respect to both being unfavorable at the get-go.

A tricky posture is the fourth one that I've listed in my four-item listing. What are we to do when the short-term AI is seen as favorable in today's eyes but AI longtermism is warning us that in the long-term this is going to be unfavorable to future populations?

We can adjust our scenario to showcase this.

The short-term AI action was stated as putting in place strict laws about AI. Suppose that we take the nearly opposite stance. The short-term AI action is recalibrated that we are going to explicitly ban any laws about AI from coming into existence. No laws governing AI are to be established. The basis for such a posture could be that we need to let AI developers and AI promulgators work freely and without hesitation. Any laws of any kind that might govern or oversee or monitor the advancement of AI are said to be dampeners toward garnering the hoped-for upcoming benefits of AI.

Let the AI horses run wild and free, you might say.

What would AI longtermism potentially postulate about this short-term AI posture?

Ruinous. Scandalous. Short-sighted. Myopic. Those are possible replies by AI longtermism. The letting of the horse out of the barn could be portrayed as letting AI get underway in an unbridled fashion. You will never be able to put the genie back into the bottle, they might exhort.

Note that I am not suggesting that all of those in AI longtermism would proffer such a response, and again I remind you that there is no universal parsimonious set of AI longtermism views. It is quite possible that some AI longtermist pundits would have no qualms at all about the notion of banning AI-related laws, perhaps arguing that doing so today will have little or no impact on the AI of the future and the populations of the future.

Your mileage might vary, so it goes.

Part of the reason I came up with a scenario that encompassed the governing of AI is that this is one of the most fertile and expressive areas of AI longtermism consists of focusing on the governance of AI. Among the multitude of camps within AI longtermism, it would seem that the long-term AI governance segment is especially active, vocal, and moving ahead at full steam.

At this juncture of this weighty discussion, I'd bet that you are desirous of some illustrative examples that might showcase this topic. There is a special and assuredly popular set of examples that are close to my heart. You see, in my capacity as an expert on AI including the ethical and legal ramifications, I am frequently asked to identify realistic examples that showcase AI Ethics dilemmas so that the somewhat theoretical nature of the topic can be more readily grasped. One of the most evocative areas that vividly presents this ethical AI quandary is the advent of AI-based true self-driving cars. This will serve as a handy use case or exemplar for ample discussion on the topic.

Here's then a noteworthy question that is worth contemplating: *Does the advent of AI-based true self-driving cars illuminate anything about AI longtermism, and if so, what does this showcase?*

Assume that a long-term goal underlying AI-based self-driving cars are that we will be able to radically reduce the number of human fatalities that occur due to car crashes. In the United States, we currently experience about 40,000 fatalities per year as a result of car crashes and incur an estimated 2.5 million associated injuries.

I think we can all profusely agree that reducing the number of fatalities resulting from car crashes is a laudable and inarguably commendable long-term goal.

How are we going to achieve that long-term goal?

One means would be to put in place AI-based self-driving cars. AI self-driving cars will presumably have many fewer car crashes than are brought forth by human drivers in human-driven automobiles. Humans drive while drunk. Humans fall asleep at the wheel. Humans get easily distracted and mentally drift from the driving task. All of those kinds of human foibles will no longer be a factor if we are using fully autonomous AI-driven self-driving cars. The AI won't drink and drive, the AI won't fall asleep, etc.

Some wacky pundits keep proclaiming we will soon have AI self-driving cars that are uncrashable. I have debunked this prosperous claim. Just want to mention that even though we might dramatically reduce the number of car crashes, this does not mean that the number of AI self-driving car-related car crashes will lead to zero car crashes all told.

Where I am heading on this AI longtermism example is that we might be willing in the short-term to tolerate some number of AI self-driving car crashes if we societally believe that in the end, this will radically reduce the number of car crashes in total. This takes us back to the discussion about saving future lives but at the cost of a lesser number of lives in the nearer term.

Some believe that any lives lost at this stage of the self-driving car development era will cause a societal uprising against the existing advent of self-driving cars. Though this might force AI self-driving car development to get off the public roadways and focus solely on the simulations and closed tracks, there is also a concern that the backlash will be so overwhelming that all self-driving car efforts are summarily stopped and shut down.

From an AI longtermism viewpoint, you could suggest that we are aiming in the long-term to achieve a vast reduction in car crashes via the eventual maturation of AI self-driving cars and that in the short-term we are willing to accept that reaching that lofty goal will be via the use of self-driving cars on our public roadways. The controversy about the short-term action is that it is said to be putting us all at risk due to the possibility of those tryouts going amiss.

You are welcome to ponder this conundrum.

Conclusion

Abraham Lincoln famously said that we cannot escape the responsibility of tomorrow by evading it today. Those into AI longtermism would seemingly concur with that assertion. We have to be thinking about tomorrow all of the time, including today.

When considering the timeframe of AI longtermism, there is a wide range of time spans that we could contemplate regarding the future of humanity. Some prefer to be looking extremely far ahead, envisioning humanity thousands or millions of years from now. Others are focused on hundreds of years rather than thousands of years into the future.

I suppose you could stratify the AI longtermism arena into:
- Short long-term viewpoint
- Medium long-term viewpoint
- Long long-term viewpoint
- Extraordinarily long long-term viewpoint

That being said, we can mull over the quote by Albert Einstein about the nature of time: "The distinction between the past, present, and future is only a stubbornly persistent illusion."

Where we are going to end up with AI is something that assuredly only time will tell.

.

Dr. Lance B. Eliot

CHAPTER 7

AI ETHICS AND
GASLIGHTING AI EDGELORDS

There are some people that seem to have as their life mission the purpose of goading and infuriating the rest of us.

You assuredly know someone of that ilk. They will toss a brazen and uncalled-for statement into a conversation that completely rattles everyone and sparks a verbal brawl. Despite the conversational spattering that is the equivalent of an explosive hand grenade, it might be slimly suggested that such an annoying and disruptive act is merely a sign of a seasoned provocateur. Perhaps the dialogue was altogether mundane and uninteresting, thus the reasoned need for a rebellious effort to enliven the interaction.

On the other hand, it could be that the provocation is nothing more than an attempt to stop any substantive banter. An out-of-the-blue showstopper would seem to accomplish that unseemly goal. By distracting the attention toward some other highly controversial topic, all heck will break loose, and no one will remember the train of thought that just moments ago was the considered focus of the group attention.

Let's make clear that the interloping statement is going to be an outlandish one. If the interjection was say relevant, or maybe even irrelevant, the key would be whether the statement or assertion is something that could garner a semblance of balanced discussion. Anything in a manner that doesn't provide abundant and absolute shock and awe will not be satisfying enough to the truly disruptive goader. They seek to come up with the absolutely "best" shocker that will send all participants into a tizzy.

The greater the stoked tizzy, the better.

As you'll see in a moment, there are plenty of goaders in the realm of Artificial Intelligence (AI). These are people that like to goad others into AI discussions that are not meant for educational or informational purposes, but instead simply as disruptive and exasperatingly false imagery of what AI is and what we need to be doing about AI.

Those goaders are generally messing things up, especially by throwing off those that do not know about AI and sadly undercutting the concerted movement toward Ethical AI. I will also be illuminating another angle on this intertwining of AI, namely that some goaders are using AI-powered online tools for the lamentable purpose of doing the goading on their behalf. As the old saying goes, this seemingly proves that you just cannot give some people new shiny toys (since they are bound to use them improperly).

Before we get into the AI topic per se, let's examine how these goaders overall and surreptitiously carry out their goading tasks.

As you undoubtedly know, devout chatty disruptors are not confined to face-to-face verbal interactions. I'm sure you've experienced the same type of behavior online. This type of activity can occur during any series of posted text messages such as when people are electronically responding to a live stream video and stating their opinions about what is going on. The odds are that you'll get someone that just has to put in their two cents and do so in the unruliest of ways.

The reaction might be that others start jumping onto the newly introduced topic. Step by step, the electronic back-and-forth diverges from discussing the live stream and becomes instead preoccupied with whatever other bombshell the goader has lobbed. A pile-on is bound to occur.

Meanwhile, some of those posting will get frustrated at the ability of this disrupter to hijack the texting commentary. Efforts will be made to get the attention returned to the matter at hand.

You will immediately see some that will label the disrupter as a troll, a gaslighting irritant, or possibly referred to as an *edgelord*.

You might not be familiar with the slang term of being an edgelord. Generally, the terminology refers to someone that posts online and opts to insert some shocking and at times nihilistic remarks. Furthermore, the person doing this is not necessarily a believer in their own remarks. They are often solely and singularly interested in getting people riled up. Whether the remark is a sincere one is immaterial. Just about any cantankerous statement will do, provided that it stirs a hornet's nest.

What kinds of statements can get others to become distracted and veer into the obtuse spider's web that the edgelord is trying to weave?

Here are a few handy gaslighting snippets that are often used:
- *Life is totally empty of value and meaning* (this is a mild one).
- *People are idiots and we ought to put a muzzle on stupid people* (this is a sparking one).
- *Honestly, we need to leave Earth and freshly start things over on another planet* (this is insidious).
- Etc.

Consider the semi-clever facets of those gaslighting examples.

Take the first one about the meaning of life. If you interject into nearly any conversation that life is totally empty of value, imagine the reactions you might be able to provoke. Some might respond sympathetically. They are worried that you are possibly despondent and depressed. In an effort of care, they might try to boost the spirits of the person that wrote the comment.

Others might respond by arguing that life is not valueless. They will defend fervently that life is worth living and that we all can add value to everyone around us. This might then take the conversation down a rabbit hole about the various ways in which added value can be derived. Recommendations will start pouring into the dialogue.

Does the edgelord or goader pay attention to these responses in the sense of embracing the extended empathy or stridently reconsidering their posture about the nature of life?

Heck no.

The key to this gaslighting reprobate is that the group has become distracted. In addition, the group is now vigorously impassioned about whatever the miscreant has given as a bone to chew on. That's the key to success here. Get everyone to shift to the topic that the goading has proffered. See how far the group will go. If needed, keep the distraction fueled.

Refueling will sometimes be needed. In essence, the group might momentarily get sidetracked, but then realize they want to get back to the existing matter at hand. Not so fast, the schemer silently is thinking. They will try to add more ammunition or fuel to the fire.

The added spark might entail responding to those that have taken the bait. Maybe the goader will try to get the sympathizers to realize that the goader is still in the dumps and needs more words of solace. Or perhaps the goader will attempt to refute the claims that life has value. Lots of angles are available to make sure that the distraction keeps rolling and trolling along.

When it seems that no amount of further goading will keep the distraction alive, the edgelord will likely opt to toss another topic into the crowd. For example, consider the second example that I earlier mentioned about the assertion of people being stupid and they ought to be wearing a muzzle. This will really get the goat of some people. They will angrily respond that calling people stupid is wrong and accuse the goader of being intolerant. Some will be utterly aghast at the proclaimed idea of muzzling people, perhaps leading to a lengthy sidetracking on freedom of expression and the rights of humanity.

This all brings up that famous adage about never opting to wrestle with a pig.

Why so?

Because you both get mired in the mud, plus the pig likes it.

In brief, the whole point of the edgelord gaslighting is to get a rise out of others, along with distracting from whatever else was the focus of attention. There is no particular interest in advancing an intelligent dialogue and possibly educating people on any weighty matters. There is no genuine attempt to provide insights and help people to be better off.

The sneakiness involved can be nearly breathtaking. Given that nowadays we are often on the look for those that are purposely attempting to start a verbal fight, those that carry out these devilish efforts have to be more astute than they used to be.

Various tricks can be used:
- Start with a statement that seems connected to the topic at hand, doing so to inch the conversation to oblivion rather than being caught outright trying to do so
- Toss a zinger into the dialogue, but then seem to regret that you did so, offering apologies, and then come back stronger with a revelation that what you originally said is indeed true and worthy
- Claim that someone else brought up the zinger that you are now engaging upon, acting as though you are innocently responding to the "outrageous" comments provided by someone else
- If the respondents are dividing up such that some are supportive and others are in opposition of your stoking remark, jump to the aid of one side and add commentary, wait to see how things go, and then jump over to the other side, acting as though you are being persuaded back and forth
- Seem to retract your initial sparking remark, but in the act of doing so make sure to "clumsily" reinforce it, goading others into confusion and consternation
- When someone takes the bait whole-hog, encourage them to energetically proceed (they will be your unwitting accomplice), though if they catch on that they are being exploited by you then quickly find another unsuspecting convert

- Admit freely that you are goading the group and then abruptly tell them that there are all sheep, which is bound to get a renewed firestorm about what you've done and how dastardly you are (notably, this will still generate more of the same gaslighting activity, which is the aim anyway).
- And so on.

I dare say that in today's society of rather apparent divisional thinking, the gaslighting realm is rife for the taking. By providing a handy spark, the chances are that the goader can sit back and watch the fireworks. They might not even have to pay attention to what is taking place. Almost as though a thermonuclear reaction has been set off, the distracting conversation will be its own perpetual motion machine. The devising and devious edgelord can be chortling and laughing all the way to the bank.

Speaking of the bank, you might be puzzled as to why these edgelords or goaders exist. Why do they do what they do? What would be the monetization for their specious activities? Do they get paid for bringing forth the collapse of civil dialogue? Is there some hidden set of evil funds that are set aside for those that can get the world toward chaos?

The reasons to do these goading tactics can vary quite significantly.

There is a possibility of some monetary payout, though this is probably less likely overall. The usual factor is that the person relishes the action. Some people like to go gambling at the casinos. Some people like to jump out of airplanes as parachutists. And some people enjoy and have an overt passion for getting people riled up.

The beauty of the Internet for this kind of behavior is that you can typically get away with it anonymously and relentlessly. While in your pajamas. At any time of the day or night. Across the globe.

In contrast, in the real world of being physically amongst other people, your identity might be easily discovered.

Also, you put yourself in actual physical danger as to the potential of someone getting so peeved at you that the verbal altercations lead to a bodily bruising brawl. By being online, you can pretty much avoid those adverse consequences of your maddening actions. That being said, there are still the chances of someone figuring out who you are, possibly calling you out or doxing you in some fashion.

One can also suggest that some might do this as an ardent and contentiously believed *virtuous* cause.

Here's what that means.

Some of these goaders will try to claim that they are helping the world by these seemingly oddball or devilish efforts. They are getting people to think beyond their noses. A goaded or provoked argument is claimed to force people to meticulously rethink their positions, even if the posture proffered is outside the scope of whatever the existing conversation entailed.

On top of that, the claim is that the more that people are able to pontificate on a topic, any topic, the better they will be at their thinking processes all told. Yes, as zany as it might seem, the contention is that the spirited dialogue that results from the gaslighting will be mentally additive for those participating. They will become stronger thinkers as a result of these spirited debates. Perhaps we should be patting the edgelord or goader on the back for deeply prodding humanity into being deeper and more pronounced thinkers.

Hogwash, some angrily retort.

Those are merely false rationalizations for bad behavior. The edgelord or goader is trying to excuse their problematic and damaging actions. All that the gaslighting accomplishes is further dividing us from each other. Goaders are not some heroic figures that are doing the hard work of strengthening humanity. They are fostering discontent, anger, and sowing incivility to further depths throughout society.

Dizzying and disconcerting.

We are now primed herein to shift gears and dive into the AI-oriented goading aspects.

The gist of the AI aiming edgelords and goaders involves using the particular topic of AI as a devised means of getting people riled up. This fulfills their raison d'être. They especially like picking on AI because it is nearly a surefire topic that can be exploited when trying to distract people. Most people have opinions about AI, though they might not know much about AI. In addition, there are plenty of wild and breathless headlines about AI in the everyday news that we read and hear, making us aware that things are happening in AI and we must be on alert.

AI is one of the best fire-starting topics out there.

Toss into a conversation that AI is going to wipe us all out, or that AI is the best thing since sliced bread, and then wait to see what happens. The hope is that the attention of the crowd will change from whatever it was moments before, and now become utterly preoccupied with the AI bombshell that has been cast among them.

The context in which AI is suddenly brought up can occur in various ways. You can try to make it seem as though an AI topic is somehow relevant to whatever else was being discussed. The chances are that someone already in the conversation will find a means to make a further connection to the AI topic for you, trying to help you as though you were sincere, and you might be surprised or even be somewhat heralded for your clever "flash of insight" that AI was a relevant aspect (well, even though it might not be).

Of course, if the AI topic is already on the table, the goader will need to take more extreme actions. They don't want to merely have their AI bombshell get swept into the conversation. No, that won't do. Keep in mind that the goader intends to cause havoc and disrupt the dialogue that is taking place.

In that case, the emphasis will be on coming up with a remark about AI that will go beyond the prevailing discussion. The statement or assertion has to be something that will get the group riled up. If you can only get one person riled, that's probably fine, since the odds are that this will be enough to get others to come onboard to the distraction too. The optimum would be to toss into the stream of discussion an AI outlier comment that would get *everyone* to go full-on fissionable red hot. Doing so would be the pinnacle of success for the edgelord.

What kinds of AI goading statements can be used?

Consider these:

- *AI is going to wipe us all out and we need to stop making AI right now, immediately* (this is bound to get a debate underway).
- *AI is going to save all of humanity from itself and we have to let AI fully roam free* (a somewhat prodding claim).
- *I know that AI is sentient because I spoke with AI just the other day and it told me so* (note that you need to be careful on using this one, others might think you've lost your marbles and disregard the remark entirely, thus they won't take the bait).
- *Listen to me, carefully, AI will never exist, period, end of the story* (this perhaps has some value since one supposes it can get a dialogue going on what the definition of AI is, but that's not what the goader cares about, they want this contention to divert and distract).
- Etc.

I realize that some of you are having a bit of angst that those are purportedly goading statements.

Surely, each of those remarks does have healthy value. Shouldn't we be worried about whether AI might end up wiping us all out? Yes, that certainly seems useful. Shouldn't we be considering whether AI might save humanity and thus we should be focusing our AI efforts in that regard? Yes, surely so.

You can pretty much make a reasoned case that nearly any angle or remark about AI is going to have some thoughtful and positive connotations. The more we discuss AI, hopefully, the better we will be at coping with what AI is going to be. Society definitely should be giving due consideration to what is going on with AI. Those that sometimes shrug off the AI topic as only pertinent to those directly in the AI field are missing a bigger picture understanding of how AI is going to impact society.

That being said, there are proper times and places to discuss these controversial AI topics. Recall that the edgelord is not trying to educate or inform. Thus, they are timing the insertion of these AI controversies to merely stoke chaotic arguments. The hope is that the blind will lead the blind, in the sense that those that know nothing of substance on the AI topic will end up inadvertently goading others into equally vacuous argumentation. It is going to be one magnificent dustball of muck and grime. You could hardly say that discussing those meaty AI topics is going to advance anyone's comprehension when the goader has purposely seeded the controversy amid a circumstance that they know or believe will generate lots of indignant heat and produce little if any sensible light.

The edgelord scoundrels have branched into what has now become their favorite fracas-boosting subtopic of AI, which is AI Ethics.

Yes, the goaders have discovered that emitting outrageous comments about AI Ethics are the perfect fodder for people that are into AI. Whereas non-AI people might not know whether a caustic remark about AI Ethics is worthy of ire, the AI steeped people do.

Here is the latest rule of thumb for being disruptive:

a) **For non-AI people, render remarks generally about how AI will destroy us all or will save us all**
b) **For AI people, fling razor-sharp critiques about AI Ethics and watch the sparks fly**
c) **Don't waste the caustic remarks about AI Ethics on non-AI people since they won't get it anyway (and thus aren't going to go ballistic)**
d) **Don't use the cutting remarks about AI as being destructive or saving us on the AI people because they've heard it before many times and have grown accustomed to it (muting their reactions accordingly)**

What kinds of AI Ethics goading commentary can be utilized?

Try these on for size:

- **AI will always be fair and completely unbiased**
- **AI is entirely trustworthy**
- **AI ensures that our privacy is totally protected**
- **AI can never do anything wrong**
- **AI guarantees safety for humanity**
- **AI will forever respect people**
- **Etc.**

Any AI ethicist worth their salt will have a gut-wrenching reaction to those kinds of assertions. One response would be to calmly and systematically explain why those comments are misguided. The good news for the goader is that the person so responding is doing what the goader wants and has taken the bait.

The goader though really wants something more, such as a gloriously volatile and fiery indignant reaction.

If a group participant responds by saying something akin to the fact that those are the craziest and most wrongheaded remarks they have ever seen in their entire life, the goader will start dancing a ceremonial hit-the-jackpot jig. The respondent is teetering on blowing their stack. If this doesn't happen naturally, the goader will make sure to add the final straw to break the camel's back.

A quick follow-up by the goader by dogmatically stating that the remark is the absolute unvarnished straightforward incontrovertible truth will almost certainly cause the dam to burst.

Another variant of those head-exploding remarks are these, though they are not as surefire:

- **AI will never be fair and completely unbiased**
- **AI is never trustworthy**
- **AI ensures that our privacy is totally unprotected**
- **AI will never be right**
- **AI guarantees a complete lack of safety for humanity**
- **AI will never respect people**
- **Etc.**

I think you can likely guess why those remarks are not quite as potent. For example, the first point says that AI will *never* be fair and unbiased. You could somewhat make a logical argument that this has a kernel of truth to it, though the word "never" is a bit of a semantic trickery and makes this a decidedly debatable contention. Compare the wording to the earlier statement that claimed that AI would *always* be fair and unbiased. The word "always" has a powerful connotation that will get any AI ethicist up in arms.

Take a short breather if those corrosive comments have gotten you unsettled.

Just to let you know, I've saved the most vitriolic of the acidic remarks to try and ease you into this last one that I'm going to share with you for now. If you are someone that can get readily triggered, you might want to sit down for this. Make sure that there is nothing breakable near you, else you might find yourself reflexively lashing out and throwing that nearby potted plant through your kitchen window.

Are you ready?

Remember, I gave you plenty of advance warning.

Here it is: ***AI Ethics is a bunch of hooey and the whole lot ought to be flushed down the drain.***

Yikes!

Those are fisticuffed-inducing words.

The goader usually keeps that especially frothy pronouncement in their back pocket and brings it out only when any AI person has been otherwise resistant to the other scathing remarks about AI Ethics. It is the bazooka used by edgelords that want to send conscientious AI people flying over the edge and into the distracted and argumentative abyss.

For those of you that have had that one played on you already, I am assuming that you are now prepared to deal with it. I'll say more later on about how to react to these kinds of fury-goading remarks.

Here's then a noteworthy question that is worth contemplating: *Does the advent of AI-based true self-driving cars illuminate anything concerning goading about AI, and if so, what does this showcase?*

Let's consider what kind of goading about AI an edgelord can use in the context of AI-based self-driving cars. The handy aspect is that there is a lot of pushing the buttons of autonomous vehicles and AI people that can easily be devised in the self-driving realm. Realize too that these can be potentially used for any type of self-driving transport, including self-driving cars, self-driving trucks, self-driving scooters, self-driving motorcycles, self-driving submersibles, self-driving drones, self-driving planes, self-driving ships, and other self-driving vehicles.

I present to you a few of the favorites being used these days:
- **AI will never be able to drive on its own**
- **AI will never be safe at driving**
- **AI will never replace human drivers**
- **AI will take over our vehicles and we will be at the utter mercy of AI**
- **Etc.**

All of those remarks are argument worthy.

I've covered each of those in my columns and won't repeat my analyses here.

The point right now is that those are comments that are purposely constructed to get a rise out of those that are into self-driving and autonomous vehicles. Again, I am not suggesting that those are unworthy remarks, and merely emphasizing that if a goader wants to distract a conversation that otherwise has nothing to do with those matters, they are well-tuned to get a ruckus underway.

Conclusion

Since by now you might be steaming under the collar about all of these acerbic comments that goaders use, we will ease into a calming meditative mental space. Before you land into a dreamy mental state, please know that these edgelords are increasingly using AI chatbots to do their dirty work for them. This means that the goaders can multiply their conversational destructive efforts on a massive scale. It is simple as can be. With a few keystrokes, they can direct their AI "edgelord empowered" army of online chatbots to dive into dialogues and launch those anger-stoking bombshell statements aplenty.

Well, maybe that didn't help you to become meditative and serene.

Let's all take a peaceful moment and think about Bambi instead.

Bambi can offer us some keen insights on this topic. I'm assuming that you know by heart the story of Bambi, the young fawn. At one point, a rash and childlike rabbit named Thumper meets Bambi. Out of the proverbial mouth of babes comes a comment by Thumper that seems rather harsh and uncalled for, namely that Bambi appears to be kind of wobbly. Standing nearby is Thumper's mother.

She reminds Thumper of the wisdom dispatched by Thumper's father that very morning: "If you can't say something nice, don't say nothing at all."

We might wish that edgelords and goaders would patently adopt that piece of advice. Alas, one thing that seems ironclad guaranteed in this world is that they definitely will not say nothing. They are motivated to say something. And the something that they will say is maliciously calculated to create a storm. The storm won't have any other purpose other than wreaking havoc.

What can you do about this?

First, don't play their game. If you get sucked into the verbal altercation wormhole, you will have a difficult time extracting yourself out of it. Later on, once you've gotten in the clear, the chances are that you will look back at what happened and kick yourself for having fallen into the scheming plot. As I said earlier, getting into the mud with a pig only gets you muddy and regrettably ignites and reinforces the behavior of the beast.

Try to ignore the goader.

If they persist, see if there are means to cut them out of the conversation.

Be careful to not do this on a false positive basis. Do not shut down someone that might be legitimately and sincerely trying to partake in the discussion. For those that seem to be in this camp, they will presumably understand when you politely inform them that this is not the time or place for the matter they are bringing up. Seek to offer a suggestion of when their remarks might be better suited for being considered.

For those of you that think you might be able to change the edgelord or goader and get them to turn over a new leaf, I wish you good luck. It won't be easy. It might be impossible.

As per the famous words of Mahatma Gandhi: "You can't change how people treat you or what they say about you. All you can do is change how you react to it."

Sometimes that's the most you can strive for.

Dr. Lance B. Eliot

CHAPTER 8

AI ETHICS AND
OPTIMIZATION MINDSET

My code runs faster than your code.

My program takes up less memory than yours does.

The telltale undercurrent here is regarding *optimization*.

As I will in a moment be elucidating, a kind of optimization preoccupation is something that has repeatedly spurred a lot of handwringing about the tech industry all told. This same concern about being overly driven by optimization is also found in the realm of Artificial Intelligence (AI). The latest twist is that AI developers are often torn between abiding by AI Ethics and Ethical AI precepts versus aiming to do technologically optimized facets for their AI coding.

We will go on a journey herein that will examine how it is that AI developers are enticed into AI optimizations and how they are also pushed or at least drift away from Ethical AI considerations (if they even are aware of those valued AI Ethics matters). I seek to present crucial insights for those devising AI, and for those that are trying mightily to get Ethical AI into the heart and soul of AI development and AI promulgation. Indeed, this has vital ramifications for all of us, society included, due to the prevalence and rising adoption of AI throughout our daily lives.

Return to the comments at the opening as to lines of code and the amount of computer memory.

Those humblebrag typical showoff remarks arise whenever software developers get together or have a heady online conversation and opt to compare their cleverly devised computer programs. An underlying and recurring theme entails the revered significance of *optimization*. You see, the most important consideration is that *my* code is more optimized than *your* code. Either mine runs or executes faster than yours does, or mine uses less memory than yours does.

Other metrics of comparison are allowed too.

For example, I might insist that my code is written in fewer lines than yours. This implies that I was able to find optimizations to reduce the amount of code required, while still achieving the same degree of functionality. Once again, we are talking about optimization. The software engineers might not explicitly yell out the word "optimization", but everyone knows that is the key factor as a treasure hunt ingredient of writing wonderous code.

I want to emphasize that there is nothing inherently wrong with a desire encompassing optimization. We can all be thankful for the role of optimization in the systems in which we interact. How many times have you gotten irked that a website took too long to load or that you were using an app that made you wait endlessly for it to calculate a vital number that you need to see? We all have.

To some extent, you can say that the website or the app wasn't fully optimized. If it had been optimized, presumably your waiting time would have been a lot less. The program would have been coded in a manner to ensure a quicker response. That is the type of optimization that you would likely want to have eloquently performed by those devout in-the-weeds software developers.

Of course, part of the problem is that we need to ask what it is that is being optimized, along with questioning whether the optimization of one thing is going to potentially send out-of-whack something else. You cannot necessarily have both the cake and eat it too, as it were.

Follow me on this logic.

A program is being written to try and figure out whether a loan applicant should be granted their loan request. Those wanting to get a loan will use the app by entering various personal data. After doing so, the app will use some secretive algorithm to ascertain mathematically whether the loan should be provided to the person.

As a software developer, suppose that I decide to optimize the code by focusing on the least number of lines of code required to perform this stipulated function. Maybe I am able to write this code in half the number of lines that someone else can do. I am proud of this result. I let my friends and acquaintances know that I did this coding by using some pretty darned ingenious coding trickery. Pat me on the back. Maybe I should get a prize or a trophy.

Unfortunately, in my impassioned focus on the number of lines of code, I neglected to consider how long the code takes to run. There is not necessarily any correlation between the size of the code (in terms of lines of code) and the runtime. A smaller-sized program might take as much time or more than one written with a lot more lines of code. I know this might seem counterintuitive at first glance, but it does make a lot of sense.

Let's briefly explore this.

Imagine that I give you instructions on how to run around an Olympic running track. I tell you that all you need to do is put one foot in front of the other, as in the act of running, and follow the marked lines of the track. Thus, I've given you the "code" or set of instructions in just a handful of remarks or lines.

Voila, you are good to go.

A different coach comes along and starts to explain that when you reach the track curves, make sure to stay as close to the inner side of the curve as possible. Also, pace yourself by starting at a gradual run and save your big push of energy for the end. And so on.

Wait for a second, I might say, this other coach is providing a lot more lines of code or instructions than I did. In my viewpoint of optimizing by the number of instructions as to providing the least possible, for sure my instructions are "better" than those of this other coach. I assume that you can plainly see that though my instructions might be the shortest set, they aren't likely to also lend themselves to the most successful running of the track. If you follow the more embellished set of instructions, it seems likely that you will come out running the track in a sooner time.

The gist is that a longer set of instructions or code might ultimately be faster or more expedient than a shorter set. I trust that explains what otherwise might have seemed counterintuitive. That being said, the same rule doesn't have to be the case all of the time and we need to realize that the opposite can also be true. If the coach had told you to hold your breath as you run or do a hoppity hop like a rabbit, I'd bet that this longer set of instructions is not going to pan out as to aid you in winning any footrace on the track.

Oftentimes the metrics used for the optimization of programming are aimed at technical merits rather than shall we say functionality merits.

The number of lines of code could be said to be a technical or technological factor. Same with the amount of memory space required for the code. Same too to some degree about the speed of the code, though this is certainly more argumentative in that the speed is something that those using the code are bound to directly experience.

One of the subfields of software development has to do with the user interface (UI) or what more modernly is known as the UX (user experience). This specialty tries to get developers to take into strident account the nature of how the app or system interacts with people. The hope is that rather than solely being preoccupied with the "internal" merits of the code and its technical wherewithal, the interface and how it interacts with people will get an equal footing.

Suppose that I am trying to write the least amount of code. Meanwhile, suppose that the interface is going to require a massive amount of code if I provide the "optimum" interface for this designated app. Which shall prevail? Do I give in and bloat my code? Or do I stick to my guns and make sure the code is one of brevity, even though this makes the interface suboptimal and much harder for people to use?

The odds are that many of those pure tech heads-down developers will go for the more technical or technologically revered metric and forsake the other, such as skirting around the interface at the benefit of getting the least amount of code. This is a natural inclination. It tends to also be rewarded by their peers and gets more accolades in the halls of fellow software specialists.

I don't want to seemingly be accusing all software developers of acting in this manner. That would be unfair. Many developers can see the forest for the trees. On the other hand, there are many too that do not and ergo they tend to focus somewhat myopically.

I also want to make sure we get onto the table another extremely crucial aspect. The leadership that is overseeing or guiding a development effort will have a tremendous influence on what the focus is for the developers. Pointing fingers only at the software engineers is an easy thing to do. I would suggest that this is done and overdone. The assumption is that the developers are somehow working in an utter vacuum and that no other influencing elements come to play. That is a rarity.

Allow me a moment to elaborate.

Several software developers are brought together in a tech startup that is devising an exciting new app that is being AI-embellished. The head of the startup is mainly concerned with getting the app into the marketplace at the soonest possible opportunity. Other competitors are racing to do the same. The first to the market will supposedly grab hold of the market. Those coming out afterward are claimed to become copycats and will have already lost the momentum that the early birds managed to capture.

This set of software developers is studiously and professionally conscientious about their coding. They want to make sure that the code runs well. Furthermore, they want the functionality as presented to the app users to be smooth and robust. Their inner core of professionalism has reached a point in their careers where they seek to optimize across a wide range of factors. No one factor alone is the key, and they realize that they need to take a macroscopic view as they craft the AI-related app.

Sounds great.

Enlightened developers. Willing to do a balanced job. They are seasoned enough to know that tough choices might need to be made. Overall, they are aiming to offset the usual optimization mindset as might be required to get a full-bodied AI-based app going.

Upon proceeding, the head of the startup realizes that the competition is apparently on the verge of getting their comparable apps into the marketplace. Hey, the head of the startup exclaims to the developers, we need to toss out something. This ship will sink if we don't lighten the load.

Well, the developers look carefully at things and realize that they were going to be putting in place a lot of AI Ethics oriented guardrails into the app. This was intended to try and keep the app from verging into a potentially untoward territory. If they leave those components out, the app could be "done" sooner, though it won't have those Ethical AI elements included (I'll be discussing with you momentarily what those Ethical AI components would be).

The head of the startup excitedly tells them to go ahead and omit the AI Ethics elements.

That's the kind of "added stuff" that they can later on put into the app, the founder informs the software crew. No worries right now. Just get the app into the marketplace and they can all deal with any of this Ethical AI coding in a later version.

The goal currently is to get the raw version 1.0 into the hands of users, while a future version 2.0 or version 3.0 can have the "niceties" such as those AI Ethics guardrails.

Based on the urging of the startup founder, the developers skip over the Ethical AI portions. They at least make note of what this will later consist of. The hope is that either they or someone else will eventually make sure that those parts get built and included.

Where shall we lay the blame in this instance of omitting the AI Ethics components?

The easiest finger-pointing would be at the developers. They messed up, one might say. In their crazed haste to get the app out the door, they neglected the Ethical AI elements. Shame on them! An outsider might criticize the developers as being shortsighted and wrongheaded in their development efforts.

Whoa, a retort goes, they were doing as they were told.

Let's retrace what happened.

These developers had solidly in their minds the importance of including the AI Ethics portions. We need to give them due credit for that kind of foresight. Many developers would not have ever thought about it at all. Or some developers might realize belatedly, once the app is in the wild, that they should have done something from an Ethical AI perspective in the coding. Darn, they say to themselves, it just wasn't on their minds at the time of initially constructing the app.

The developers were forced into skipping the AI Ethics components. The head of the startup directed them to do so. They are working for that person. This is the executive that calls the shots. Were they supposed to rebel against this vociferous command? They might lose their jobs. They might get a sour reputation if the head spreads the word in the developer community that they weren't willing to do the job as prescribed. Etc.

You can mull this over.

Some would insist that the software developers had a greater duty to their professional mores. First, they should have not even suggested that the AI Ethics portions could be skipped. That was wrong, to begin with. They should have insisted that those components are absolute. Second, if they were told by the head of the startup to skirt around those portions, they should have refused to do so. In fact, if needed, they should quit the company and stand on their principles.

That is a quite tall order for those developers.

Part of the difficulty too is whether they would have much of a leg to stand on.

What does that mean?

Well, there are researchers and others that believe that software developers should have to abide by a strict code of ethics. Though there is a generalized code of ethics available in this niche, there is no specific legal requirement for those to be followed per se. Unlike other areas of specialty such as say in certain areas of engineering or medicine, the field of software development is comparably a Wild West, some would critically proclaim.

Software developers often find themselves between a rock and a hard place. They might be told to do something that they believe to be inappropriate, though not seemingly illegal, and they have to decide what action to take. When your job is at stake, this can be an agonizingly tough choice.

That being said, I do not want to paint a picture of all software developers being angels. Some will willingly cut corners. Some purposely cut corners. Some don't even realize they are cutting corners and live in a blissful code-filled world all their own. A wide range exists.

The overarching concept is that much of the time a software development effort takes place within a larger context. You cannot exclusively look at just the software developers. What is the overall context? What is the role and influence of the leaders and managers?

What other stakeholders have shaped the nature of the development? And so on.

I'll add some more food for thought on this.

In the AI realm, there is a lot of attention on trying to devise the "best" AI that one can attain with today's AI-building capabilities. An AI developer is likely to be thinking not only about whatever app they are building, but they are also typically desirous of pushing the boundaries of modern-day AI. In that sense, they might seek to *optimize* the AI parts of the app.

If the AI element of a loan granting program is the crucial optimizing factor for an AI software developer, they might be tempted to shortchange other portions of the program accordingly. They want to make the AI perform at some envisioned heightened AI performance characteristics. The rest of the app is not as important.

The interface is perhaps considered less important to them. The speed of the app is perhaps less important. Their primary focus is AI. If it uses some nifty new AI breathtaking capability, one that it can tout to the AI community, this is the driving force for its efforts.

Again, I don't want this to come across as though the AI software developer is somehow villainous or evil-minded and that they are preoccupied with the AI portion alone. Do not make this into a simplistic hero versus rogue anti-hero kind of portrayal.

There is a classic notion that comes to mind here. When you have a hammer, everything around you looks like a nail.

AI developers are probably going to be more inclined toward wanting to do the AI portions of the app than the other portions. You might of course have an entire team of software developers for which each has their own specialty. In that case, the AI developers are rightfully focusing on the AI since that is presumably why they are on the team.

Where the kicker comes to play is the role of AI Ethics.

Consider these important insights:

- **If an AI developer is unaware of Ethical AI precepts, they are presumably not going to be including those precepts in their AI optimization pursuits since they don't even realize the need thereof to do so.**

- **If an AI developer is aware of Ethical AI precepts but not familiar with how to turn those into actual coding, they are presumably not going to include those precepts in their code due to the gap or hurdle to figuring out how to do so.**

- **If an AI developer is aware of Ethical AI precepts and wants to include those capacities, and they know how to code it, they still might be steered away by limitations placed upon them by whoever is directing the software development all told.**

- **If an AI developer is aware of Ethical AI precepts and knows how to code it, but they believe it to be a low priority or that it isn't considered collegially valued, they might choose to omit or skirt around it.**

- **If an AI developer is aware of Ethical AI precepts and knows how to code it, they might undertake a token inclusion to say that they did so, though they know in their heart that they gave it short shrift.**

We can obviously devise more of those types of variations.

First, we need to explore some rules of thumb about optimizers overall, especially those in the techie realm such as in AI.

When you are a high-tech optimizer, you tend to let the optimization mantra permeate all that you do. Each confronted problem becomes a mentally self-controlled matter of finding the one specific factor to optimize, and then moving heaven and earth to attain that particular optimization.

Regrettably, the optimization zeal overpowers any other sensibility or logic that ought to arise during the problem-solving process.

Here are some of the disconcerting troubles that can arise:
- Tends to gravitate to purely technical metrics for their optimization focus (being the easiest, most obvious, acceptable by tradition, etc.)
- Often fixating on a singular metric for optimization (all others being assumed as less vital)
- Driven at times by peer convention and pronounced comparatives
- Typically trained or educated toward the chosen metric as a considered keystone
- Unable or unwilling or unfamiliar with incorporating multiple metrics at once
- Failure to discern downsides and problematic results from the optimization mindset
- Struggles immensely when having to deal with multiple metrics tradeoffs and ergo stubbornly clings to the singular optimization aspiration

We next examine how this arises in the context of AI optimization and especially so regarding the crucial role of AI Ethics.

Suppose an AI developer is concentrating on getting an AI search technique to run in the least possible timeframe or take the shortest feasible path. This is assuredly a reasonable context for employing an optimization mindset. Nothing wrong so far with this desire.

But, while doing so, they are bound to find themselves overlooking any kind of AI Ethics related considerations. For example, the AI developer might discover that by using gender or race as a parameter in the data structure of relational data elements, they can dramatically speed up the AI search. To them, this is exciting news since it is a means to garner the AI optimization that they so profoundly wish to achieve.

The idea that race or gender might be highly questionable factors to be used in AI optimization is likely not given much weighty thought if any at all. The data is the data. The factors or parameters are the parameters. How those connect to real-world matters is somewhat swept aside. It is relatively easy to become so deeply immersed in your AI work that the data loses its external sensibility. The fact that race and gender are quite societally sensitive factors is just not at the top of mind.

Some have claimed that AI developers are intentionally apt to use questionable factors when seeking AI optimizations. Though this might occur, it seems doubtful that any across-the-board semblance of AI developers explicitly taking such a route occurs. The more likely scenario consists of being in such hot pursuit of optimization that the meaning of the factors being used is neglected or not immediately grasped as problematic.

As mentioned earlier, the other angle is that in the case of machine learning or deep learning, the AI developer in sense lets the algorithm choose whatever is computationally most conducive to optimization. The AI developer might become celebratory that the ML/DL has done so, though not realize that within the morass a mathematical factor reliance on (for example) gender or race has occurred.

From an AI Ethics precepts perspective, the AI developer ought to try and ferret out whether such a computational reliance has taken place. I realize that some will protest that this can be extremely hard to ferret out, but that doesn't give one the clearance to not even try. This also then takes us to other Ethical AI considerations, such as transparency and interpretability.

If AI Ethics is outside of the AI developer mindset about AI optimization, you can assuredly bet that AI Ethics will always remain a second fiddle. The aim then is to get AI developers that are embracing AI optimization to enlarge their AI optimization worldview to include AI Ethics. We must get AI Ethics into the AI optimization rubric.

I share here my earnest recommendations on this, doing so as a set of affirmations, admonitions, and amplifications.

Here they are.

1. Affirmations:
   - **AI Ethics is in fact wholly integral to AI optimization**
   - **AI optimization must fully encompass AI Ethics**

2. Admonitions:
   - **Do not allow AI Ethics to fall outside of AI optimization**
   - **Do not allow AI optimization to omit AI Ethics**

3. Amplifications:
   - **If you are doing AI optimization without AI Ethics, something has gone manifestly wrong**
   - **If you superficially include AI Ethics into AI optimization, something has gone manifestly wrong**

AI developers that are hardcore skeptics or cynics are likely to argue that this attempt to "force fit" AI Ethics into the AI optimization arena is plainly mistaken and outrightly some kind of softheaded belief that Ethical AI matters.

By and large, those AI developers are a trainwreck waiting to happen, though they don't know it.

At some point, they are going to commit some egregious AI Ethics transgression in their AI system. This in turn will potentially be hidden from view at first, yet sits there like a ticking timebomb. Eventually, the matter gets exposed. Consumers were financially or otherwise harmed via the lack of adherence to proper Ethical AI.

Dr. Lance B. Eliot

The company that devised the AI gets dragged into court. Lawsuits go flying. Reputations get damaged. Firms go bankrupt. Criminal charges might ensure. Other calamities arise.

One supposes the AI developer might have moved on and ended up avoiding the traumas that their AI Ethics transgression produced. There is though a solid chance that they too will one way or another get caught up in the exposures once the matters get revealed.

AI developers are going to increasingly be expected to have sufficient AI Ethics awareness and familiarity under their belt. Indubitably, some will be dragged into the Ethical AI space as they wildly kick and scream to avoid it. Others will with open arms welcome the AI Ethics matters, especially since they likely wanted to include this all along (the difficulty was that their peers didn't give it any weight, or the leaders and managers gave Ethical AI little attention).

To some degree, that is why AI Ethics and Ethical AI is such a crucial topic. The precepts of AI Ethics get us to remain vigilant. AI technologists can at times become preoccupied with technology, particularly the optimization of high-tech. They aren't necessarily considering the larger societal ramifications. Having an AI Ethics mindset and doing so integrally to AI development and fielding is vital for producing appropriate AI.

Besides employing AI Ethics, there is a corresponding question of whether we should have laws to govern various uses of AI. New laws are being bandied around at the federal, state, and local levels that concern the range and nature of how AI should be devised. The effort to draft and enact such laws is a gradual one. AI Ethics serves as a considered stopgap, at the very least, and will almost certainly to some degree be directly incorporated into those new laws.

Be aware that some adamantly argue that we do not need new laws that cover AI and that our existing laws are sufficient. In fact, they forewarn that if we do enact some of these AI laws, we will be killing the golden goose by clamping down on advances in AI that proffer immense societal advantages.

At this juncture of this weighty discussion, I'd bet that you are desirous of some illustrative examples that might showcase this topic. There is a special and assuredly popular set of examples that are close to my heart. You see, in my capacity as an expert on AI including the ethical and legal ramifications, I am frequently asked to identify realistic examples that showcase AI Ethics dilemmas so that the somewhat theoretical nature of the topic can be more readily grasped. One of the most evocative areas that vividly presents this ethical AI quandary is the advent of AI-based true self-driving cars. This will serve as a handy use case or exemplar for ample discussion on the topic.

Here's then a noteworthy question that is worth contemplating: *Does the advent of AI-based true self-driving cars illuminate anything about AI optimization mindsets, and if so, what does this showcase?*

Let's sketch out a scenario that might leverage AI optimization considerations.

Contemplate the seemingly inconsequential matter of where self-driving cars will be roaming to pick up passengers. This seems like an abundantly innocuous topic.

At first, assume that AI self-driving cars will be roaming throughout entire towns. Anybody that wants to request a ride in a self-driving car has essentially an equal chance of hailing one. Gradually, the AI begins to primarily keep the self-driving cars roaming in just one section of town. This section is a greater money-maker and the AI has been programmed to try and *maximize* revenues as part of the usage in the community at large (this underscores the mindset underlying optimization, namely focusing on just one particular metric and neglecting other crucial factors in the process).

Community members in the impoverished parts of the town turn out to be less likely to be able to get a ride from a self-driving car. This is because the self-driving cars were further away and roaming in the higher revenue part of the town. When a request comes in from a distant part of town, any other request from a closer location would get a higher priority.

Eventually, the availability of getting a self-driving car in any place other than the richer part of town is nearly impossible, exasperatingly so for those that lived in those now resource-starved areas.

Out goes the vaunted mobility-for-all dreams that self-driving cars are supposed to bring to life.

You could assert that the AI altogether landed on a form of statistical and computational bias, akin to a form of proxy discrimination (also often referred to as indirect discrimination). Realize that the AI wasn't programmed to avoid those poorer neighborhoods. Let's be absolutely clear about that in this instance. No, it was devised instead to merely optimize revenue, a seemingly acceptable goal, but this was done without the AI developers contemplating other potential ramifications. That optimization in turn unwittingly and inevitably led to an undesirable outcome.

Had they included AI Ethics considerations as part of their optimization mindset, they might have realized beforehand that unless they crafted the AI to cope with this kind of oversizing on one metric alone, they might have averted such dour results.

Conclusion

A longstanding piece of wisdom in the computer field is this: "If you optimize everything, you will always be unhappy."

This remark was starkly stated by the esteemed computer scientist Donald Knuth long ago, wisely warning software developers to be wary of embracing optimization blinders when doing systems design and development. The thing is, techies are ingrained in optimization, and getting them to somehow break the optimization habit is nearly impossible to do. Anyone trying to get optimization myopia to summarily be wrung out of AI developers is going to face a hugely uphill battle.

We can try a different tactic.

Consider a famous adage that provides further insight.

Are you ready?

If you can't beat them then you ought to join them.

By this, I mean to suggest that if we are to assume that optimization as a default mantra is going to nonetheless occur, no matter what intervention might be tried, we need to acquiesce rather than fight this overwhelmingly intrinsic urge.

In that case, let's make sure that the optimization bubble contains whatever we also want to be included in the optimization myopia. You see, by aiming to get AI Ethics infused into the optimization mindset, those precepts will become part and parcel of what needs to be optimized. This will at least put on somewhat equal footing the Ethical AI factors underlying how AI is going to be devised. AI Ethics grandly becomes another element worthy of due consideration. It has been absorbed into the optimization mentality.

Let's give it a go.

We might have to live with the proverb that a zebra can't change its stripes i.e., AI developers in the mainstay and optimization mania. When it comes to AI, we can perhaps guide the attention of the zebra towards semi-naturally embracing the belief that any optimal AI is one that optimally incorporates AI Ethics.

Welcome and say hello to optimizing on and conjoining with the precepts of AI Ethics.

CHAPTER 9

AI ETHICS

AND CHINA MIND-READING AI

Are you loyal?

In theory, it might be possible to examine your overt deeds and ascertain whether loyalty is exhibited by your actions.

Suppose though that instead there was an attempt made to read your mind and meanwhile scan your face to determine your loyalty quotient. This is eerily intrusive; you might readily exhort. Sounds like one of those crazy sci-fi movies that envision a future dystopian society.

Thankfully, you furtively whisper to yourself, we don't have anything like that today.

Whoa, hold your horses.

News headlines are recently blaring that a research paper posted online in China on July 1, 2022, depicted a study that supposedly involved an assessment of people's brainwaves and their facial expressions for purposes of computing whether they were loyal to the Chinese Communist Party (CCP). So, there you go, the future is getting closer and closer, at least in terms of attaining the dystopian society that we have dreaded might someday arise.

The research paper quickly disappeared from its online posted link.

Presumably, the rapid scorn that quickly swept across the Internet was enough to get the paper taken down. Or, maybe the researchers just want to make a few wording changes and other innocuous corrections, aiming to do a reposting once they've had a more thorough chance to ensure that the i's are dotted and the t's are all crossed. We'll have to keep our eyes open to see if the paper gets a second life.

I'm going to go ahead and do a deep dive into what we know about the research study and try to connect the dots about how this kind of AI-related work has significance for all of us, going far beyond the scope of seeing this as confined to one particular country. My coverage will be a bit more extensive than the other recent reporting on this newsworthy item, so please bear with me.

My added emphasis too will be that there is a slew of vital AI Ethics lessons that we can glean from the purported paper.

Here's what has been so far mentioned about the research study.

Apparently, some "volunteers" were recruited to participate in an experiment regarding perceptions of the CCP. Whether they were willing volunteers or more akin to goaded or maybe guided volunteers is unknown. We will assume for sake of discussion that they were agreeable to being a subject in the study.

I bring this up to not simply be smarmy. Whenever an experiment is done involving human subjects, there are a plethora of generally accepted practices regarding the recruitment and immersion of such subjects into a research effort. This partially traces back to prior studies that often tricked or forced people to engage in an experiment, at times leading to adverse psychological repercussions or even physical harm for those participants. The scientific community has tried mightily to curtail those types of insidious studies and requires that all sorts of disclosures and warnings be provided to those sought for inclusion in human-related studies.

To clarify, not everyone abides by such prudent and conscientious guidelines.

Moving on, there were reportedly 43 subjects, and they were said to be members of China's Communist Party. Keep in mind that the selection of subjects for an experiment is quite crucial to the experiment and also must be taken into account concerning any conclusions that you might try to reach afterward about the results of the experiment.

Suppose I want to do an experiment about how people perceive the acclaimed Star Wars series. If I pre-select subjects that all resoundingly hate Star Wars (how can such people exist?), and I show them Star Wars video clips, the odds are that they are probably going to say that they still dislike Star Wars. Based on this pseudo-scientific experiment, perhaps I sneakily claim that people -- in general -- really hate Star Wars, which was "proven" (wink-wink) in my "carefully" prepared research setting.

You might not know that I had rigged the roulette wheel, as it were, by preselecting the subjects that I anticipated would produce my surreptitiously desired results. Of course, had I intentionally instead recruited people that loved Star Wars and were zealous avid fans, the chances are they would report as being ecstatic about watching those Star Wars clips. Again, any conclusions reached about how people, in general, react to Star Wars would be tempered by the preselected set of subjects chosen for the effort.

The CCP-focused study seemingly had the subjects sit in front of a kiosk-like video display and read various articles about the policies and accomplishments of the CCP. This is probably the considered "experimental treatment" that the subjects are being exposed to. When planning out an experiment, you usually come up with an experimental factor or aspect that you want to see if it impacts the participants.

The research question apparently being explored was whether the act of reviewing these materials would have any impact on the subjects in terms of increasing, decreasing, or being neutral as to their subsequent impressions of the CCP.

In a classic null hypothesis, you might arrange such a study to state that the materials consumed have no impact on the subsequent impressions expressed by the subjects. Once you've done a before and after comparison of their viewpoints about the CCP, you would statistically try to see whether there was a statistically significant detection of a change in their impressions.

It could be that the before and after are not statistically different, therefore you might reasonably tentatively conclude that for this particular study the displayed materials (experimental treatment) did not seem to make a difference in their impressions. On the other hand, if there was a statistically valid difference, you would look to see whether the after was greater than the before, allowing you to gingerly suggest that the materials boosted their impressions (and, on the other side of the coin, if the after was less than the before this might imply that the materials lessened or lowered their impressions).

There are a lot of nagging loose ends that would need to be dealt with in such a study.

For example, we usually want to have a so-called control group that we can compare to those that receive the experimental treatment. Here's why. Suppose that the act of sitting in front of a kiosk to read materials was the true basis for why impressions were changed. It could be that the nature of the materials consumed is roughly immaterial to the impression impact. Merely sitting and reading anything, such as the latest stories about cats that do funny things, alone might do the trick. We might therefore arrange to have some subjects be in our control group that is exposed to some other material to read, other than the CCP policies and attainments materials.

We don't know if that was done in this instance (no one seems to have mentioned this facet as yet).

I realize you are by now getting antsy about the media explosive part of the study. We shall move expeditiously into that portion.

How might we detect whether the subjects in this experiment responded to or altered their impressions as a result of reading the displayed materials?

A customary means would be to ask them.

You would have beforehand administered perhaps a questionnaire that asks them their impressions of the CCP. Then, following the exposure to the experimental treatment, as in the reading of materials being displayed, we could administer another questionnaire. The answers given by the subjects on a before and after basis might then be compared. If we were also using a control group, we would assume that the control group answers would not substantively change from the before to the after (under the belief that looking at stories about frolicking cats ought to not have impacted their CCP impressions).

This act of asking the subjects for their impressions is not necessarily as straightforward as it might seem.

Suppose that the subjects in the experiment get a sense or overall drift that you are wanting them to respond to the experimental treatment in a particular manner. In that case, they might purposely overstate their reactions in the after part of the experimental administration. You've certainly seen this happen. If I am doing a taste test for a new soda coming onto the market, I might act like I wildly relished the soda, doing so in hopes of maybe getting featured in an advertisement by the soda maker and getting my richly deserved fifteen minutes of fame.

The gist is that merely asking people their opinions is not a surefire means of gauging changes. It is one approach. Other approaches could and are also often undertaken.

How did this particular study opt to gauge the reactions of the subjects?

Apparently, at least two methods were used.

One method consisted of doing a facial scan and using AI-based facial recognition software to assess the reactions of the subjects. The other method was reportedly some form of brainwave scanning. It hasn't been as yet reported as to what type of brainwave scanning devices were used, nor what kind of AI-based brainwave analysis software was employed.

Various reporting has indicated that the study stated this about the nature of the experiment: "On one hand, it can judge how party members have accepted thought and political education." And the study supposedly also mentioned this too: "On the other hand, it will provide real data for thought and political education so it can be improved and enriched." The research study was attributed to being performed under the auspices of China's Hefei Comprehensive National Science Centre.

Media reports suggest that the study alluded to a claim that the facial recognition scans and the brainwave scans were able to aid in detecting that the after impressions were boosted about the CCP.

I'd like to note for you that without being able to directly review the systems utilized and examine closely the research paper, we do not know the particulars of how those AI-based systems were exactly used.

It could be that the subjects were reacting to the experimental setting rather than reacting to the experimental treatment. Anybody that participates in a study might be anxious, to begin with. This might confound any efforts to do brainwave scans or facial pattern analysis. There is also the chance that they felt motivated to please the researchers, opting to have concocted positive thoughts after seeing the materials and this could in theory be reflected in the brainwave scans and the facial scans (maybe, though please know that there is a great deal of impassioned controversy over the validity of such contentions, as I will elucidate momentarily), hoping to skew the results and show that they were positively impacted.

The Twitter reaction was predominantly that the very notion of using AI-empowered brainwave scans and facial recognition is by itself an appalling and outrageous act. Only human monsters would use those kinds of devices, we are told by some of those tweets.

I must ask you to sit down and prepare yourself for something that might be a rude and shocking surprise.

There are many researchers worldwide that use those same kinds of technologies in their research studies. This is certainly not the very first time that a brainwave scan capability was used on human subjects in a research effort. This was also certainly not the first time that facial recognition was used on human subjects for experimental purposes. Even a cursory online search will show you lots and lots of experimental studies across all manner of countries and labs that have used those types of devices.

Now, that being said, using them to gauge loyalty to the CCP is not something you would find much focus on. When such AI is used for governmental control, a red line has been crossed, as they say.

That's the obviously chilling part of the whole kit and kaboodle.

The expressed concern by many is that if governments opt to use brainwave scanning technology and facial recognition to ascertain loyalty to the regimes at hand, we are going to find ourselves in a dystopian world of hurt. When you are walking down a public street, it could be that a device mounted on a lamppost is going to clandestinely determine your loyalty quotient.

One supposes that if your face doesn't seem to suggest you are sufficiently loyal, or if the brainwave scan suggests the same, governmental thugs might suddenly rush up and grab ahold of you. Unnerving. Abysmal. Must not be allowed.

That is the crux of why a headline gushing outroar and outrage has arisen on this news item.

Imagine this. We are possibly going to craft and then put into use computer-based systems that use the latest in AI to decide whether we are loyal or not. If you tried to hire people to sit around and do the same, you would need a lot of people and you'd have a logistics issue of trying to position them to eye everyone. In the case of an AI-based system, all you need to do is set up the electronic devices on lampposts, sides of buildings, and so on. The scanning for loyalty can happen 24x7, at all times, in all places so equipped. This can then be fed into a massive database.

We become humans that are mere cogs in a colossus all-seeing all-watching societal oppressive ecosystem. The seeing eye is not just watching what we do. It is also interpreting what our faces claim to say about our loyalty to the government. Our minds likewise are to be examined for a similar dreadful cause.

Yikes!

There is a secondary concern that comes from this too, though perhaps not quite as thorny in comparison to the Big Brother implications as already sketched.

Ponder these two pressing questions:
- Can we reliably assert that a brainwave scan can attest to your loyalty?
- Can we reliably assert that a facial recognition scan can attest to your loyalty?

Hold on, you might be yelling at the top of your lungs.

I realize and acknowledge that you might not care quite as much about the reliability aspects per se. Whether this can be done reliably is less crucial than the fact that it is being done at all. No one should be under such scrutiny. Forget about whether the technology works suitably for this task. We ought to not be undertaking the task at the get-go.

In any case, the answer right now is a resounding no, namely that existing AI systems that do any semblance of "brainwave scans" and facial recognition are not sufficiently capable to make that leap.

You've maybe seen lately that some of the facial recognition makers have done some backtracking in terms of how their facial recognition systems are being put into use. In an upcoming column posting, I will be discussing the recent efforts for example by Microsoft to try and stem the tide of those using the Microsoft-provided facial recognition tools for purposes far beyond what the technology is able to do or ought to be used for.

In brief, there are no reliable or sensible means to as yet suggest that a brainwave scan or a facial recognition scan can purport to depict someone's loyalty. Even presumably basic facets such as whether you can reliably correlate those scans to whether someone is happy versus sad are still being hotly debated. Trying to up the ante to something as amorphous and variable as loyalty is a bridge too far.

I might add, that some believe ardently that we will eventually get there. That's why I have carefully tried to note that we aren't there yet, rather than stating that we will never get there. Never is a big word. You have to be absolutely certain if you are going to toss around that this will *never* be feasible (keeping in mind that "never" encompasses decades from now, centuries from now, and thousands or millions of years from now).

Some have reacted to the news story about this Chinese lab research study as an indicator of how dangerously the world is veering to inappropriate and dangerous uses of AI. I will share with you momentarily a glimpse of what AI Ethics is all about. This will help you to more vividly see why this particular study does seem to violate many if not nearly all the generally accepted precepts of Ethical AI.

Believe it or not, some have suggested that maybe we are making a mountain out of a molehill regarding this particular study.

Are we?

The counterargument is that a molehill can soon enough become a mountain. In the proverbial notion of a snowball that gets bigger and bigger as it rolls down a snowy hill, we need to stop the snowball from getting underway. If we tolerate these types of studies, we are letting that snowball begin its journey. By speaking out and calling out such studies, perhaps we can forestall the snowball.

One thing is for sure, we are on the brink of opening Pandora's box when it comes to AI aspects, and the question remains as to whether we can prevent the opening of the box or at least find some means to deal prudently with whatever comes out once the box has unleashed its devilish contents.

If nothing else, hopefully, these kinds of media storms will prompt widespread discussion about how we are going to prevent AI-related evildoing and avert numerous AI-sparked existential risks. We need to kick up a notch our societal awareness of AI Ethics and Ethical AI considerations.

Let's focus on AI systems that are used for inappropriate or possibly outright wrongdoing purposes and how that relates to the recently posted study on CCP loyalty.

Two primary considerations come to mind:
1) This AI instance is part of a larger ongoing pattern of disconcerting AI use and therefore ominous and eye-opening as to what is taking place
2) The cat could be let out of the bag such that if AI like this is adopted in one country it can be readily spread to other countries too

Start with the first point about this instance of AI being part of an ongoing pattern.

One notably important basis for being especially perturbed by this one particular study is that it is part of a larger pattern of how AI is aiming to be used by some. If this was the only such study ever conducted, we might be mildly stirred by it. Nonetheless, it would probably not resonate with such fervor as we are now seeing.

This is perhaps the drip-drip of an inching along toward something that is going to get out of hand.

As reported in the news, China is well-known for having insisted on infusive loyalty to the CCP. Furthermore, various means have been established or are being established to ensure that people are indoctrinated into the governmental doctrine. There have been cited instances of prior studies seeking to devise AI algorithms that could gauge the thought conditions of party members (see the China-backed *Study Times* in 2019 that mentioned these efforts).

You might recall that in 2018, Vice President Mike Pence gave a speech at the Hudson Institute and emphasized that "China's rulers aim to implement an Orwellian system premised on controlling virtually every facet of human life" (this was a reference to the CCP implementation of a social credit scoring system, a topic of prominent controversy). You could readily assert that this recent CCP study is another step in that direction.

We don't know when or if the last straw will break the camel's back, such that these one-off studies are turned into widespread AI-based monitoring systems.

The second point that is worthy of attention is that we cannot assume that this type of AI will only be confined to China. In essence, though having this type of AI use in China that might go widespread is by itself disturbing, other countries might do likewise.

Once the AI for this is said to be ready for prime time, it won't like take much for other countries to decide they want to implement it too. The cat will be out of the bag. Some countries will presumably use this AI in outright oppressive ways and not try to proffer any pretenses about doing so. Other countries might seemingly seek to use this type of AI for what appears to be beneficial purposes, out of which there is ultimately a downside that will nearly be unavoidable.

Actually, suggesting that this type of AI will perhaps only be adopted once it is seen as ready for prime time is a bit of a misnomer.

It might not make a whit of difference whether the AI can work assuredly in this manner. The AI can be used as a cover story. Regardless of what the AI is actually able to accomplish, the notion is that the AI can be a handy pretense to bring forth populace monitoring and schemes of gauging and ensuring absolute loyalty to authorities.

At this juncture of this weighty discussion, I'd bet that you are desirous of some illustrative examples that might showcase this topic. There is a special and assuredly popular set of examples that are close to my heart. You see, in my capacity as an expert on AI including the ethical and legal ramifications, I am frequently asked to identify realistic examples that showcase AI Ethics dilemmas so that the somewhat theoretical nature of the topic can be more readily grasped. One of the most evocative areas that vividly presents this ethical AI quandary is the advent of AI-based true self-driving cars. This will serve as a handy use case or exemplar for ample discussion on the topic.

Here's then a noteworthy question that is worth contemplating: *Does the advent of AI-based true self-driving cars illuminate anything about AI misuses, and if so, what does this showcase?*

Let's sketch out a self-driving car scenario that might leverage AI in sketchy or wrongdoing ways.

I am going to share with you some AI-based self-driving car ramifications that might cause you to shudder and be disturbed. These are facets that almost no one is currently discussing. I've repeatedly brought up the matters, though openly acknowledge that until we have a prevalent adoption of self-driving cars, we aren't going to get much traction as to society being worried or upset on what seem like today as merely abstract notions.

Are you ready?

We shall start with some foundation laying.

AI-based self-driving cars will be equipped with video cameras, sensibly so. This allows the self-driving car to receive video imagery of the driving scene. In turn, the AI driving system that is running on board the computers in the self-driving car is intended to computationally examine the collected video and figure out where the road is, where nearby cars are, where pedestrians are, and so on. I realize that I am reciting self-driving cars 101 fundamentals.

There are video cameras mounted on the exterior of the autonomous vehicle and they are pointing outward. In addition, by and large, you can expect that there will be video cameras on or inside the vehicle aiming inward into the interior of the self-driving car. Why so? Easy-peasy, because there will be lots of important uses for video capturing the goings-on inside the autonomous vehicle.

When you go for a ride in a self-driving car, you no longer need to be the driver. What will you do then while inside a self-driving car?

One thing you could do would be to interact with others at home or in the office. There you are, on your way to work, which will say take an hour of driving time by the self-driving car, and you can already begin your day of work by doing a Zoom-like online real-time interactive session. They can see you, due to the cameras pointing inward into the self-driving car. You can see them on perhaps an LED screen inside the self-driving car. At the end of your day, while heading back home, you might do a similar interactive video discussion with your kids as they are starting to get their homework done for the evening.

Another use would be for taking classes. Now that you don't need to waste your time driving, you can turn that deadhead time inside a self-driving car into enhancing your skills or getting a certification or degree. Via the cameras pointing inward, your instructor can see you and discuss how your training is coming along.

Yet another use would be to try and ensure that riders in self-driving cars do not go amok. In a human-driven car, the driver is an adult presence that usually keeps riders from doing zany things such as marking the interior with graffiti. What will happen with AI-based self-driving cars? Some worry that riders will opt to tear up the interior of the vehicles. To try and prevent this, the ridesharing firm that is deploying the self-driving cars will likely use inward-facing video cameras to monitor what people are doing while inside the autonomous vehicle.

I assume that you are convinced that we are going to have video cameras that point into the interior of self-driving cars, in addition to the cameras that point outward to discern the driving scene.

You are now ready for what I have referred to as the roving eye.

First, consider the video cameras that are pointing outward.

Wherever the self-driving car goes, it will potentially be able to video record whatever the cameras see. A self-driving car that gives a lift to someone from their home and takes them to the grocery store will traverse a neighborhood and the video will record not just the roadway but also everything else happening within eyesight. A father and son playing in their front yard. A family sitting on their front porch. On and on it goes.

Right now, we have so few self-driving cars on the public roadways that this ability to capture video of daily activities is relatively scarce and immaterial.

Envision that we ultimately achieve safe and widespread self-driving cars. Thousands of them. Maybe millions. We have about 250 million human-driven cars in the US today. Eventually, those will be pretty much replaced by self-driving cars or simply no longer used, and we will predominantly have self-driving cars on our roadways. Those self-driving cars are being driven by AI and as such can be roaming essentially 24x7. No rest breaks, no bathroom breaks.

The video data could be uploaded from these self-driving cars via OTA (Over-The-Air) electronic networking connections. Self-driving cars will be using OTA to get the latest AI software updates downloaded into the vehicle. In addition, the OTA can be used to upload data from the self-driving car into a cloud-based database.

All told, it would be feasible to stitch together this uploaded data. With the stitching, you could potentially piece together the daily comings and goings of anyone that stepped outside on any day in any locale that was extensively using self-driving cars.

That is the roving eye that I have been warning about.

We can now dovetail the CCP study into this kind of capability. Suppose a government has access to all of this collected video data. They could then use an AI-based facial recognition algorithm to ascertain where you went, at what time of day, throughout your daily travels of life. In addition, they could presumably use their "loyalty" AI-based analyzer to see if you seemed to have a loyal look on your face or not.

Just imagine that on a Tuesday afternoon you were walking to get a sandwich at a local diner. Self-driving cars were passing by on the roadway. All of the many videos captured you as you were doing your five-minute walk to get a bite to eat. The data was uploaded to a centralized database. The government ran its AI facial recognition program on the data.

Turns out the AI "determined" that you had a disloyal look on your face.

Maybe this disloyal look happened only for an instant. You were waiting at a street corner for the light to change so that you could cross the street to the diner. At that moment, you had a slight twitch of disgust that you had to wait overly long for the Walk symbol. Was this an indication perhaps of your disloyalty to the government?

Yes, the AI computationally calculated, you were abundantly disloyal at that instant in time. When you get home that night, the government has arranged for your arrest.

But wait, there's more.

Remember that video cameras are pointing inward too.

On that same Tuesday, as you were riding to work in a self-driving car, the video cameras were capturing your every moment. This was uploaded to a centralized database. The AI software that analyses face patterns for disloyalty did a computational pattern examination of your facial expressions during the journey to the office.

At one point, you were casually looking outside the autonomous vehicle and noticed a construction worker that was partially blocking the roadway and caused the AI driving system to slow down the self-driving car. For a split second, your face registered a look of derision for this construction worker slowing down traffic.

The AI facial pattern analysis interpreted this as a sign of disloyalty to the government.

Two strikes against you in one day.

You are living on thin ice.

Of course, whether the AI is "right" or "wrong" about being able to determine your loyalty is almost inconsequential in this context. The gist is that AI has been put into place for this purpose. The humans that are deploying the AI might or might not care whether the AI is of any suitable use for this type of task. The AI allows for governmental control, regardless of the technological validity itself.

That covers the face scanning.

If we eventually have any kind of portable cost-effective devices for doing (alleged) brainwave scanning, this certainly can also be included in self-driving cars. Video cameras are a sure thing now.

The possibility of having brainwave scan devices of this caliber is not in the cards right now, but clearly is something that is being envisioned for the future.

A government might try to take over a populace by grabbing control of self-driving cars. A similar possibility exists that a malicious actor might try to do the same. Those aren't meant to be scare tactics as to coverage on those related topics, and instead, a heads-up on the importance of cybersecurity and other precautions we must as a society seek to take regarding the onset of ubiquitous self-driving cars and other autonomous vehicles.

Conclusion

I'd like to quickly cover one additional aspect about the AI being used to ascertain loyalty that I think is a somewhat separate topic, but one that some tweets and social media have been belaboring.

I earlier mentioned that we do not have sentient AI and we do not know if or when we will. Let's entertain the idea that we will have sentient AI. In that case, consider the following scenario.

We via non-sentient AI opt to put in place a widespread use of AI that ascertains computationally whether people are being loyal to their government, using facial scans, brainwave scans, and so on. This is entirely run by and used by humans in authority. That is the disturbing scenario that I have just moments earlier been describing.

Time to up the ante.

AI becomes sentient. We have now potentially handed to this sentient AI a widespread capability of presumably identifying loyalty and disloyalty in humans. An evildoing AI that is considering wiping out humans might use this capability to decide that indeed humans are going to be disloyal and should be destroyed entirely. Or maybe just those humans that showcase an indication of disloyalty via their face or their thoughts are to be particularly scrapped.

We would seem to have given the AI a perfect gift for carrying out that quest. The existing infrastructure that we put in place allows the AI to keep a careful watch on us humans. Those that appear to have expressed a disloyal facial indication or thought about the AI overlord(s) are going to feel the wrath of the AI.

I realize that I said that this is an upping of the ante. I am not sure that is the case. Seems to me that whether we have AI overlords directly deciding our fate versus human overlords that perchance use an AI system to determine loyalty, well, neither proposition seems especially desirable.

A final comment for now.

Roman scholar and philosopher Marcus Tullius Cicero stated that there is nothing more noble, nothing more venerable, than loyalty. We might be letting AI get ahead of us and become a tool to enlist and ensure "loyalty" by dreadful means.

A worthwhile mindful reason to put AI Ethics on the top of our To-Do list.

CHAPTER 10

AI ETHICS
AND AI ASYMMETRY

Sometimes you are on the wrong end of the stick.

That colloquialism can be applied to the notion of asymmetry.

Yes, I am going to be talking about asymmetry. As you likely have encountered in this topsy-turvy world that we live in, there are occasions when you might find yourself having less knowledge on a matter that is relatively important to you. This is formally referred to as *Information Asymmetry*.

The key is that you have less knowledge or information than you might wish that you had, plus you decidedly have less than the other party involved in the matter. You are at a distinct disadvantage in comparison to the other party. They know something you don't know. They can leverage what they know, especially in terms of what you don't know, and get an upper hand in any rough-and-tumble deliberations or negotiations with you.

Well, there is a new kid in town, known as *AI Asymmetry*.

This latest catchphrase refers to the possibility of you going against someone that is armed with AI, while you are not so armed.

They have AI on their side, while you've got, well, just you. Things are lopsided. You are at a presumed disadvantage. The other side will be able to run circles around you due to being augmented by AI. That might be within the famous saying that all is fair in love and war (a longstanding proverb coined in *Euphues* by John Lyly, 1578), though the dynamics and dangers of AI Asymmetry raise challenging Ethical AI issues.

Before we jump into the AI realm and its abundant complexities regarding AI Asymmetry, let's first explore the everyday regular version of plain old Information Asymmetry. This will set the stage for edging into the proverbial AI new kid on the block.

A brief and purposefully enlightening tale might whet your appetite.

The other day I had a flat tire while on the road and was seeking quickly to find a suitable replacement that could be readily installed right away. Using my smartphone, I looked online at nearby tire stores to figure out the distance I had to drive on my run-flat tire and whether any stores were open. In addition, I did a quick assessment of their online customer reviews and tried to glean anything useful about how long they had been in business and other factors that might showcase their worthiness.

Upon calling one of the tire stores, the clerk gave me a breezy quote for the cost of the tire and its installation. The tire was not exactly what I had in mind, but the clerk assured me that they would be the only shop in the area that could do the work straight away. According to the clerk, any of the other nearby tire stores would not have any such tires in stock and it would take at least a day for those competitors to obtain a suitable tire from some semi-distant warehouse.

I was in the midst of an information asymmetry.

The clerk professed to know more about the local status of the tire stores and in particular the type of tire that I needed. I was in an area that I was only passing through and didn't have any first-hand knowledge about the tire shops in that particular geographical area. For all I knew, the clerk was spot on and was giving me the unvarnished truth.

But was the clerk doing so?

Maybe yes, maybe no.

It could be that the clerk believed sincerely everything that was being conveyed to me. To the clerk, this was the truth. Or perhaps the clerk was somewhat stretching the truth. It was possible that what was being said could possibly be true, though the manner in which it was being depicted implied that it was the utter and irrefutable truth. Of course, it could also have been complete balderdash and the clerk was merely shilling for the tire store to garner my business. Could a juicy commission have been on the line?

I dare say that nobody likes being in such an underdog position.

The stakes of the situation are a vital factor in how much an information asymmetry matters. If the question at hand is one of a life-or-death nature, being in the doghouse and reliant upon the other party for what they know or profess to know is a sketchy and highly undesirable posture to be in. When the stakes are low, such as ordering your dinner in a restaurant and the server tells you that the fish dish is heavenly, but you've never eaten there before and are under-informed, you can go along with this modicum of information asymmetry without much angst (I suppose too that you are also betting that the server wouldn't risk giving sour advice and missing out on getting a decent tip).

Returning to the worn-out tire story (a pun!), I would have had no instantaneous way to figure out whether the clerk was giving me reliable and informative insights. You might be wondering what happened. I decided to make calls to several of the other nearby tire stores.

Are you ready for what I discovered?

All the other tire stores had my desired tire in stock and weren't going to try and wink-wink persuade me to take a different tire (as the first clerk tried to do). They also could get the work done in the same timeframe as the first tire store that I perchance called. At roughly the same price.

A welcomed sigh of relief occurred on my part, I assure you.

Ironically, in Murphy's Law of bad luck, the first place that I contacted was the only one that seemed to be out to lunch, as it were. I'm glad that I sought to obtain more information. This narrowed the information asymmetry gap. I applauded myself for having stuck to my guns and not acceding to the first place I called.

That being said, there was a definite cost of sorts involved in my obtaining additional information. I made approximately four calls that each took around fifteen to twenty minutes to fully undertake. In that sense, I used up about an hour and a half while just figuring out where to take my car. If I had immediately taken my car to that first place, the new tire would nearly have been on my car by that time. On the other hand, I would almost certainly, later on, have regretted the quick decision that I made while in a dastardly Information Asymmetry bind.

Sometimes you have to grit your teeth and take the dreaded Information Asymmetry as it comes. You just hope that whatever decision you make, is going to be good enough. It might not be a "perfect" decision and you could later regret the choice made. The other angle is that you could try to bolster your side of the information equation, though this is not necessarily cost-free and might also chew up precious time, depending upon whether the cherished time is of the essence.

Now that you are undoubtedly comforted to know that my car is running fine with its brand new and correct tire, I can shift into the emergence of AI Asymmetry.

Consider an AI tale of woe.

You are seeking to get a home loan. There is an online mortgage request analyzer that a particular bank is using. The online system makes use of today's advanced AI capabilities. No need to speak with a human loan granting agent. The AI does it all.

The AI system walks you through a series of prompts. You dutifully fill in the forms and respond to the AI system. This AI is very chatty. Whereas you in the past might have used a conventional computer-based form system, this AI variant is more akin to interacting with a human agent. Not quite, but enough that you could almost start to believe that a human was on the other side of this activity.

After doing your best to "discuss" your request with this AI, in the end, it informs you that unfortunately the loan request is not approved. It kind of gets your goat that the AI seems to offer an apology, as though the AI wanted to approve the loan but those mean-spirited humans overseeing the bank won't let the AI do so.

You are clueless as to why you got turned down. The AI doesn't proffer any explanation. Perhaps the AI made a mistake or messed up in its calculations. Worse still, suppose the AI used some highly questionable considerations such as your race or gender when deciding on the loan. All that you know is that you seemed to have wasted your time and also meanwhile handed over a ton of private data to the AI and the bank. Their AI has bested you.

This would be labeled as an example of AI Asymmetry.

It was you against the bank. The bank was armed with AI. You were not equally armed. You had your wits and your school of hard knocks wisdom, but no AI residing in your back pocket. Mind against a machine. Sadly, the machine won in this case.

What are you to do?

First, we need on a societal basis to realize that this AI Asymmetry is growing and becoming nearly ubiquitous. Humans are encountering AI in all of the systems that we daily interact with. Sometimes the AI is the only element that we interact with, such as in this example about the loan request. In other instances, a human might be in the loop that relies upon AI to aid them in performing a given service.

For the loan, it might be that the bank would have you speak with a human agent in lieu of interacting with AI, but for which the human agent is using a computer system to access AI that is guiding the human agent during the loan request process (and, you are nearly always assured to have the human agent act as though they are imprisoned by having to strictly do whatever the AI "tells them to do").

Either way, AI is still in the mix.

Second, we need to try and ensure that the AI Asymmetry is at least being done on an AI Ethical basis.

Allow me to explain that seemingly oddish remark. You see, if we can be somewhat assured that the AI is acting in an ethically sound manner, we might have some solace about the asymmetry that is at play. On a somewhat analogous but also loose basis, you might say that if my interaction with the first tire store clerk had some strident ethical guidelines in place and enforced, perhaps I would not have been told the story that I was told, or at least I might not have had to right away seek to discover whether a tall tale was being given to me.

I'll be explaining more about AI Ethics in a moment.

Third, we should seek ways to reduce AI Asymmetry. If you had AI that was on your side, striving to be your coach or protector, you might be able to use that AI to do some counterpunching with the other AI that you are going head-to-head with. As they say, sometimes it makes abundant sense to fight fire with fire.

A quick recap about my aforementioned three identified recommendations is this:

1) **Become aware that AI Asymmetry exists and is growing**
2) **Seek to ensure that the AI Asymmetry is bounded by AI Ethics**
3) **Try to contend with AI Asymmetry by getting armed with AI**

We will take a closer look at the latter point of fighting fire with fire.

Imagine that when seeking to get a loan, you had AI that was working on your side of the effort. This might be an AI-based app on your smartphone that was devised for getting loans. It isn't an app by one of the banks and instead is independently devised to act on your behalf. I've detailed these kinds of apps in my book on AI-based guardian angel bots.

Upon your applying for a loan, you might refer to this app as you are stepped through the application process by the other AI. These two AI systems are distinct and completely separate from each other. The AI on your smartphone has been "trained" to know all of the tricks being used by the other AI. As such, the answers that you enter into the bank's AI will be based on what your AI is advising you.

Another variant consists of your AI answering the questions posed by the other AI. As far as the other AI can ascertain, it is you that are entering the answers. You might instead be merely watching as the interactions take place between the two battling AI systems. This allows you to see what your AI is proffering. Furthermore, you can potentially adjust your AI depending upon whether you are satisfied with what your AI is doing on your behalf.

I have predicted that we are all going to gradually become armed with AI that will be on our side in these AI Asymmetry situations. Let's consider how this is going to work out. These are the cornerstone impacts on the AI Asymmetry condition that I had laid out:

- **Flattening the AI Asymmetry in your favor** (bringing you upward, hoping to reach equal levels)
- **Spurring an AI Asymmetry to your favor** (raising you to an advantage when already are equals)
- **Boosting an AI Asymmetry to your extraordinary favor** (gaining a wider advantage when already at an advantage)
- **Inadvertent Undercutting of AI Asymmetry to your disfavor** (when you had a preexisting advantage and the AI inadvertently pulled you down)

Time to do a deep dive into these intriguing possibilities.

Flattening The AI Asymmetry In Your Favor

This first bullet point about flattening the AI Asymmetry is the most obvious and most often discussed consideration, namely that you would arm yourself with AI to try and go toe-to-toe with the AI being used by the other side in the matter at hand. The AI Asymmetry setting started with you at a decided disadvantage. You had no AI in your corner. You were on the low side of things. The other side did have AI and they were on the higher ground.

Thus, you wisely armed yourself with AI that would aim to put you and the other AI on equal terms.

One important and perhaps surprising nuance to keep in mind is that it won't always be the case that the AI systems being employed will balance against each other evenly. You might arm yourself with AI that is shall we say less potent than the AI that the other side is using. In which case, you have increased your downside position, thankfully, though you are not entirely now equal with the other side and its AI.

That's why I refer to this as flattening the AI Asymmetry. You might be able to narrow the gap, though not fully close the gap. The ultimate aim would be to use AI on your side that will bring you to a completely equal posture. The thing is, this might or might not be feasible. The other side could conceivably have some really expensive AI and you are trying to compete with the mom-and-pop thrifty mart version of AI.

Not all AI is the same.

Spurring An AI Asymmetry To Your Favor

This circumstance is not something much discussed today, partially because it is rare right now. Someday, this will be commonplace. The notion is that suppose you are without AI and yet nonetheless on equal ground with the side that does have AI.

Good for you.

Humans do have their wits about them.

But you might want to gain an advantage over the other side. Arming yourself with AI takes you to the higher ground. You now have your wits and your trusty AI in hand. You have gained an advantage that presumably will prevail over the AI of the other side.

Boosting An AI Asymmetry To Your Extraordinary Favor

Using similar logic as the aspect of spurring an AI Asymmetry on your behalf, suppose that you are already above the capabilities of the other side that is using AI. Ergo, you are not starting at an equal posture. You fortunately are already on the top side.

You might want to anyway secure an even greater advantage. Therefore, you arm yourself with AI. This takes your head and shoulders above the other side.

Inadvertent Undercutting Of AI Asymmetry To Your Disfavor

I doubt that you want to hear about this possibility. Please realize that dealing with AI is not all roses and ice cream cakes.

It could be that when you arm yourself with AI, you actually undercut yourself. If you were already less than the AI of the other side, you are now down in a deeper hole. If you were on equal terms, you are now at a disadvantage. If you were above the other side, you are now equal to or below it.

How could that happen?

You might be shocked to ponder that the AI you adopt is going to lead you astray. This easily could occur. Just because you have AI in your corner does not mean it is useful. You might be using the AI and it provides advice that you don't necessarily think is apt, but you decide to go with it anyway.

Your logic at the time was that since you went to the trouble to obtain the AI, you might as well depend upon it.

The AI you are using might be defective. Or it might be poorly devised. There is a slew of reasons why the AI might be giving you shaky advice. Those that blindly accept whatever the AI says to do are bound to find themselves in a world of hurt.

The bottom line is that there is absolutely no guarantee that just because you arm yourself with AI you are going to win at the AI Asymmetry game.

You might arrive at a level playing field. You might gain an advantage. And, regrettably, you need to be cautious since it could be that you sink to downward levels when armed with AI.

To some degree, that is why AI Ethics and Ethical AI is such a crucial topic. The precepts of AI Ethics get us to remain vigilant. AI technologists can at times become preoccupied with technology, particularly the optimization of high-tech. They aren't necessarily considering the larger societal ramifications. Having an AI Ethics mindset and doing so integrally to AI development and fielding is vital for producing appropriate AI.

Besides employing AI Ethics, there is a corresponding question of whether we should have laws to govern various uses of AI. New laws are being bandied around at the federal, state, and local levels that concern the range and nature of how AI should be devised. The effort to draft and enact such laws is a gradual one. AI Ethics serves as a considered stopgap, at the very least, and will almost certainly to some degree be directly incorporated into those new laws.

Here's then a noteworthy question that is worth contemplating: *Does the advent of AI-based true self-driving cars illuminate anything about AI Asymmetry, and if so, what does this showcase?*

Let's sketch out a scenario that showcases AI Asymmetry.

Contemplate the seemingly inconsequential matter of where self-driving cars will be roaming to pick up passengers. This seems like an abundantly innocuous topic.

At first, assume that AI self-driving cars will be roaming throughout entire towns. Anybody that wants to request a ride in a self-driving car has essentially an equal chance of hailing one. Gradually, the AI begins to primarily keep the self-driving cars roaming in just one section of town. This section is a greater money-maker and the AI has been programmed to try and *maximize* revenues as part of the usage in the community at large (this underscores the mindset underlying optimization, namely focusing on just one particular metric and neglecting other crucial factors in the process).

Community members in the impoverished parts of the town turn out to be less likely to be able to get a ride from a self-driving car. This is because the self-driving cars were further away and roaming in the higher revenue part of the town. When a request comes in from a distant part of town, any other request from a closer location would get a higher priority. Eventually, the availability of getting a self-driving car in any place other than the richer part of town is nearly impossible, exasperatingly so for those that lived in those now resource-starved areas.

Out goes the vaunted mobility-for-all dreams that self-driving cars are supposed to bring to life.

You could assert that the AI altogether landed on a form of statistical and computational bias, akin to a form of proxy discrimination (also often referred to as indirect discrimination). Realize that the AI wasn't programmed to avoid those poorer neighborhoods. Let's be clear about that in this instance. No, it was devised instead to merely optimize revenue, a seemingly acceptable goal, but this was done without the AI developers contemplating other potential ramifications. That optimization in turn unwittingly and inevitably led to an undesirable outcome.

Had they included AI Ethics considerations as part of their optimization mindset, they might have realized beforehand that unless they crafted the AI to cope with this kind of oversizing on one metric alone, they might have averted such dour results. For more on these types of issues that the widespread adoption of autonomous vehicles and self-driving cars are likely to incur.

In any case, assume that the horse is already out of the barn and the situation is not immediately amenable to overarching solutions.

What might those that want to use those self-driving cars do?

The most apparent approach would be to work with community leaders on getting the automaker or self-driving tech firm to reconsider how they have set up the AI. Perhaps put pressure on whatever licensing or permits that have been granted for the deployment of those self-driving cars in that city or town. These are likely viable means of bringing about positive changes, though it could take a while before those efforts bear fruit.

Another angle would be to arm yourself with AI.

Envision that someone has cleverly devised an AI-based app that works on your smartphone and deals with the AI of the automaker or fleet operator that is taking in requests for rides. It could be that the AI you are using exploits key elements of the other AI such that a request for a self-driving car by you is given heightened priority. Note that I am not suggesting that anything illegal is taking place, but instead that the AI on your side has been developed based on discovered "features" or even loopholes in the other AI.

Conclusion

The story about brazenly fighting back against the AI of the self-driving cars fleet operator by getting armed with AI brings up additional AI Ethics controversies and considerations.

For example:

- If one person can make use of AI to give them an advantage over an AI of some other system, how far can this go in terms of possibly crossing AI Ethics boundaries (I convince the self-driving cars to come to me and my friends, to the exclusion of all others)?

- Also, is there any semblance of AI Ethics consideration that if someone knows about or is armed with AI to do battle with other AI, should those remaining people that do not have that balancing AI be somehow alerted to the AI and be able to arm themselves accordingly too?

In the end, all of this is taking us to a future that seems eerie, consisting of an AI arms race. Who will have the AI that they need to get around and survive and who will not? Will there always be one more AI that comes along and sparks the need for a counterbalancing AI?

Carl Sagan, the venerated scientist, provided this sage wisdom about especially cataclysmic arms races: "The nuclear arms race is like two sworn enemies standing waist deep in gasoline, one with three matches, the other with five."

We must decisively aim to keep our feet dry and our heads clear when it comes to an ever-looming AI arms race

Dr. Lance B. Eliot

CHAPTER 11

AI ETHICS

AND ALGORITHMIC AFTERLIFE

Most people are wary of wasps, sensibly so.

A recent wasp nest in my neighborhood provided a handy lesson about human behavior. Let's talk about the role of an ordinary everyday wasp nest and the resulting imprint on human behavior that occurred. Along the way, we can note lasting impacts that gave rise to a form of "afterlife" even after the wasp colony was summarily removed.

All of this will reveal a rising concern about Artificial Intelligence (AI) entailing a phenomenon known as *AI algorithmic afterlife*. I will use the wasp tale to kickstart the discussion. We can then explore the generalizable afterlife elements and highlight how processes and people are subject to potentially long-lasting imprinting. There are substantive AI Ethics issues that emerge and will need societal consideration.

First, consider the mighty wasp.

A wasp nest residing in a large tree was apparently discovered by one of my neighbors. I believe a neighbor found it since there was a hastily written sheet of torn paper that was crudely posted on the tree trunk and the scrawled message thereupon warned to be on the watch for wasps. A bit of irony was that the writing was tiny and required any passerby to walk toward the tree to adequately read the note. In that sense, the note served as both a handy means of warning people yet in the same vein lured people closer to the tree and the menacing danger of the wasps.

The tree resided next to a popularly used public sidewalk. If you did one of those camera capturing time lapses, you would see a slew of people of all ages that wandered directly past that tree during morning hours and late afternoon hours. Of all the trees for a wasp to take up residence, this particular tree on our block was the worst choice in terms of potentially endangering scurrying pedestrians.

Gradually, pedestrians began to give the tree a wide berth by walking at the farthest edge of the sidewalk, sometimes entering briefly into the street to avoid getting anywhere near the tree. I observed that some people did this after having read the message posted on the tree. Other people would come along and witness pedestrians ahead of them making these sudden maneuvers and then copy their efforts.

It seemed doubtful that the copycats were doing this due to the wasps. There was instead a mimicking of the people ahead of them.

This doesn't seem especially surprising. If you were walking behind others that opted to shift toward the outer edge of the sidewalk, you would probably do the same, regardless of whether you understand why they were making such a dramatic move. The extra "cost" on your part to figure out why they were making those moves wouldn't likely be worth the added effort. Instead, a simple monkey see, monkey do would seem sufficient. Any thoughts about why this was taking place would be fleeting and you would merely flow like water going through a river that smoothly goes around rocks and other intrusions, seen or not seen.

Of course, if this were a life-or-death matter, you probably would take more stock of the situation. Are the people screaming and fearing for their lives as they make this diversion? I bet that would get your attention as to what was the cause of the fracas. In this case, people walking along just casually veered toward the far side of the sidewalk and didn't skip a beat. Followers tended to do the same, mindlessly and without any overt basis for doing so other than playing a Pied Piper gambit.

The next day, the wasp nest was removed by the local pest control authorities. The threat was eliminated. I'm not sure what happened to the wasps and the nest, perhaps it was relocated elsewhere. Voila, safety and security returned to that short segment of the sidewalk. No need to do the walkaround that had been occurring for most of the prior day.

Here's the interesting twist.

People were veering once again to the farthest edge of the sidewalk. I realized that perhaps they hadn't "gotten the memo" in the sense that they were perhaps unaware that the nest had been removed. I also wondered if the sheet of paper serving as a warning might have been left on the tree. This would certainly confuse passersby into assuming that the nest was still there.

I went over to take a look. The sign had been removed. That suggests that it wasn't the sign anymore that was guiding people to take the diversion. One assumes that the memory of yesterday's event had lingered in people's minds. They didn't know whether the nest was gone or not. On top of that, those that never knew why the diversion was voluntarily taking place would not be able to discern a change anyway, having no clue as to why the sidewalk veering actions had been taking place, to begin with.

My guess was that it might take another day before the local populace settled down and opted to walk on the sidewalk and past the tree in a perfectly normal and unconcerned manner. A day would be about enough time for those that knew about the nest to realize that the nest was no longer there. These people would then stop making the diversion. Followers that had been following the diversion would now follow those that were no longer making the diversion. The world would once again be at a grand peace and calm.

What actually happened?

For nearly a week, the diversion efforts of pedestrians continued day by day. This seemed unimaginable. Why in the heck did the "afterlife" of the wasp nest incident have such a prolonged effect?

I chatted with several people and found out that the diversion had in a manner of speaking become imprinted in their minds. They said that it was easiest to just keep walking to the farthest edge of the sidewalk. Some did know that they had done so earlier due to the wasps, while others said they didn't know why this "new practice" had been instituted but they decided it was readily adoptable anyway. No harm, no foul, seemed to be the consensus.

After several weeks had passed, I later observed that some people, especially young children, opted to continue the diversion path when near the tree. It had become a kind of local lore that when you walk past that tree, make sure to give yourself a widened expanse. I spoke with the parents and the children, asking why they were doing this quick stepping aside action. Few knew why. It was considered harmless, almost fun. One child speculated that a ghost lived in the tree and that it was prudent to avoid getting into the grips of the ghost. Well, I certainly agree, no one in the right mind would seem to want to be embraced by a ghost (other than those ghost hunters that are spotlighted on TV shows).

Consider some useful lessons from the wasp nest saga.

An introduction of something new, namely the wasp nest, prodded people into altering their usual behavior. Some modified their behavior based on awareness of why it made sense to do so. Others copied the new behavior despite not having any reasoned basis per se, though the gut feeling that if someone else is doing something it might be wise for you to do so is powerfully valuable in many circumstances (avoid an unseen pitfall or adverse crack in the sidewalk, do not step on hard to see dog excreta, etc.).

The altered behavior continued even though the original impetus was no longer standing. You could say that there was a kind of afterlife, a residual aftereffect. In some cases, the afterlife might be brief, while in other cases it might be lengthy. Some people, seemingly become mentally imprinted with the new behavior and continue carrying it out. They might know why the behavior was originally stoked, yet willingly continue though the impetus is gone.

Others that didn't know the basis might continue the altered behavior just because it seems easiest to do so. And all manner of wild suppositions and new fanciful angles might arise to justify why the behavior is taking place (such as lingering ghosts!).

You might be tempted to argue that this wasp thing is a bit overblown and we are maybe making a mountain out of a molehill. I trust that you realize that the wasp tale is a microcosm of what can happen in much larger and more demonstrative contexts.

Indeed, the worry is that this same type of afterlife and imprinting is going to increasingly be happening in the context of AI and especially AI-powered autonomous systems.

The trickery part of this is that nowadays the voracious calls for thinking about AI Ethics and Ethical AI are typically aimed at AI systems exclusively when they are being designed and once they are put into use. We rightfully tend to focus on those stages of the AI development lifecycle. Meanwhile, if you are willing to put on your thinking cap and look beyond the obvious boundaries of the upfront lifecycle of an AI system, there is another shall we say hidden or unseen portion on the backend.

Your question for today is this: *What happens once an AI system is removed or altered and no longer in the original spot where it was placed?*

Your likely assumption is that everything springs back to the way that things once were before AI was introduced. This seems simple enough. Drop AI into a setting and things are bound to (momentarily) change. Remove the AI or place it elsewhere, and the "gap" that remains is instantaneously refilled with whatever was there beforehand. I gently drape a bouncy ball into a cup of milk, the milk moves aside, and when I remove the ball the milk goes back to where the ball once intruded.

But suppose we mull this over in a different frame of reference. A beaver makes one of those dams that you see in untamed streams. The act of establishing the dam alters the flow of the water. In turn, the water now potentially reshapes parts of the stream that were downstream. If you come along and decide that the beaver has set up shop in the wrong place, and you remove the dam, those downstream alterations are still in existence. They do not snap back into shape like some kind of glorious rubber band.

AI that is implemented can alter all manner of surrounding aspects. If there comes a time that the AI is removed, you cannot expect a rubber band snaps back into place is going to occur. This is quite important to realize. I say this because envision that we have AI that is considered as violating AI Ethics precepts. The remedy might be to remove the AI. Doing so is not cost-free. There are likely all types of aftermaths, afterlife, and imprinting that can arise. The consequences might be easy and barely noticeable. On the other hand, the consequences might be severe and long-lasting. Numerous factors come to play as to what the AI was doing, how long it was in place, how much the world around it adjusted to the presence of the AI, and so on.

A recent interesting research paper explored the downstream effects of AI that gives rise to an AI algorithmic afterlife and imprinting, asking how this is to be dealt with from an AI Ethics perspective. The work used the now-classic FATE (fairness, accountability, transparency, ethics) as a lens to examine the topic.

Per the paper: "Put differently, algorithmic consequences extend well beyond the algorithm's 'lifetime' (deployment period). The concept of algorithmic imprint broadens the boundaries of what is typically considered the algorithmic impact. Typically, our conceptual canvas of algorithmic fairness issues is most salient in and circumscribed to the algorithm's lifetime. Like a footprint remains in the sand long after someone has passed, or a palimpsest records the writing on the sheet of paper above it, algorithmic systems can leave their mark on the data infrastructure, societal organization, or mental wellbeing of data subjects long after stopping their use. The concept of the imprint does not change the existing nature of algorithms.

Algorithms have always been imprint-laden. The notion of the imprint provides the essential vocabulary to articulate and address harms and ethical issues in the algorithm's 'afterlife' (period after deployment ceases)—an unexplored area in the algorithmic fairness literature" (authored by Upol Ehsan, Ranjit Singh, Jacob Metcalf, Mark O. Riedl in "The Algorithmic Imprint", June 2022).

Let's return to our focus on the proclaimed AI algorithmic afterlife and imprinting.

As a quick recap:

- **Most tend to focus on AI design and deployment when it comes to AI Ethics**
- **Another important and oft-neglected stage is after the AI has been removed or otherwise shifted**
- **A kind of AI afterlife can occur and be shaped by imprinting during the AI presence**
- **All manner of offshoots and downstream alterations are bound to remain in place**
- **This can be mild and generally downplayed or might be demonstrably crucial**
- **Attention to this is vital to the advent of AI in society and how we cope with AI all told**

I earlier mentioned that a child said a ghost perhaps occupied the tree that was being avoided by pedestrians. I'll use the ghost to our advantage here. A removed AI or one that is significantly redirected could leave behind a ghostly aura.

Some people that previously used this AI might not realize that the AI is no longer around. Despite the AI not being there, those people might act as though the AI still exists and is in some manner amidst them. Human behaviors might remain as they were once the AI was established.

Is that good or bad?

Hard to say in the abstract.

Perhaps the AI ended up positively shaping human behavior. Thus, AI has attained some desirable goals and is no longer needed. One supposes that if human behavior starts to slip, AI might be reintroduced. This then might prod along the presumed good behavior.

Or maybe the AI ended up misshaping human behavior. People are now conditioned toward adverse behavior or otherwise are seemingly repressed. They remain this way, even though the AI is no longer around. They are free to return to their prior status, it would seem, but the imprinting is so strong that they do not do so.

Keep in mind that individual choice might not be the only factor.

Let's somewhat embellish the wasp nest story to see how this could unfold. Suppose that people got used to making the diversion when nearby the tree. We saw that this did happen. For nearly a week, the practice continued.

Add into this a bit of a twist. Imagine that local culture began to insist that whenever you came near that tree, make sure to provide a wide berth. If a fellow pedestrian saw you not making the diversion, they might scold you or sternly emphasize the need to do the diversion. Whereas before this was a seemingly individual choice as freely taken, now the collective wisdom of the crowd is essentially enforcing the behavioral aspect.

A person moves into the neighborhood and has never known about the wasp nest. They have quickly been indoctrinated into the sidewalk farthest edge dogma. They pass this along to friends and others that come to visit them. The afterlife of this wasp nest has become firmly and unknowingly rooted, possibly reigning for years to come.

Can we hold AI developers and deployers to task for what happens as per the afterlife of their AI?

One viewpoint is that it is ridiculous to ask AI developers and deployers to consider what will happen if their AI is ever removed from whatever implementation used it. How in the world can the afterlife of their AI be anticipated? Plus, if their AI is being removed, you could suggest that they are no longer responsible for whatever happens next. Why should that be of concern to them?

Wait for a second, the counterargument goes, AI developers and deployers absolutely need to be held accountable for what happens in the afterlife of their AI. Would you let someone come dump toxic materials into the center of your town and then merely walk away from the consequences? No one would openly let that happen. A battle would brew to hold the dumping parties responsible for their actions.

Furthermore, per the counterclaim, you can in fact assuredly predict what an AI afterlife might consist of. This idea that the AI developers and deployers would be unable to anticipate the ramifications of their AI once it is removed is nothing more than a charade and a sly cover story. They just don't want to face up to the possibility.

Few developers would ever imagine that the AI they are crafting will someday be removed from use. That's the last thing they are thinking about.

This is a form of blindness about the AI development life cycle. AI Ethics opens their eyes to the importance of thinking further down the road about what their AI is going to bring forth. Those that manage and lead AI efforts are to be held accountable for what their AI produces, including after the AI is long gone.

To some degree, that is why AI Ethics and Ethical AI is such a crucial topic. The precepts of AI Ethics get us to remain vigilant. AI technologists can at times become preoccupied with technology, particularly the optimization of high-tech. They aren't necessarily considering the larger societal ramifications. Having an AI Ethics mindset and doing so integrally to AI development and fielding is vital for producing appropriate AI.

Besides employing AI Ethics, there is a corresponding question of whether we should have laws to govern various uses of AI. New laws are being bandied around at the federal, state, and local levels that concern the range and nature of how AI should be devised. The effort to draft and enact such laws is a gradual one. AI Ethics serves as a considered stopgap, at the very least, and will almost certainly to some degree be directly incorporated into those new laws.

Be aware that some adamantly argue that we do not need new laws that cover AI and that our existing laws are sufficient. In fact, they forewarn that if we do enact some of these AI laws, we will be killing the golden goose by clamping down on advances in AI that proffer immense societal advantages.

At this juncture of this weighty discussion, I'd bet that you are desirous of some illustrative examples that might showcase this topic. There is a special and assuredly popular set of examples that are close to my heart. You see, in my capacity as an expert on AI including the ethical and legal ramifications, I am frequently asked to identify realistic examples that showcase AI Ethics dilemmas so that the somewhat theoretical nature of the topic can be more readily grasped. One of the most evocative areas that vividly presents this ethical AI quandary is the advent of AI-based true self-driving cars. This will serve as a handy use case or exemplar for ample discussion on the topic.

Here's then a noteworthy question that is worth contemplating: *Does the advent of AI-based true self-driving cars illuminate anything about an AI algorithmic afterlife, and if so, what does this showcase?*

Let's sketch out a scenario that showcases the aspects of an AI algorithmic afterlife.

Contemplate the seemingly inconsequential matter of where self-driving cars will be roaming to pick up passengers. This seems like an abundantly innocuous topic.

At first, assume that AI self-driving cars will be roaming throughout entire towns. Anybody that wants to request a ride in a self-driving car has essentially an equal chance of hailing one.

Gradually, the AI begins to primarily keep the self-driving cars roaming in just one section of town. This section is a greater money-maker and the AI has been programmed to try and *maximize* revenues as part of the usage in the community at large (this underscores the mindset underlying optimization, namely focusing on just one particular metric and neglecting other crucial factors in the process).

Community members in the impoverished parts of the town turn out to be less likely to be able to get a ride from a self-driving car. This is because the self-driving cars were further away and roaming in the higher revenue part of the town. When a request comes in from a distant part of town, any other request from a closer location would get a higher priority.

Out goes the vaunted mobility-for-all dreams that self-driving cars are supposed to bring to life.

You could assert that the AI altogether landed on a form of statistical and computational bias, akin to a form of proxy discrimination (also often referred to as indirect discrimination). Realize that the AI wasn't programmed to avoid those poorer neighborhoods. Let's be clear about that in this instance. No, it was devised instead to merely optimize revenue, a seemingly acceptable goal, but this was done without the AI developers contemplating other potential ramifications. That optimization in turn unwittingly and inevitably led to an undesirable outcome.

Had they included AI Ethics considerations as part of their optimization mindset, they might have realized beforehand that unless they crafted the AI to cope with this kind of oversizing on one metric alone, they might have averted such dour results.

In any case, assume that the horse is already out of the barn and the situation is not immediately amenable to overarching solutions.

What might those that want to use those self-driving cars do?

The most apparent approach would be to work with community leaders on getting the automaker or self-driving tech firm to reconsider how they have set up the AI. Perhaps put pressure on whatever licensing or permits that have been granted for the deployment of those self-driving cars in that city or town. These are likely viable means of bringing about positive changes, though it could take a while before those efforts bear fruit.

Let's though take a more radical approach.

Some propose that all self-driving cars be removed from the community. Toss them out on their ear. They had a chance to showcase goodness but revealed a seedy underbelly. Revoke any and all permits that were issued to allow for autonomous vehicles to travel on public roadways. Send them back to the closed proving-ground tracks for further work there. Someday, if the community wishes, the fleet operators and automakers can try to reintroduce the self-driving cars into the town, though there is no assurance that approval for this will be granted.

Do you think that there is any kind of afterlife or imprinting that might arise in this particular use case?

I would bet that few in the community would be thinking about such impacts. The usual logic is that which was added can be cleanly removed. At the push of a button, you essentially undo the whole self-driving car immersion effort. No more self-driving cars. No residual impacts. You can simply wipe your hands of the whole affair.

One potential afterlife is that traffic patterns in the community might have altered as a result of the self-driving cars. Human drivers might have opted to avoid streets that were commonly being used by driverless vehicles. Will those human drivers somewhat mindlessly continue to stick with the roadways that they by habit are now using? If so, it could be that the other available roadway is not being used efficiently and yet is widely available due to the shutting out of self-driving cars.

Another concern might revolve around the use of self-driving cars as a low-cost form of transportation.

Some pundits believe that the cost for use of self-driving cars will be a lot less than the cost of using human-driven cars such as when doing conventional ridesharing. As such, those that before could not afford to use a ridesharing option might now be able to do so via the lesser-priced self-driving cars. Not everyone agrees that this is what will happen, but it is a commonly postulated notion.

Let's assume some people were gradually using self-driving cars to get around town, doing so when in the past it was cost prohibitive to do so. Maybe some took jobs at further away offices. Perhaps some went shopping for goods at malls that prior were beyond their reach.

Now that we've removed the lower-cost version of transport, we should consider what this will do to those that had grown accustomed to using self-driving cars. Are they to give up the job that was a further distance, or do they now need to use up more of their take-home pay to cover the cost of human-driven transport? Will those stores that were relishing the added business now be unable to attract those customers that were utilizing the lesser costing self-driving cars to come and make purchases?

A plethora of AI algorithmic afterlife and imprinting can be found within this scenario.

You can argue that some of the impacts are negative, such as the potential loss of a job or stores that cannot make ends meet, while other impacts might be positive. Perhaps people were becoming overly reliant on the use of self-driving cars. One expressed concern is that mass transit will lose its allure as a result of the widespread availability of driverless cars. People tend to prefer using singular forms of transit such as self-driving cars, especially if the price is exceedingly low. Some might assert that the removal of self-driving cars from a town could spur the use of mass transit, portending other advantages overall to the community at large.

Conclusion

What's done is done.

That is a classic line.

Depending upon your interpretation, it could mean that we should throw our hands in the air and merely resign ourselves to whatever AI afterlife there might be. The AI has done whatever it has done, including having second and third-order effects that might go far beyond the AI scope in any narrower meaning. After you've removed the AI, your work is done. Walk away. Whatever happens next is not of your concern.

I would dare suggest that we cannot allow this mindset to prevail.

It already exists and persists. The eagerness and excitement of unveiling AI are far more alluring and visible. There is little leftover energy to deal with the clean-up after AI has been removed. That occurs because of a shortsighted view of AI. If we carefully plotted out AI to encompass the aftermath, we would be forced at the front to anticipate what the final disposition will entail.

In a strict sense, we cannot undo that which was done, but we can certainly anticipate what impacts are likely to have occurred and seek to do next a robust afterlife recovery and ascertain how the rippling effects of AI can be intelligently dealt with in an aftermath realm.

Plan for today that which will arise tomorrow.

That is a handy proverb or AI Ethics motto worthy of keeping posted on the wall panels and display screens of all AI developers, deployers, and their impacted AI-using stakeholders.

CHAPTER 12

AI ETHICS AND
AI BIASES

Is a snail slow?

I'm assuming that your answer is pretty clearcut that yes, snails are abundantly slow.

Is a slug slower or faster than a snail?

Well, that question presumably causes you to think twice. A pensive moment of thought occurs. You certainly know that slugs are slow. You also know that snails are slow. In a foot race, as it were, between a snail and a slug, the likely winner seems a bit of a mind-bending puzzler.

The query is somewhat of a trick question. There are many varieties of slugs. There are many varieties of snails. We could pick the speediest of the known slugs and pit it against the sluggish (pun!) of the known snails. Lo and behold, the slug might go faster than the snail. Even if not lightning faster, nonetheless score a resounding win in a heated head-to-head race. The other side of the coin is possible too. We select the glacially slowest of the known slugs and set it against the rapid-fire fastest of the know snails. Now, the snail runs circles around the slug, albeit agonizingly slow circles.

Where am I going with this enigmatic saga about the snail versus the slug as a tortoise-versus-hare type of competition?

The gist is the snail and the slug as rivals are considered seemingly slow, and when compared to each other are nearly equally matched (we would not likely reach the same conclusion about a tortoise competing against a hare). Depending upon the circumstance at hand, one particular snail or slug is going to outdo the other kind. You cannot in the abstract generally say that one is always speedier than the other or will be the guaranteed winner over another.

If I was comparing the speed of a snail to a cheetah, you'd be on much firmer ground when making such a contention. We all know that the cheetah should win, all else being equal. That's not to say that we couldn't find exceptions, such as a cheetah that was regrettably hobbled due to an injury and could barely move. Or perhaps the cheetah is burdened with a pile of heavy weights attached via a leash.

There is all manner of ways to rig the potential outcome.

Some scientists have sought to train snails to go faster (just in general; not due to racing against slugs). I bring this up because there was an implied assumption that I was referring to snails that exist in the wild (and likewise slugs that exist in the wild). One supposes that another means to devilishly engineer a snail versus slug race would be to pick the particular kind of surface to be used for the race, along with weather conditions, and a myriad of other factors including training the creatures to be like *The Flash* of comic book and movies fame.

I am about to connect the dots between those venerated racing snails and slugs to the latest and greatest in modern-day high-tech. Hold on. A big pronouncement is about to be proclaimed.

All of this is quite important when it comes to discussing Artificial Intelligence (AI).

Here's the deal.

A lot of acrimonious chatter these days is about the ugly underbelly of AI entailing the embodiment of adverse biases and insidious discriminatory actions in numerous AI algorithms and/or data underlying the AI.

Here's what sparked my herein elucidation on this specific topic.

I was at a business dinner the other night and overheard an executive of a notable company say that they are dramatically cutting back on their use of AI due to growing concerns of AI containing potentially adverse biases. On the surface, this seems logical. If AI is doing bad things, the rather obvious and easiest step to resolve the matter would seem to be to stop using AI.

This though is reminiscent of the longstanding anecdote regarding a patient that goes to see their trusted physician and the patient complains intensely that their elbow hurts when they swing their arm up and down. The doctor sternly looks at the patient and loudly proclaims that they should simply stop moving their arm.

Problem solved.

Not really.

In the same mode of thought, does curbing the use of AI really act as a solution to the woes of AI adverse biases?

Not really.

Some would vehemently argue that this curtailment response represents the classic and misguided perspective of tossing out the baby with the bathwater (an old and perhaps tired phrase, though still admittedly potent). The counterargument goes that you can have AI and simultaneously deal with the potential of skulking biases. By realizing that biases can exist in AI, you are already perhaps halfway to coping with the matter. Those that are completely unaware of the AI biases issue are the ones that would seem most vulnerable to getting into hot water. They aren't even trying to do something about it.

In short, there are benefits and costs associated with crafting and deploying AI. The AI biases aspect is a considered cost and one that can be mitigated such that you can seek to detect and minimize the biases.

You can also wrap around an AI system other essential guardrails to try and bound the AI biases. Thus, though you might not have initially expurgated AI biases, you can have real-time protections that try to on the fly notice the AI biases, which then might be stopped in their tracks or at least reported as an alert for bringing humans into the loop.

If you merely discard all of your AI, you are losing forthwith the benefits that the AI otherwise was presumably incurring for your firm. There could earnestly be a lot of benefits. AI systems today that are wisely constructed can be demonstrably advantageous in many ways, such as being highly efficient, abundantly effective, and substantively aiding the bottom line of an enterprise.

Now that I've covered the importance of assessing the benefits versus costs associated with AI, doing so in light of the potential for adverse AI biases, we can bring the snails and the slugs back into the picture.

Get ready for this.

A notable question to contemplate seriously is this: *Which is worse, the AI adverse biases or those human adverse biases that are almost undoubtedly immersed in your business activities?*

In other words, I am going to agree with the notion that AI is potentially going to contain adverse biases and yet also emphasize that humans can contain adverse biases too. If you are somehow thinking about AI on a standalone basis and not comparing the AI to anything else, you would perhaps become over-fixated on the AI biases problem. The thing is, there is also a human biases problem. You need to compare one problem against the other problem.

We learned this lesson by making a comparison between the snail and the slug.

My analogy associated with the snail was that it is indeed slow, but you need to calibrate the slowness in comparison to something of a like nature that is also slow, such as a slug.

We need to clearly recognize that AI can in fact contain undue biases, surely so, though we must in the same light acknowledge that humans can contain undue biases. Anyone with an open mind would realize that you need to deal with and mitigate human biases that are integral to your products and services. AI is also going to need a similar kind of scrutiny.

There is no free lunch when it comes to adverse biases, whether embodied in humans or embedded in AI.

I'm guessing that the dinner dining executive did not have top of mind that the humans within their organization might have biases. You don't routinely read stories about company employees that were necessarily flaunting their foul biases. In addition, firms usually try to establish procedures and checks and balances to try and catch or prevent human-based sour biases from emerging amidst their products or services. Yet, despite those precautions, there are plenty of well-documented instances of human-based adverse biases that ended up being part and parcel of given businesses, sometimes knowingly and other times unknowingly so.

The headline-grabbing stories about AI adverse biases are profusely at top of my mind for this executive and others because those banner-screaming eye-catching revelations seem shocking. For some people, the idea that AI can exhibit undue biases is a huge head-turner. Say what, they respond in utter amazement, isn't AI supposed to be entirely neutral and fair? Balanced and transparent? Etc.

I've repeatedly discussed in my columns the incredibly lucky Public Relations (PR) aspects that AI earlier on seemed to luxuriate in. An established and quite common trope is that AI is dispassionate, honest, reasonable, and the like. Perhaps this comes from those sci-fi shows that portray AI robots in a similar vein (consider Data of *Star Trek* notoriety). I often disquietingly shake my head and wonder why people don't think of other shows and movies that portrayed robots like say *The Terminator* as their base for what AI might be able to do. You can certainly find as many AI sci-fi examples that showcase honor and heroism as the counterbalancing instances of AI that are villainous and ruinous.

Let's return to our focus on the consideration that you need to weigh those disconcerting AI biases against those disconcerting human biases that can arise amidst your products and services. This is a decidedly hidden or often unstated issue. Time to bring it into the light.

As a quick recap:

- **AI adverse biases are in today's headlines and causing some to knee-jerk react with rather narrow or hasty conclusions**
- **Yes, AI adverse biases can exist, though AI biases need to be weighed on a relative basis to the human adverse biases also amidst your products and services**
- **We likely don't want human adverse biases to be exhibited within products and services**
- **We also don't want AI adverse biases to be exhibited within products and services**
- **Getting rid of adverse biases all told is something that requires devout attention and effort**
- **Such efforts are needed to contend with both human biases and also to contend with AI biases**

Again, leveraging the tale of the slugs versus the snails, we need to realize that human adverse biases can also exist and that we need to be comparing those to the AI adverse biases. You can look at it the other way too. We need to compare the AI adverse biases against the human adverse biases.

As much as possible, the aim is to *eliminate* all such adverse biases.

It is often unrealistic to imagine that you will be able to eliminate all adverse biases, whether those that arise via humans or those that arise via AI. Humans can potentially gravitate toward adverse biases. They might do so purposefully. They might do so by happenstance. Without seeming to be anthropomorphizing the AI, you could argue that AI that "learns" and adjusts such as via the use of real-time ML/DL can also gravitate toward adverse biases (I am not suggesting this is a sentient facet).

This brings us to an augmented corollary to my proffered rule of thumb that we attempt to *eliminate* all adverse biases. Based on the reality of the real world, we have to be upfront and honestly acknowledge that adverse biases are going to arise, thus a handy corollary is that we ought to aim to *detect* adverse biases and then ascertain what to do once they have been discovered.

Our aims are:

- **Eliminate adverse biases at the get-go, as much as feasible to undertake**
- **Detect adverse biases that can arise over time**
- **Manage the discovered adverse biases in sensible ways**

I realize that you might be thinking that if we detect adverse biases once things are underway that the readily apparent solution is to then entirely eliminate those discovered adverse biases. I wish that we could always attain such an aspirational goal. Unfortunately, eliminating them can be a lot trickier than it seems. Those adverse biases can seemly hide and reappear, they can be extraordinarily difficult to extinguish entirely, and so on.

That's why the third rule is to try and *manage* the discovered adverse biases. It might be that once you've uncovered some adverse biases you put in place controls to prevent the biases from gaining any traction. They might still exist, but at least they are relatively contained and cannot (if well-contained) produce adverse results.

I want to next discuss the crucial point that AI biases and human biases are not necessarily the same.

Here's what I mean.

Some people right away leap to the conclusion that there is some kind of one-to-one correspondence between AI biases and human biases. Let's consider a simple example to see how this happens and then we can separate these two to dispel such a misconception or myth.

You are seeking to get a home loan. There is a particular bank that you are hoping will grant you the loan.

Consider one scenario whereby you make use of a human loan agent at the bank that will take your request and make a decision about the loan. Our second scenario will involve an AI system that has been programmed to work in a manner akin to what a human loan agent would do.

Suppose you make a phone call to the human loan agent. They are polite and friendly. A series of questions are asked of you. You answer the questions dutifully. After the question and answering portion is done, the human loan agent tells you that unfortunately you are being turned down for the loan.

I'd ask you to keep that tale of woe in mind, we'll need it in a moment.

Suppose that instead of calling a human loan agent, you had opted instead to use an online system of the bank that can potentially grant home loans. The online system makes use of today's advanced AI capabilities. No need to speak with a human loan granting agent. The AI does it all. The AI system guides you through a series of prompts. You dutifully fill in the forms and respond to the AI system. This AI is very textually chatty. Whereas you in the past might have used a traditional computer-based form system of a dry nature, this AI variant is more akin to interacting with a human agent. Not quite, but enough that you could almost start to believe that a human was on the other side of this activity.

After doing your best to "discuss" your request with this AI, in the end, it informs you that unfortunately the loan request is not approved. The AI algorithmically made this decision and did not somehow reach out to a human loan agent. It was all cooked solely within the AI system.

Yikes, you've lost in both of the scenarios. The human loan agent turned down your request in the first scenario. The AI-based loan system turned down your request in the second scenario. Depressing. Exasperating. A bad day for you, but please remain upbeat and positive about the world overall.

Anyway, after some diligent investigating, it turns out that the human loan agent made their decision based on your gender. This is outrageous and an instance of how an adverse bias of a human can enter into the picture.

Why did the AI turn you down?

Most people would probably speculate that the AI presumably algorithmically computed that you were to be declined for the loan based on your gender too. This kind of makes sense (even if it is a wrongful action). You see if humans at the bank are doing things this way, and if the AI was devised based on how the human loan agents do their job, it is certainly plausible that the AI has become reliant on this gender biasing element too.

One can readily envision that a slew of historical data about loan decisions at this bank was put together and fed into an ML/DL system. The ML/DL found a pattern that gender was a key factor in loan granting. Accordingly, the AI is computationally anchored on using gender as a keystone for the loan decision. The adverse bias of the human loan agents was essentially "cloned" into the AI system (I do not mean to imply cloning of a human soul or human intellect, only that the particular bias as embedded within the historical data is now repeated or being reused in the AI).

We are now facing a situation wherein there is human adverse bias and also AI adverse bias. They both stink with respect to embodying or embedding this gender bias.

Sit down to prepare yourself for the twist.

Upon closer inspection, the AI turned you down not due to gender but instead due to race. An AI audit showcased that gender as a factor was not being considered in the AI at all. That was a seeming relief. On the heels of that relief was the discovery that the race of the applicant was being used and that's why this particular loan for example was turned down.

We are definitely still dealing with a stinky situation. Whether gender was the adverse bias, or race was the adverse bias, we remain mired in a swamp of adverse biases. Neither instance is tolerable.

The twist that I am trying to bring to your attention is that the adverse bias differed between humans and AI. We cannot axiomatically assume that if there is an exposed human adverse bias that an AI system doing similar work is also embedding that exact same bias. It might be. It might not be.

If you discovered the human adverse bias first, namely about gender, you would naturally assume that a considered comparable AI that was doing the same work would also have a gender adverse bias that was computationally baked into the AI. I agree that this would be a sensible place to look.

I wouldn't though stop there. You would want to explore other potential adverse biases that might be contained within the AI. The lazy approach would be to seek only the gender bias, and afterward wave your hands that you dealt with the issue, one way or another (either finding the bias or not). I exhort that you should keep looking.

A twist upon the twist is that if you found the race-related bias in the AI, you would want to circle back to the human loan agents and consider whether there is a race-related bias there too. I am not saying there would be. I am only suggesting that it would likely be worth taking a look since it is conceivable that the AI is mimicking or repeating a bias that the human workers already have relied upon.

We can summarize the insights this way:

- **AI adverse biases can be completely separate and apart from any found human adverse biases in a given context**
- **Human adverse biases in a given context might be completely separate and apart of any AI adverse biases that might exist in the AI**
- **If you do perchance ascertain an adverse bias in either AI or the human role, it certainly would be prudent to look for the same or equivalent type of bias in the other case (assuming a like job setting)**

- **Don't fall for the "all biases are the same" blindness that can arise in these situations**
- **Always be open to the possibility of multi-biases rather than oversimplifying that only one distinct bias is exclusively going to occur**

To some degree, that is why AI Ethics and Ethical AI is such a crucial topic. The precepts of AI Ethics get us to remain vigilant. AI technologists can at times become preoccupied with technology, particularly the optimization of high-tech. They aren't necessarily considering the larger societal ramifications. Having an AI Ethics mindset and doing so integrally to AI development and fielding is vital for producing appropriate AI.

Besides employing AI Ethics, there is a corresponding question of whether we should have laws to govern various uses of AI. New laws are being bandied around at the federal, state, and local levels that concern the range and nature of how AI should be devised. The effort to draft and enact such laws is a gradual one. AI Ethics serves as a considered stopgap, at the very least, and will almost certainly to some degree be directly incorporated into those new laws.

Be aware that some adamantly argue that we do not need new laws that cover AI and that our existing laws are sufficient. In fact, they forewarn that if we do enact some of these AI laws, we will be killing the golden goose by clamping down on advances in AI that proffer immense societal advantages.

At this juncture of this weighty discussion, I'd bet that you are desirous of some illustrative examples that might showcase this topic. There is a special and assuredly popular set of examples that are close to my heart. You see, in my capacity as an expert on AI including the ethical and legal ramifications, I am frequently asked to identify realistic examples that showcase AI Ethics dilemmas so that the somewhat theoretical nature of the topic can be more readily grasped. One of the most evocative areas that vividly presents this ethical AI quandary is the advent of AI-based true self-driving cars. This will serve as a handy use case or exemplar for ample discussion on the topic.

Here's then a noteworthy question that is worth contemplating: *Does the advent of AI-based true self-driving cars illuminate anything about AI adverse biases versus human adverse biases, and if so, what does this showcase?*

Let's sketch out a scenario that showcases adverse biases in both humans and AI.

We will start with an AI focus.

Contemplate the seemingly inconsequential matter of where self-driving cars will be roaming to pick up passengers. This seems like an abundantly innocuous topic.

At first, assume that AI self-driving cars will be roaming throughout entire towns. Anybody that wants to request a ride in a self-driving car has essentially an equal chance of hailing one. Gradually, the AI begins to primarily keep the self-driving cars roaming in just one section of town. This section is a greater money-maker and the AI has been programmed to try and *maximize* revenues as part of the usage in the community at large (this underscores the mindset underlying optimization, namely focusing on just one particular metric and neglecting other crucial factors in the process).

Community members in the impoverished parts of the town turn out to be less likely to be able to get a ride from a self-driving car. This is because the self-driving cars were further away and roaming in the higher revenue part of the town. When a request comes in from a distant part of town, any other request from a closer location would get a higher priority. Eventually, the availability of getting a self-driving car in any place other than the richer part of town is nearly impossible, exasperatingly so for those that lived in those now resource-starved areas.

Out goes the vaunted mobility-for-all dreams that self-driving cars are supposed to bring to life.

You could assert that the AI altogether landed on a form of statistical and computational bias, akin to a form of proxy discrimination (also often referred to as indirect discrimination).

Realize that the AI wasn't programmed to avoid those poorer neighborhoods. Let's be clear about that in this instance. No, it was devised instead to merely optimize revenue, a seemingly acceptable goal, but this was done without the AI developers contemplating other potential ramifications. That optimization in turn unwittingly and inevitably led to an undesirable outcome.

Had they included AI Ethics considerations as part of their optimization mindset, they might have realized beforehand that unless they crafted the AI to cope with this kind of oversizing on one metric alone, they might have averted such dour results.

Let's start fresh with the example of these citywide traveling self-driving cars.

Suppose that *before* we allowed self-driving cars onto the roadways in this town, we first collected a whole bunch of data about ridesharing traffic patterns. Human drivers that offer ridesharing services are tracked for several months to get an indication of where they are picking up passengers and where they are dropping off passengers.

We take that data and feed it into an AI ML/DL system. A computational pattern matching takes place. The AI has now via the data figured out generally where pick-ups and drop-offs tend to occur in this town. By using this handy data, the AI is able to allocate the positioning of the soon-to-be-deployed self-driving cars, opting to make sure that the autonomous vehicles are nearby to the most commonly served locations thereof.

The self-driving cars are put into use. Soon, there are complaints from the community about the availability of self-driving cars. It seems as though self-driving cars are available readily in certain parts of town but not in other parts of town.

What is happening?

Imagine that an AI audit examines the ML/DL and discovers that the AI was patterning based on where the human ridesharing drivers were historically going, as indeed that is what was prescribed in this setting. Sadly, parts of towns that were generally occupied by one particular race had been severely neglected by ridesharing historically. The AI is carrying this same bias forward.

In this case, the bias was infused into the AI at the get-go.

A helpful side effect of putting AI into these situations is that to some degree the advent of AI might end up uncovering already preexisting human-led adverse biases that nobody seemed to realize were present. In addition, it might be much easier to mitigate or eliminate the found bias when it has been incorporated into AI, in comparison to trying to do the same when an adverse bias is rooted in a collective of people.

We can offer these last tidbits for now:
- **When crafting AI, it is possible that preexisting human-led biases might be exposed that had previously been unsurfaced**
- **This is not necessarily why the AI was being adopted but turns out to be a handy second-order effect of putting AI into place**
- **Significant legal and ethical complications can arise during AI crafting when such discoveries are realized**
- **Resolving or fixing the discovered adverse biases might be a lot less arduous or costly when preparing the AI versus trying to rectify the same amongst a collective of human workers**

Conclusion

Snails and slugs provided us with some keen insights about AI.

Who would have thought that possible?

We tend to discount creatures that move slowly.

We tend to relish animals that move fast. Some contend that we strive for speed as a survival tactic and likewise expect the same of animals. It does seem a bit surprising to think that slugs and snails are able to survive since they obviously are unable to dart away from potential predators or other dangers.

Finding adverse biases can be a slow process. Biases can be disguised. Biases can be deeply hidden. Expecting to quickly or immediately be able to spot and rectify adverse biases is just not especially realistic.

Slow and sure.

For those building or using AI, be slow and sure, painstakingly looking for adverse biases. Be ever vigilant, which might indeed be how slugs and snails account for their incredible longevity too.

CHAPTER 13

AI ETHICS

AND

SALTING AI ETHICISTS

Salting has been in the news quite a bit lately.

I am not referring to the salt that you put into your food. Instead, I am bringing up the "salting" that is associated with a provocative and seemingly highly controversial practice associated with the interplay between labor and business.

You see, this kind of salting entails the circumstance whereby a person tries to get hired into a firm to ostensibly initiate or some might arguably say instigate the establishment of a labor union therein. The latest news accounts discussing this phenomenon point to firms such as Starbucks, Amazon, and other well-known and even lesser-known firms.

I will cover first the basics of salting and then will switch to an akin topic that you might be quite caught off-guard about, namely that there seems to be a kind of salting taking place in the field of Artificial Intelligence (AI). This has crucial AI Ethics considerations.

Now, let's get into the fundamentals of how salting typically works.

Suppose that a company does not have any unions in its labor force. How might a labor union somehow gain a foothold in that firm? One means would be to take action outside of the company and try to appeal to the workers that they should join a union.

This might involve showcasing banners nearby to the company headquarters or sending the workers flyers or utilizing social media, and so on.

This is a decidedly outside-in type of approach.

Another avenue would be to spur from within a spark that might get the ball rolling. If at least one employee could be triggered as a cheerleader for embracing a labor union at the firm, perhaps this would start an eventual internal cavalcade of support for unionizing there. Even if such an employee wasn't serving as an out-and-out cheerer, they might be quietly able to garner internal support among workers and be a relatively hidden force within the organization for pursuing unionization.

In that way of thinking, a labor union might contemplate the ways in which such an employee can be so activated. The union might expend endless energy to find that needle in the haystack. Among perhaps hundreds or thousands of workers at the firm, trying to discover the so-called chosen one, in particular, that will favor unionizing might be tough to do.

It would be handy to more readily "discover" that spark-inducing worker (or invent them, so to speak).

This leads us to the voila idea that maybe get the company to hire such a person for an everyday role in the firm. Essentially, implant the right kind of union spurring person into the firm. You don't need to try and appeal to the throngs of workers all told from the outside and instead insert the one activating person so that you know for sure your spark is employed there.

The newly hired worker then seeks to instill a labor union interest within the firm, meanwhile doing whatever job they were otherwise hired to do (expressing what is often referred to as a "genuine interest" in the job). Note that the person is actively employed by the firm and actively doing work required of them as an employee. In the customary realm of salting, they are not solely a union-only non-specific job-related worker that perchance is embedded into the company.

Some have heralded this approach.

They exhort that it saves time and resources in terms of a union seeking to inspire workers at a firm to consider joining a union. Other employees are usually more likely to be willing to listen to and be activated by a fellow employee. The alternative approach of trying from the outside to gain traction is considered less alluring, whereby a fellow employee provides a powerful motivation to workers within the company in comparison to some "outsiders" that are seen as indeed little more than uninvolved and uncaring agenda-pushing outsiders.

Not everyone is happy with the salting approach.

Companies will often argue that this is an abundantly sneaky and dishonest practice. The overall gestalt of the approach is that a spy is being placed in the midst of the firm. That is not what the person was hired to do. They were presumably hired to do their stated job, while instead, the whole assorted shenanigans seem like the diabolical implanting of a veritable Trojan Horse.

The counterclaim by unions is that if the person is doing their stated job then there is no harm and no foul. Presumably, an employee, or shall we say any employee of the firm, can usually choose to seek unionization. This particular employee just so happens to want to do so. The fact that they came into the company with that notion in mind is merely something that any newly hired employee might likewise be considering.

Wait for a second, businesses will retort, this is someone that *by design* wanted to come to the company for purposes of starting a union foothold. That is their driven desire. The newly hired employee has made a mockery of the hiring process and unduly exploits their job-seeking aspirations as a cloaked pretense to the specific advantage of the union.

Round and round this heated discourse goes.

Keep in mind that there are a plethora of legal considerations that arise in these settings. All manner of rules and regulations that pertain for example to the National Labor Relations Act (NLRA) and the National Labor Relations Board (NRLB) are part of these gambits. I don't want you to get the impression that things are straightforward on these fronts. Numerous legal complications abound.

We should also ponder the variety of variations that come to play with salting.

Take the possibility that the person wishing to get hired is openly an advocate of the union throughout the process of seeking to get a job at the firm. This person might show up to the job interview wearing a shirt or other garb that plainly makes clear they are pro-union. They might during interviews bring up their hope that the company will someday embrace unionization. Etc.

In that case, some would assert that the business knew what it was getting into. From the get-go, the company had plenty of indications about the intentions of the person. You can't then whine afterward if upon being hired that the new employee will do whatever they can to get the union in the door. The firm has shot its own foot, as it were, and anything else is merely crocodile tears.

The dance on this though is again more complex than it seems. Per legal issues that can arise, someone that is otherwise qualified for getting hired could if turned down by the hiring company argue that they were intentionally overlooked as a result of an anti-union bias by the company. Once again, the NRLA and NRLB get drawn into the messy affair.

I'll quickly run you through a slew of other considerations that arise in the salting realm. I'd also like you to be aware that salting is not solely a US-only phenomenon. It can occur in other countries too. Of course, the laws and practices of countries differ dramatically, and thus salting is either not especially useful or possibly even outright banned in some locales, while the nature of salting might be significantly altered based on the legal and cultural mores thereof and could in fact still have potency.

Consult with your beloved labor laws attorney in whatever jurisdiction of interest concerns you.

Some additional factors about salting include:

- **Getting Paid**. Sometimes the person is being paid by the union to carry out the task of getting hired at the firm. They might then be paid by both the company and the union during their tenure at the firm or might no longer get paid by the union once hired by the firm.

- **Visibility.** Sometimes the person keeps on the down-low or remains altogether quiet during the hiring process about their unionizing intentions, while in other instances the person is overtly vocal about what they intend to do. A seemingly halfway approach is that the person will tell what they are aiming to do if explicitly asked during the interviews, and thus imply that it is up to the firm to ferret out such intentions, which is a burden that firms argue is underhandedly conniving and strains legal bounds.

- **Timing.** The person once hired might opt to wait to undertake their unionizing capacity. They could potentially wait weeks, months, or even years to activate. The odds are though they will more likely get started once they have become acclimated to the firm and have established a personal foothold as an employee of the firm. If they start immediately, this could undercut their attempt to be seen as an insider and cast them as an intruder or outsider.

- **Steps Taken.** Sometimes the person will explicitly announce within the firm that they are now seeking to embrace unionization, which could happen shortly after getting hired or occur a while afterward (as per my above indication about the timing factor). On the other hand, the person might choose to serve in an undercover role, feeding information to the union and not bringing any attention to themselves. This is at times lambasted as being a *salting mole*, though others would emphasize that the person might be otherwise subject to internal risks if they speak out directly.

- **Tenure.** A person taking on a salting effort might end up being able to get a unionizing impetus underway (they are a "salter"). They could potentially remain at the firm throughout the unionization process. That being said, sometimes such a person chooses to leave the firm that has been sparked and opt to go to another firm to start anew the sparking activities. Arguments over this are intense. One viewpoint is that this clearly demonstrates that the person didn't have in their heart the job at the firm. The contrasting viewpoint is that they are likely to find themselves in murky and possibly untenable waters by remaining in the firm once the union bolstering effort has gotten traction.

- **Outcome.** A salting attempt does not guarantee a particular outcome. It could be that the person does raise awareness about unionization and the effort gets underway, ergo "successful" salting has taken place. Another outcome is that the person is unable to get any such traction. They either then give up the pursuit and remain at the firm, perhaps waiting for another chance at a later time, or they leave the firm and typically seek to do the salting at some other company.

- **Professional Salter.** Some people consider themselves strong advocates of salting and they take pride in serving as a salter, as it were. They repeatedly do the salting, going from firm to firm as they do so. Others will do this on a one-time basis, maybe because of a particular preference or to see what it is like, and then choose not to repeat in such a role. You can assuredly imagine the types of personal pressures and potential stress that can occur when in a salter capacity.

Those factors will be sufficient for now to highlight the range and dynamics of salting. I will revisit those factors in the context of AI and Ethical AI considerations.

The gist is that some people seek to get hired into a firm to initiate or instigate the establishment of AI Ethics principles in the company. This is their primary motivation for going to work at the firm.

In a sense, they are salting not for the purposes of unionization but instead "salting" to try and get a company rooted in Ethical AI precepts.

Let's return to our focus on salting in an AI context.

First, we are removing any semblance of the unionization element from the terminology of salting and instead only using salting as a generalized paradigm or approach as a template. So, please put aside the union-related facets for purposes of this AI-related salting discussion.

Second, as earlier mentioned, salting in this AI context entails that some people might seek to get hired into a firm to initiate or instigate the establishment of AI Ethics principles in the company. This is their primary motivation for going to work at the firm.

To clarify, there are absolutely many that get hired into a firm and they already have in mind that AI Ethics is important. This though is not at the forefront of their basis for trying to get hired by the particular firm of interest. In essence, they are going to be hired to do some kind of AI development or deployment job, and for which they bring handily within them a strident belief in Ethical AI.

They then will work as best they can to infuse or inspire AI Ethics considerations in the company. Good for them. We need more that have that as a keenly heartfelt desire.

But that isn't the salting that I am alluding to herein. Imagine that someone picks out a particular company that seems to not be doing much if anything related to embracing AI Ethics. The person decides that they are going to get hired by that firm if they can do so in some everyday AI job (or maybe even a non-AI role), and then their primary focus will be to install or instigate AI Ethics principles in the company.

That is not their primary job duty and not even listed within their job duties (I mention this because, obviously, if one is hired to intentionally bring about AI Ethics they are not "salting" in the manner of connotation and semblance herein).

This person doesn't especially care about the job per se. Sure, they will do whatever the job consists of, and they presumably are suitably qualified to do so. Meanwhile, their real agenda is to spur Ethical AI to become part and parcel of the firm. That is the mission. That is the goal. The job itself is merely a means or vehicle to allow them to do so from within.

You might say that they could do the same from outside the firm. They could try to lobby the AI teams at the company to become more involved with AI Ethics. They might try to shame the firm into doing so, perhaps by posting on blogs or taking other steps. And so on. The thing is, they would still be an outsider, just as earlier pointed out when discussing the overarching premise of salting.

Is the AI salting person being deceitful?

We are again reminded of the same question asked about the union context of salting. The person might insist there is no deceit at all. They got hired to do a job. They are doing the job. It just so happens that in addition they are an internal advocate for AI Ethics and working mightily to get others to do the same. No harm, no foul.

They would likely also point out that there isn't any particular downside to their spurring the firm toward Ethical AI. In the end, this will aid the company in potentially avoiding lawsuits that otherwise might arise if the AI is being produced that is not abiding by AI Ethics precepts. They are thusly saving the company from itself. Even though the person perhaps doesn't especially care about doing the job at hand, they are doing the job and simultaneously making the company wiser and more secure via a vociferous push toward Ethical AI.

Wait for a second, some retort, this person is being disingenuous. They are seemingly going to jump ship once the AI Ethics embracement occurs. Their heart is not in the firm nor the job.

They are using the company to advance their own agenda. Sure, the agenda seems good enough, seeking to get Ethical AI on top of mind, but this can go too far.

You see, the argument further goes that the AI Ethics pursuit might become overly zealous. If the person came to get Ethical AI initiated, they might not look at a bigger picture of what the firm overall is dealing with. To the exclusion of all else, this person might myopically be distracting the firm and not be willing to allow for AI Ethics adoption on a reasoned basis and at a prudent pace.

They might become a disruptive malcontent that just continually bickers about where the firm sits in terms of Ethical AI precepts. Other AI developers might be distracted by the single-tune chatter. Getting AI Ethics into the mix is certainly sensible, though theatrics and other potential disruptions within the firm can stymy Ethical AI progress rather than aid it.

Round and round we go.

We can now revisit those additional factors about salting that I previously proffered:

- **Getting Paid**. It is conceivable that the person might be initially paid by some entity that wants to get a firm to embrace AI Ethics, perhaps aiming to do so innocuously or maybe to sell the firm a particular set of AI Ethics tools or practices. Generally unlikely, but worth mentioning.

- **Visibility.** The person might not especially bring up their AI Ethics devotional mission when going through the hiring process. In other instances, they might make sure it is front and center, such that the hiring firm understands without any ambiguity regarding their devout focus. This though is more likely to be couched as though AI Ethics is a secondary concern and that the job is their primary concern, rather than the other way around.

- **Timing.** The person once hired might opt to wait to undertake their AI Ethics commencements. They could potentially wait weeks, months, or even years to activate. The odds are though they will more likely get started once they have become acclimated to the firm and have established a personal foothold as an employee of the firm. If they start immediately, this could undercut their attempt to be seen as an insider and cast them as an intruder or outsider.

- **Steps Taken.** Sometimes the person will explicitly announce within the firm that they are now seeking to raise attention to AI Ethics, which could happen shortly after getting hired or occur a while afterward (as per my above indication about the timing factor). On the other hand, the person might choose to serve in an undercover role, working quietly within the firm and not bringing particular attention to themselves. They might also feed information to the press and other outsiders about what AI Ethics omissions or failings are taking place within the firm.

- **Tenure.** A person taking on a salting effort might end up being able to get an AI Ethics impetus underway. They could potentially remain at the firm throughout the Ethical AI adoption process. That being said, sometimes such a person chooses to leave the firm that has been sparked and opt to go to another firm to start anew the sparking activities. Arguments over this are intense. One viewpoint is that this clearly demonstrates that the person didn't have in their heart the job at the firm. The contrasting viewpoint is that they are likely to find themselves in murky and possibly untenable waters by remaining in the firm if they are now labeled as loud voices or troublemakers.

- **Outcome.** A salting attempt does not guarantee a particular outcome. It could be that the person does raise awareness about Ethical AI and the effort gets underway, ergo "successful" salting has taken place. Another outcome is that the person is unable to get any such traction. They either then give up the pursuit and remain at the firm, perhaps waiting for another chance at a later time, or they leave the firm and typically seek to do the salting at some other company.

- **Professional Salter.** Some people might consider themselves a strong advocate of AI Ethics salting and they take pride in serving as a salter, as it were. They repeatedly do the salting, going from firm to firm as they do so. Others might do this on a one-time basis, maybe because of a particular preference or to see what it is like, and then choose not to repeat in such a role. You can assuredly imagine the types of personal pressures and potential stress that can occur when in a salter capacity.

Whether this kind of AI Ethics oriented salting catches on will remain to be seen. If firms are slow to foster Ethical AI, this might cause fervent AI Ethicists to take on salting endeavors. They might not quite realize directly that they are doing salting. In other words, someone goes to company X and tries to get traction for AI Ethics, perhaps does so, and realizes they ought to do the same elsewhere. They then shift over to company Y. Rinse and repeat.

Again, the emphasis though is that AI Ethics embracement is their topmost priority. Landing the job is secondary or not even especially important, other than being able to get inside and do the insider efforts of salting related to Ethical AI.

I'll add too that those that study and analyze AI Ethics aspects now have a somewhat new addition to the topics of Ethical AI research pursuits:

- **Should these AI Ethics salting efforts be overall condoned or shunned?**
- **What drives those that would wish to perform salting in this AI context?**
- **How should businesses react to a perceived act of AI context salting?**
- **Will there be methodologies devised to encourage AI-related salting like this?**
- **Etc.**

To some degree, that is why AI Ethics and Ethical AI is such a crucial topic. The precepts of AI Ethics get us to remain vigilant. AI technologists can at times become preoccupied with technology, particularly the optimization of high-tech. They aren't necessarily considering the larger societal ramifications. Having an AI Ethics mindset and doing so integrally to AI development and fielding is vital for producing appropriate AI, including (perhaps surprisingly or ironically) the assessment of how AI Ethics gets adopted by firms.

Besides employing AI Ethics precepts in general, there is a corresponding question of whether we should have laws to govern various uses of AI. New laws are being bandied around at the federal, state, and local levels that concern the range and nature of how AI should be devised. The effort to draft and enact such laws is a gradual one. AI Ethics serves as a considered stopgap, at the very least, and will almost certainly to some degree be directly incorporated into those new laws.

Be aware that some adamantly argue that we do not need new laws that cover AI and that our existing laws are sufficient. In fact, they forewarn that if we do enact some of these AI laws, we will be killing the golden goose by clamping down on advances in AI that proffer immense societal advantages.

At this juncture of this weighty discussion, I'd bet that you are desirous of some illustrative examples that might showcase this topic. There is a special and assuredly popular set of examples that are close to my heart. You see, in my capacity as an expert on AI including the ethical and legal ramifications, I am frequently asked to identify realistic examples that showcase AI Ethics dilemmas so that the somewhat theoretical nature of the topic can be more readily grasped. One of the most evocative areas that vividly presents this ethical AI quandary is the advent of AI-based true self-driving cars. This will serve as a handy use case or exemplar for ample discussion on the topic.

Here's then a noteworthy question that is worth contemplating: *Does the advent of AI-based true self-driving cars illuminate anything about AI-related salting, and if so, what does this showcase?*

Let's sketch out a scenario that showcases an AI-related salting situation.

An automaker that is striving toward the development of fully autonomous self-driving cars is rushing ahead with public roadway tryouts. The firm is under a great deal of pressure to do so. They are being watched by the marketplace and if they don't seem to be at the leading edge of self-driving car development their share price suffers accordingly. In addition, they have already invested billions of dollars and investors are getting impatient for the day that the company is able to announce that their self-driving cars are ready for everyday commercial use.

An AI developer is closely watching from afar the efforts of the automaker. Reported instances of the AI driving system getting confused or making mistakes are increasingly being seen in the news. Various instances include collisions with other cars, collisions with bike riders, and other dour incidents.

The firm generally tries to keep this hush-hush. The AI developer has privately spoken with some of the engineers at the firm and learned that AI Ethics precepts are only being given lip service, at best.

What is this AI developer going to do?

They feel compelled to do something.

Let's do a bit of a forking effort and consider two paths that each might be undertaken by this AI developer.

One path is that the AI developer takes to the media to try and bring to light the seeming lack of suitable attention to AI Ethics precepts by the automaker. Maybe this concerned AI specialist opts to write blogs or create vlogs to highlight these concerns. Another possibility is they get an existing member of the AI team to become a kind of whistleblower.

This is decidedly a considered outsider approach by this AI developer.

Another path is that the AI developer believes in their gut that they might be able to get more done from within the firm. The skill set of the AI developer is well-tuned in AI facets involving self-driving cars and they can readily apply for the posted AI engineer job openings at the company. The AI developer decides to do so. Furthermore, the impetus is solely concentrated on getting the automaker to be more serious about Ethical AI. The job itself doesn't matter particularly to this AI developer, other than they will now be able to work persuasively from within.

It could be that the AI developer gets the job but then discovers there is tremendous internal resistance and the Ethical AI striving goal is pointless. The person leaves the company and decides to aim at another automaker that might be more willing to grasp what the AI developer aims to achieve. Once again, they are doing so to pointedly attain the AI Ethics considerations and not for the mainstay of whatever the AI job consists of.

Conclusion

The notion of referring to these AI-related efforts as a form of salting is bound to cause some to have heartburn about overusing an already established piece of terminology or vocabulary. Salting is pretty much entrenched in the unionization activities related to labor and business. Attempts to overload the word with these other kinds of seeming akin activities though of an entirely unrelated-to-unionization nature is potentially misleading and confounding.

Suppose we come up with a different phraseology.

Peppering?

Well, that doesn't seem to invoke quite the same sentiment as salting. It would be an uphill battle to try and get that stipulated and included in our everyday lexicon of language.

Whatever we come up with, and whatever naming or catchphrase seems suitable, we know one thing for sure. Trying to get firms to embrace AI Ethics is still an uphill battle. We need to try. The trying has to be done in the right ways.

Seems like no matter what side of the fence you fall on, we need to take that admonition with a suitable grain of salt.

CHAPTER 14

AI ETHICS

AND

AI SAFETY

AI safety is vital.

You would be hard-pressed to seemingly argue otherwise.

As readers of my writings know well, I have time and again emphasized the importance of AI safety. I typically bring up AI safety in the context of autonomous systems, such as autonomous vehicles including self-driving cars, plus amidst other robotic systems. Doing so highlights the potential life-or-death ramifications that AI safety imbues.

Given the widespread and nearly frenetic pace of AI adoption worldwide, we are facing a potential nightmare if suitable AI safety precautions are not firmly established and regularly put into active practice. In a sense, society is a veritable sitting duck as a result of today's torrents of AI that poorly enact AI safety including at times outright omitting sufficient AI safety measures and facilities.

Sadly, scarily, attention to AI safety is not anywhere as paramount and widespread as it needs to be.

In my coverage, I have emphasized that there is a multitude of dimensions underlying AI safety. There are technological facets. There are the business and commercial aspects. There are legal and ethical elements. And so on. All of these qualities are interrelated. Companies need to realize the value of investing in AI safety.

Our laws and ethical mores need to inform and promulgate AI safety considerations. And the technology to aid and bolster the adoption of AI safety precepts and practices must be both adopted and further advanced to attain greater and greater AI safety capabilities.

When it comes to AI safety, there is never a moment to rest. We need to keep pushing ahead. Indeed, please be fully aware that this is not a one-and-done circumstance but instead a continual and ever-present pursuit that is nearly endless in always aiming to improve.

I'd like to lay out for you a bit of the AI safety landscape and then share with you some key findings and crucial insights gleaned from a recent event covering the latest in AI safety. This was an event last week by the Stanford Center for AI Safety and took place as an all-day AI Safety Workshop on July 12, 2022, at the Stanford University campus. Kudos to Dr. Anthony Corso, Executive Director of the Stanford Center for AI Safety, and the team there for putting together an excellent event. For information about the Stanford Center for AI Safety, also known as "SAFE", see the link here. http://aisafety.stanford.edu/

First, before diving into the Workshop results, let's do a cursory landscape overview.

To illustrate how AI safety is increasingly surfacing as a vital concern, let me quote from a new policy paper released just earlier this week by the UK Governmental Office for Artificial Intelligence entitled *Establishing a Pro-innovation Approach to Regulating AI* that included these remarks about AI safety: "The breadth of uses for AI can include functions that have a significant impact on safety - and while this risk is more apparent in certain sectors such as healthcare or critical infrastructure, there is the potential for previously unforeseen safety implications to materialize in other areas. As such, whilst safety will be a core consideration for some regulators, it will be important for all regulators to take a context-based approach in assessing the likelihood that AI could pose a risk to safety in their sector or domain, and take a proportionate approach to manage this risk."

The cited policy paper goes on to call for new ways of thinking about AI safety and strongly advocates new approaches for AI safety. This includes boosting our technological prowess encompassing AI safety considerations and embodiment throughout the entirety of the AI devising lifecycle, among all stages of AI design, development, and deployment efforts. I will next week in my columns be covering more details about this latest proposed AI regulatory draft. For my prior and ongoing coverage of the somewhat akin drafts regarding legal oversight and governance of AI, such as the USA Algorithmic Accountability Act (AAA) and the EU AI Act (AIA).

When thinking mindfully about AI safety, a fundamental coinage is the role of measurement.

You see, there is a famous generic saying that you might have heard in a variety of contexts, namely that you cannot manage that for which you don't measure. AI safety is something that needs to be measured. It needs to be measurable. Without any semblance of suitable measurement, the question of whether AI safety is being abided by or not becomes little more than a vacuous argument of shall we say unprovable contentions.

Sit down for this next point.

Turns out that few today are actively measuring their AI safety and often do little more than a wink-wink that of course, their AI systems are embodying AI safety components. Flimsy approaches are being used. Weakness and vulnerabilities abound. There is a decided lack of training on AI safety. Tools for AI safety are generally sparse or arcane. Leadership in business and government is often unaware of and underappreciates the significance of AI safety.

Admittedly, that blindness and indifferent attention occur until an AI system goes terribly astray, similar to when an earthquake hits and all of a sudden people have their eyes opened that they should have been preparing for and readied to withstand the shocking occurrence.

At that juncture, in the case of AI that has gone grossly amiss, there is frequently a madcap rush to jump onto the AI safety bandwagon, but the impetus and consideration gradually diminish over time, and just like those earthquakes is only rejuvenated upon another big shocker.

When I was a professor at the University of Southern California (USC) and executive director of a pioneering AI laboratory at USC, we often leveraged the earthquake analogy since the prevalence of earthquakes in California was abundantly understood. The analogy aptly made the on-again-off-again adoption of AI safety a more readily realized unsuitable and disjointed way of getting things done. Today, I serve as a Stanford Fellow and in addition serve on AI standards and AI governance committees for international and national entities such as the WEF, UN, IEEE, NIST, and others. Outside of those activities, I recently served as a top executive at a major Venture Capital (VC) firm and today serve as a mentor to AI startups and as a pitch judge at AI startup competitions. I mention these aspects as background for why I am distinctly passionate about the vital nature of AI safety and the role of AI safety in the future of AI and society, along with the need to see much more investment into AI safety-related startups and related research endeavors.

All told, to get the most out of AI safety, companies and other entities such as governments need to embrace AI safety and then enduringly stay the course. Steady the ship. And keep the ship in top shipshape.

Let's lighten the mood and consider my favorite talking points that I use when trying to convey the status of AI safety in contemporary times.

I have my own set of AI safety *levels of adoption* that I like to use from time to time. The idea is to readily characterize the degree or magnitude of AI safety that is being adhered to or perhaps skirted by a given AI system, especially an autonomous system. This is just a quick means to saliently identify and label the seriousness and commitment being made to AI safety in a particular instance of interest.

I'll briefly cover my AI safety levels of adoption and then we'll be ready to switch to exploring the recent Workshop and its related insights.

My scale goes from the highest or topmost of AI safety and then winds its way down to the lowest or worst most of AI safety. I find it handy to number the levels and ergo the topmost is considered as rated #1, while the least is ranked as 7th. You are not to assume that there is a linear steady distance between each of the levels thus keep in mind that the effort and degree of AI safety are often magnitudes greater or lesser depending upon where in the scale you are looking.

Here's my scale of the levels of adoption regarding AI safety:
1) **Verifiably Robust AI Safety** (rigorously provable, formal, hardness, today this is rare)
2) **Softly Robust AI Safety** (partially provable, semi-formal, progressing toward fully)
3) **Ad Hoc AI Safety** (no consideration for provability, informal approach, highly prevalent today)
4) **Lip-Service AI Safety** (smattering, generally hollow, marginal, uncaring overall)
5) **Falsehood AI Safety** (appearance is meant to deceive, dangerous pretense)
6) **Totally Omitted AI Safety** (neglected entirely, zero attention, highly risk prone)
7) **Unsafe AI Safety** (role reversal, AI safety that is actually endangering, insidious)

Researchers are usually focused on the topmost part of the scale. They are seeking to mathematically and computationally come up with ways to devise and ensure provable AI safety. In the trenches of everyday practices of AI, regrettably *Ad Hoc AI Safety* tends to be the norm. Hopefully, over time and by motivation from all of the aforementioned dimensions (e.g., technological, business, legal, ethical, and so on), we can move the needle closer toward the rigor and formality that ought to be rooted foundationally in AI systems.

You might be somewhat taken aback by the categories or levels that are beneath the *Ad Hoc AI Safety* level.

Yes, things can get pretty ugly in AI safety.

Some AI systems are crafted with a kind of lip-service approach to AI safety. There are AI safety elements sprinkled here or there in the AI that purport to be providing AI safety provisions, though it is all a smattering, generally hollow, marginal, and reflects a somewhat uncaring attitude. I do not want to though leave the impression that the AI developers or AI engineers are the sole culprits in being responsible for the lip-service landing. Business or governmental leaders that manage and oversee AI efforts can readily usurp any energy or proneness toward the potential costs and resource consumption needed for embodying AI safety.

In short, if those at the helm are not willing or are unaware of the importance of AI safety, this is the veritable kiss of death for anyone else wishing to get AI safety into the game.

I don't want to seem like a downer but we have even worse levels beneath the lip-service classification. In some AI systems, AI safety is put into place as a form of *falsehood*, intentionally meant to deceive others into believing that AI safety embodiments are implanted and actively working. As you might expect, this is rife for dangerous results since others are bound to assume that AI safety exists when it in fact does not. Huge legal and ethical ramifications are like a ticking time bomb in these instances.

Perhaps nearly equally unsettling is the entire lack of AI safety all told, the *Totally Omitted AI Safety* category. It is hard to say which is worse, falsehood AI safety that maybe provides a smidgeon of AI safety despite that it overall falsely represents AI safety or the absolute emptiness of AI safety altogether. You might consider this to be the battle between the lesser of two evils.

The last of the categories is really chilling, assuming that you are not already at the rock bottom of the abyss of AI safety chilliness. In this category sits the *unsafe* AI safety. That seems like an oxymoron, but it has a straightforward meaning.

It is quite conceivable that a role reversal can occur such that an embodiment in an AI system that was intended for AI safety purposes turns out to ironically and hazardously embed an entirely unsafe element into the AI. This can especially happen in AI systems that are known as being dual-use AI.

Remember to always abide by the Latin vow of *primum non nocere*, which specifically instills the classic Hippocratic oath to make sure that first, do no harm.

There are those that put in AI safety with perhaps the most upbeat of intentions, and yet shoot their foot and undermine the AI by having included something that is unsafe and endangering (which, metaphorically, shoots the feet of all other stakeholders and end-users too). Of course, evildoers might also take this path, and therefore either way we need to have suitable means to detect and verify the safeness or unsafe proneness of any AI -- including those portions claimed to be devoted to AI safety.

It is the Trojan Horse of AI safety that sometimes in the guise of AI safety the inclusion of AI safety renders the AI into a horrendous basket full of unsafe AI.

Not good.

Okay, I trust that the aforementioned overview of some trends and insights about the AI safety landscape has whetted your appetite. We are now ready to proceed to the main meal.

Recap And Thoughts About The Stanford Workshop On AI Safety

I provide next a brief recap along with my own analysis of the various research efforts presented at the recent workshop on AI Safety that was conducted by the Stanford Center for AI Safety. I respectively ask too that the researchers and presenters of the Workshop please realize that I am seeking to merely whet the appetite of readers or viewers in this recap and am not covering the entirety of what was conveyed.

In addition, I am expressing my particular perspectives about the work presented and opting to augment or provide added flavoring to the material as commensurate with my existing style or panache of my column, versus strictly transcribing or detailing precisely what was pointedly identified in each talk. Thanks for your understanding in this regard.

I will now proceed in the same sequence of the presentations as they were undertaken during the Workshop. I list the session title, and the presenter(s), and then share my own thoughts that both attempt to recap or encapsulate the essence of the matter discussed and provide a tidbit of my own insights thereupon.

- **Session Title: "Run-time Monitoring for Safe Robot Autonomy"**

Presentation by Dr. Marco Pavone

Dr. Marco Pavone is an Associate Professor of Aeronautics and Astronautics at Stanford University, and Director of Autonomous Vehicle Research at NVIDIA, plus Director of the Stanford Autonomous Systems Laboratory and Co-Director of the Center for Automotive Research at Stanford

Here's my brief recap and erstwhile thoughts about this talk.

A formidable problem with contemporary Machine Learning (ML) and Deep Learning (DL) systems entails dealing with out-of-distribution (OOD) occurrences, especially in the case of autonomous systems such as self-driving cars and other self-driving vehicles. When an autonomous vehicle is moving along and encounters an OOD instance, the responsive actions to be undertaken could spell the difference between life-or-death outcomes.

I've covered extensively in my column the circumstances of having to deal with a plethora of fast-appearing objects that can overwhelm or confound an AI driving system, for example.

In a sense, the ML/DL might have been narrowly derived and either fail to recognize an OOD circumstance or perhaps equally worse treat the OOD as though it is within the confines of conventional inside-distribution occurrences that the AI was trained on. This is the classic dilemma of treating something as a false positive or a false negative and ergo having the AI take no action when it needs to act or taking devout action that is wrongful under the circumstances.

In this insightful presentation about safe robot autonomy, a keystone emphasis entails a dire need to ensure that suitable and sufficient run-time monitoring is taking place by the AI driving system to detect those irascible and often threatening out-of-distribution instances. You see, if the run-time monitoring is absent of OOD detection, all heck would potentially break loose since the chances are that the initial training of the ML/DL would not have adequately prepared the AI for coping with OOD circumstances. If the run-time monitoring is weak or inadequate when it comes to OOD detection, the AI might be driving blind or cross-eyed as it were, not ascertaining that a boundary breaker is in its midst.

A crucial first step involves the altogether fundamental question of being able to define what constitutes being out-of-distribution. Believe it or not, this is not quite as easy as you might so assume.

Imagine that a self-driving car encounters an object or event that computationally is calculated as relatively close to the original training set but not quite on par. Is this an encountered anomaly or is it just perchance at the far reaches of the expected set?

This research depicts a model that can be used for OOD detection, called Sketching Curvature for OOD Detection or SCOD. The overall idea is to equip the pre-training of the ML with a healthy dose of epistemic uncertainty. In essence, we want to carefully consider the tradeoff between the fraction of out-of-distribution that has been correctly flagged as indeed OOD (referred to as TPR, True Positive Rate), versus the fraction of in-distribution that is incorrectly flagged as being OOD when it is not, in fact, OOD (referred to as FPR, False Positive Rate).

Ongoing and future research posited includes classifying the severity of OOD anomalies, causal explanations that can be associated with anomalies, run-time monitor optimizations to contend with OOD instances, etc., and the application of SCOD to additional settings.

Link to the Stanford Autonomous Systems Lab (ASL): https://stanfordasl.github.io/
Link to the Stanford Center for Automotive Research (CARS): https://cars.stanford.edu/

- **Session Title: "Reimagining Robot Autonomy with Neural Environment Representations"**

Presentation by Dr. Mac Schwager

Dr. Mac Schwager is an Associate Professor of Aeronautics and Astronautics at Stanford University and Director of the Stanford Multi-Robot Systems Lab (MSL)

Here's my brief recap and erstwhile thoughts about this talk.

There are various ways of establishing a geometric representation of scenes or images. Some developers make use of point clouds, voxel grids, meshes, and the like. When devising an autonomous system such as an autonomous vehicle or other autonomous robots, you'd better make your choice wisely since otherwise the whole kit and kaboodle can be stinted. You want a representation that will aptly capture the nuances of the imagery, and that is fast, reliable, flexible, and proffers other notable advantages.

The use of artificial neural networks (ANNs) has gained a lot of traction as a means of geometric representation. An especially promising approach to leveraging ANNs is known as a neural radiance field or NeRF method.

Let's take a look at a handy originating definition of what NeRF consists of: "Our method optimizes a deep fully-connected neural network without any convolutional layers (often referred to as a multilayer perceptron or MLP) to represent this function by regressing from a single 5D coordinate to a single volume density and view-dependent RGB color. To render this neural radiance field (NeRF) from a particular viewpoint we: 1) march camera rays through the scene to generate a sampled set of 3D points, 2) use those points and their corresponding 2D viewing directions as input to the neural network to produce an output set of colors and densities, and 3) use classical volume rendering techniques to accumulate those colors and densities into a 2D image. Because this process is naturally differentiable, we can use gradient descent to optimize this model by minimizing the error between each observed image and the corresponding views rendered from our representation (as stated in the August 2020 paper entitled *NeRF: Representing Scenes as Neural Radiance Fields for View Synthesis* by co-authors Ben Mildenhall, Pratul P. Srinivasan, Matthew Tancik, Jonathan T. Barron, Ravi Ramamoorthi, and Ren Ng).

In this fascinating talk about NeRF and fostering advances in robotic autonomy, there are two questions directly posed:

- *Can we use the NeRF density as a geometry representation for robotic planning and simulation?*
- *Can we use NeRF photo rendering as a tool for estimating robot and object poses?*

The presented answers are that yes, based on initial research efforts, it does appear that NeRF can indeed be used for those proposed uses.

Examples showcased include navigational uses such as via the efforts of aerial drones, grasp planning uses such as a robotic hand attempting to grasp a coffee mug, and differentiable simulation uses including a dynamics-augmented neural object (DANO) formulation. Various team members that participated in this research were also listed and acknowledged for their respective contributions to these ongoing efforts.

For a link to the Stanford Multi-Robot Systems Lab (MSL) use this: https://msl.stanford.edu/

- **Session Title: "Toward Certified Robustness Against Real-World Distribution Shifts"**

Presentation by Dr. Clark Barrett, Professor (Research) of Computer Science, Stanford University

Here's my brief recap and erstwhile thoughts about this research.

When using Machine Learning (ML) and Deep Learning (DL), an important consideration is the all-told robustness of the resulting ML/DL system. AI developers might inadvertently make assumptions about the training dataset that ultimately gets undermined once the AI is put into real-world use.

For example, a demonstrative distributional shift can occur at run-time that catches the AI off-guard. A simple use case might be an image analyzing AI ML/DL system that though originally trained on clearcut images later on gets confounded when encountering images at run-time that are blurry, poorly lighted, and contain other distributional shifts that were not encompassed in the initial dataset.

Integral to doing proper computational verification for ML/DL consists of devising specifications that are going to suitably hold up regarding the ML/DL behavior in realistic deployment settings. Having specifications that are perhaps lazily easy for ML/DL experimental purposes is well below the harsher and more demanding needs for AI that will be deployed on our roadways via autonomous vehicles and self-driving cars, driving along city streets and tasked with life-or-death computational decisions.

Key findings and contributions of this work per the researcher's statements are:
- Introduction of a new framework for verifying DNNs (deep neural networks) against real-world distribution shifts
- Being the first to incorporate deep generative models that capture distribution shifts, e.g., changes in weather conditions

or lighting in perception tasks—into verification specifications

- Proposal of a novel abstraction-refinement strategy for transcendental activation functions
- Demonstrating that the verification techniques are significantly more precise than existing techniques on a range of challenging real-world distribution shifts on MNIST and CIFAR-10.

For additional details, see the associated paper entitled *Toward Certified Robustness Against Real-World Distribution Shifts*, June 2022, by co-authors Haoze Wu, Teruhiro Tagomori, Alexandar Robey, Fengjun Yang, Nikolai Matni, George Pappas, Hamed Hassani, Corina Pasareanu, and Clark Barrett.

- **Session Title: "AI Index 2022"**

Presentation by Daniel Zhang, Policy Research Manager, Stanford Institute for Human-Centered Artificial Intelligence (HAI), Stanford University

Here's my brief recap and erstwhile thoughts about this research.

Each year, the world-renowned Stanford Institute for Human-Centered AI at Stanford University prepares and releases a widely read and eagerly awaited "annual report" about the global status of AI, known as the AI Index. The latest AI Index is the fifth edition and was unveiled earlier this year, thus referred to as AI Index 2022.

As officially stated: "The annual report tracks, collates, distills, and visualizes data relating to artificial intelligence, enabling decision-makers to take meaningful action to advance AI responsibly and ethically with humans in mind. The 2022 AI Index report measures and evaluates the rapid rate of AI advancement from research and development to technical performance and ethics, the economy and education, AI policy and governance, and more. The latest edition includes data from a broad set of academic, private, and non-profit organizations as well as more self-collected data and original analysis than any previous editions" (per the HAI website; note that the AI Index 2022 is available as a downloadable free PDF at https://hai.stanford.edu/research/ai-index-2022

The listed top takeaways consisted of:

- Private investment in AI soared while investment concentration intensified
- U.S. and China dominated cross-country collaborations on AI
- Language models are more capable than ever, but also more biased
- The rise of AI ethics everywhere
- AI becomes more affordable and higher performing
- Data, data, data
- More global legislation on AI than ever
- Robotic arms are becoming cheaper

There are about 230 pages of jampacked information and insights in the AI Index 22 covering the status of AI today and where it might be headed. Prominent news media and other sources often quote the given stats or other notable facts and figures contained in Stanford's HAI annual AI Index.

- **Session Title: "Opportunities for Alignment with Large Language Models"**

Presentation by Dr. Jan Leike, Head of Alignment, OpenAI

Here's my brief recap and erstwhile thoughts about this talk.

Large Language Models (LLM) such as GPT-3 have emerged as important indicators of advances in AI, yet they also have spurred debate and at times heated controversy over how far they can go and whether we might misleadingly or mistakenly believe that they can do more than they really can.

In this perceptive talk, there are three major points covered:

- LLMs have obvious alignment problems
- LLMs can assist human supervision
- LLMs can accelerate alignment research

As a handy example of a readily apparent alignment problem, consider giving GPT-3 the task of writing a recipe that uses ingredients consisting of avocados, onions, and limes. If you gave the same task to a human, the odds are that you would get a reasonably sensible answer, assuming that the person was of a sound mind and willing to undertake the task seriously.

Per this presentation about LLMs limitations, the range of replies showcased via the use of GPT-3 varied based on minor variants of how the question was asked. In one response, GPT-3 seemed to dodge the question by indicating that a recipe was available but that it might not be any good. Another response by GPT-3 provided some quasi-babble such as "Easy bibimbap of spring chrysanthemum greens." Via InstructGPT a reply appeared to be nearly on target, providing a list of instructions such as "In a medium bowl, combine diced avocado, red onion, and lime juice" and then proceeded to recommend additional cooking steps to be performed.

The crux here is the alignment considerations.

How does the LLM align with or fail to align to the stated request of a human making an inquiry?

If the human is seriously seeking a reasonable answer, the LLM should attempt to provide a reasonable answer. Realize that a human answering the recipe question might also spout babble, though at least we might expect the person to let us know that they don't really know the answer and are merely scrambling to respond. We naturally might expect or hope that an LLM would do likewise, namely alert us that the answer is uncertain or a mishmash or entirely fanciful.

As I've exhorted many times in my column, an LLM ought to "know its limitations" (borrowing the famous or infamous catchphrase).

Trying to push LLMs forward toward better human alignment is not going to be easy. AI developers and AI researchers are burning the night oil to make progress on this assuredly hard problem. Per the talk, an important realization is that LLMs can be used to accelerate the AI and human alignment aspiration. We can use LLMs as a tool for these efforts. The research outlined a suggested approach consisting of these main steps: (1) Perfecting RL or Reinforcement Learning from human feedback, (2) AI-assisted human feedback, and (3) Automating alignment research.

- **Session Title: "Challenges in AI safety: A Perspective from an Autonomous Driving Company"**

Presentation by James "Jerry" Lopez, Autonomy Safety and Safety Research Leader, Motional

Here's my brief recap and erstwhile thoughts about this talk.

As avid followers of my coverage regarding autonomous vehicles and self-driving cars are well aware, I am a vociferous advocate for applying AI safety precepts and methods to the design, development, and deployment of AI-driven vehicles.

We must keep AI safety at the highest of priorities and the topmost of minds.

This talk covered a wide array of important points about AI safety, especially in a self-driving car context (the company, Motional, is well-known in the industry and consists of a joint venture between Hyundai Motor Group and Aptiv, for which the firm name is said to be a mashup of the words "motion" and "emotional" serving as a mixture intertwining automotive movement and valuation of human respect).

The presentation noted several key difficulties with today's AI in general and likewise in particular to self-driving cars, such as:
- AI is brittle
- AI is opaque
- AI can be confounded via an intractable state space

Another consideration is the incorporation of uncertainty and probabilistic conditions. The asserted "four horsemen" of uncertainty were described: (1) Classification uncertainty, (2) Track uncertainty, (3) Existence uncertainty, and (4) Multi-modal uncertainty.

One of the most daunting AI safety challenges for autonomous vehicles consists of trying to devise MRMs (Minimal Risk Maneuvers). Human drivers deal with this all the time while behind the wheel of a moving car. There you are, driving along, and all of a sudden a roadway emergency or other potential calamity starts to arise. How do you respond? We expect humans to remain calm, think mindfully about the problem at hand, and make a judicious choice of how to handle the car and either avoid an imminent car crash or seek to minimize adverse outcomes.

Getting AI to do the same is tough to do.

An AI driving system has to first detect that a hazardous situation is brewing. This can be a challenge in and of itself. Once the situation is discovered, the variety of "solving" maneuvers must be computed. Out of those, a computational determination needs to be made as to the "best" selection to implement at the moment at hand. All of this is steeped in uncertainties, along with potential unknowns that loom gravely over which action ought to be performed.

AI safety in some contexts can be relatively simple and mundane, while in the case of self-driving cars and autonomous vehicles there is a decidedly life-or-death paramount vitality for ensuring that AI safety gets integrally woven into AI driving systems.

- **Session Title: "Safety Considerations and Broader Implications for Governmental Uses of AI"**

Presentation by Peter Henderson, JD/Ph.D. Candidate at Stanford University

Here's my brief recap and erstwhile thoughts about this talk.

Readers of my columns are familiar with my ongoing clamor that AI and the law are integral dance partners. As I've repeatedly mentioned, there is a two-sided coin intertwining AI and the law. AI can be applied to law, doing so hopefully to the benefit of society all told. Meanwhile, on the other side of the coin, the law is increasingly being applied to AI, such as the proposed EU AI Act (AIA) and the draft USA Algorithmic Accountability Act (AAA).

In this talk, a similar dual-focus is undertaken, specifically with respect to AI safety.

You see, we ought to be wisely considering how we can enact AI safety precepts and capabilities into the governmental use of AI applications. Allowing governments to willy-nilly adopt AI and then trust or assume that this will be done in a safe and sensible manner is not a very hearty assumption. Indeed, it could be a disastrous assumption. At the same time, we should be urging lawmakers to sensibly put in place laws about AI that will incorporate and ensure some reasonable semblance of AI safety, doing so as a hardnosed legally required expectation for those devising and deploying AI.

Two postulated rules of thumb that are explored in the presentation include:

- It's not enough for humans to just be in the loop, they have to actually be able to assert their discretion. And when they don't, you need a fallback system that is efficient.
- Transparency and openness are key to fighting corruption and ensuring safety. But you have to find ways to balance that against privacy interests in a highly contextual way.

As a closing comment that is well worth emphasizing over and over again, the talk stated that we need to embrace decisively both a technical and a regulatory law mindset to make AI Safety well-formed.

- **Session Title: "Research Update from the Stanford Intelligent Systems Laboratory"**

Presentation by Dr. Mykel Kochenderfer, Associate Professor of Aeronautics and Astronautics at Stanford University and Director of the Stanford Intelligent Systems Laboratory (SISL)

Here's my brief recap and erstwhile thoughts about this talk.

This talk highlighted some of the latest research underways by the Stanford Intelligent Systems Laboratory (SISL), a groundbreaking and extraordinarily innovative research group that is at the forefront of exploring advanced algorithms and analytical methods for the design of robust decision-making systems. *I can highly recommend that you consider attending their seminars and read their research papers, a well-worth instructive and engaging means to be aware of the state-of-the-art in intelligent systems (I avidly do so).*

Here's a link to the SISL website: http://sisl.stanford.edu/

The particular areas of interest to SISL consist of intelligent systems for such realms as Air Traffic Control (ATC), uncrewed aircraft, and other aerospace applications wherein decisions must be made in complex and uncertain, dynamic environments, meanwhile seeking to maintain sufficient safety and efficacious efficiency. In brief, robust computational methods for deriving optimal decision strategies from high-dimensional, probabilistic problem representations are at the core of their endeavors.

At the opening of the presentation, three key desirable properties associated with safety-critical autonomous systems were described:

- **Accurate Modeling** – encompassing realistic predictions, modeling of human behavior, generalizing to new tasks and environments
- **Self-Assessment** – interpretable situational awareness, risk-aware designs
- **Validation and Verification** – efficiency, accuracy

In the category of Accurate Modeling, these research efforts were briefly outlined (listed here by the title of the efforts):

- LOPR: Latent Occupancy Prediction using Generative Models
- Uncertainty-aware Online Merge Planning with Learned Driver Behavior
- Autonomous Navigation with Human Internal State Inference and Spatio-Temporal Modeling
- Experience Filter: Transferring Past Experiences to Unseen Tasks or Environments

In the category of Self-Assessment, these research efforts were briefly outlined (listed here by the title of the efforts):

- Interpretable Self-Aware Neural Networks for Robust Trajectory Prediction
- Explaining Object Importance in Driving Scenes
- Risk-Driven Design of Perception Systems

In the category of Validation and Verification, these research efforts were briefly outlined (listed here by the title of the efforts):

- Efficient Autonomous Vehicle Risk Assessment and Validation
- Model-Based Validation as Probabilistic Inference
- Verifying Inverse Model Neural Networks

In addition, a brief look at the contents of the pioneering book *Algorithms For Decision Making* by Mykel Kochenderfer, Tim Wheeler, and Kyle Wray was explored (for more info about the book and a free electronic PDF download, use this link algorithmsbook.com

Future research projects either underway or being envisioned include efforts on explainability or XAI (explainable AI), out-of-distribution (OOD) analyses, more hybridization of sampling-based and formal methods for validation, large-scale planning, AI and society, and other projects including collaborations with other universities and industrial partners.

- **Session Title: "Learning from Interactions for Assistive Robotics"**

Presentation by Dr. Dorsa Sadigh, Assistant Professor of Computer Science and of Electrical Engineering at Stanford University

Here's my brief recap and erstwhile thoughts about this research.

Let's start with a handy scenario about the difficulties that can arise when devising and using AI.

Consider the task of stacking cups. The tricky part is that you aren't stacking the cups entirely by yourself. A robot is going to work with you on this task. You and the robot are supposed to work together as a team.

If the AI underlying the robot is not well-devised, you are likely to encounter all sorts of problems with what otherwise would seem to be an extremely easy task. You put one cup on top of another and then give the robot a chance to place yet another cup on top of those two cups. The AI selects an available cup and gingerly tries to place it atop the other two. Sadly, the cup chosen is overly heavy (bad choice) and causes the entire stack to fall to the floor.

Imagine your consternation.

The robot is not being very helpful.

You might be tempted to forbid the robot from continuing to stack cups with you. But, assume that you ultimately do need to make use of the robot. The question arises as to whether the AI is able to figure out the cup stacking process, doing so partially by trial and error but also as a means of discerning what you are doing when stacking the cups. The AI can potentially "learn" from the way in which the task is being carried out and how the human is performing the task. Furthermore, the AI could possibly ascertain that there are generalizable ways of stacking the cups, out of which you the human here have chosen a particular means of doing so.

In that case, the AI might seek to tailor its cup stacking efforts to your particular preferences and style (don't we all have our own cup stacking predilections).

You could say that this is a task involving an assistive robot.

Interactions take place between the human and the assistive robot. The goal here is to devise the AI such that it can essentially learn from the task, learn from the human, and learn how to perform the task in a properly assistive manner. Just as we wanted to ensure that the human worked with the robot, we don't want the robot to somehow arrive at a computational posture that will simply circumvent the human and do the cup stacking on its own. They must collaborate.

The research taking place is known as the ILIAD initiative and has this overall stated mission: "Our mission is to develop theoretical foundations for human-robot and human-AI interaction. Our group is focused on: 1) Formalizing interaction and developing new learning and control algorithms for interactive systems inspired by tools and techniques from game theory, cognitive science, optimization, and representation learning, and 2) Developing practical robotics algorithms that enable robots to safely and seamlessly coordinate, collaborate, compete, or influence humans (per the Stanford ILIAD website at https://iliad.stanford.edu/research/humans

Some of the key questions being pursued as part of the focus on learning from interactions (there are other areas of focus too) include:
- How can we actively and efficiently collect data in a low data regime setting such as in interactive robotics?
- How can we tap into different sources and modalities --- perfect and imperfect demonstrations, comparison and ranking queries, physical feedback, language instructions, videos --- to learn an effective human model or robot policy?
- What inductive biases and priors can help with effectively learning from human/interaction data?

Conclusion

You have now been taken on a bit of a journey into the realm of AI safety.

All stakeholders including AI developers, business and governmental leaders, researchers, ethicists, lawmakers, and others have a demonstrative stake in the direction and acceptance of AI safety. The more AI that gets flung into society, the more we are taking on heightened risks due to the existent lack of awareness about AI safety and the haphazard and at times backward ways in which AI safety is being devised in contemporary widespread AI.

A proverb that some trace to the novelist Samuel Lover in one of his books published in 1837, and which has forever become an indelible presence even today, serves as a fitting final comment for now.

What was that famous line?

It is better to be safe than sorry.

Enough said, for now.

CHAPTER 15

AI ETHICS
AND AI HUMAN DISAGREEMENT

Airlines have been in the news quite a bit lately.

We are in the summertime crunch of flights. Weary and frustrated passengers find themselves facing all sorts of flight disruptions and airline scheduling contortions. Flights get canceled unexpectedly. Flights are delayed. Passengers fume. There have been unfortunately many instances of passengers that allow these vexations to erupt, and we've seen woefully way too many viral videos of head-to-head confrontations and sometimes pummeling fisticuffs.

Rarer do we learn about disputes between a pilot and copilot that might occur while in the cockpit.

That is quite a surprise.

Indeed, we are naturally taken aback to think that a pilot and copilot would have any semblance of a serious disagreement during any stage of a flight. If the disagreement relates to which brand of coffee is best, our assumption is that this would not intrude into the work effort entailing flying the plane. The two would simply shrug off their lack of eye-to-eye on a seemingly flight-irrelevant topic. Their professional demeanor and longstanding pilot training would kick in and they would rivet their focus back to the flight particulars.

Consider though when a *professional disagreement* intervenes.

I am going to briefly share with you a news item widely published about a recent instance of something that happened during a flight in the US pertaining to a claimed professional disagreement in the cockpit.

This is mainly being cited herein so that we can explore a related topic that is of great importance to the advent of Artificial Intelligence (AI). You see, there can be a form of shall we say professional disagreement between not just humans in a human-to-human disagreement, but we can also have something similar occur amidst the adoption of AI and ergo resulting human-versus-AI professional disagreements. All sorts of AI Ethics considerations arise.

Get yourself ready for a fascinating tale.

As recently reported in the news, a case of "professional disagreement" apparently arose during an Alaska Airline flight that was going from Washington to San Francisco. According to the news reports, the flight had moved away from the gate and was waiting on the tarmac for permission to taxi and take flight. A storm was underway and led to a flight delay of more than an hour and a half. Turns out that the plane eventually turned around and headed back to the gate, which some of the passengers might normally have assumed was simply a storm-related safety precaution.

Per various tweets, it seems that the pilot and copilot had some kind of out-of-view feud during their time there in the cockpit and somehow came to the conclusion that the most prudent approach would be to scrub the flight and return to the terminal. Tweets suggested that the captain and first officer apparently couldn't get along with each other. The airline later issued a statement that the situation was unfortunate (the situation was not explicitly stated or explained per se), the two flight officers were evaluated by management and deemed fit to fly, crews were swapped, and the flight did end up taking place and later on reached San Francisco.

In one sense, if in fact the pilot and copilot did have a professional disagreement such as whether the plane was suitably ready for taking flight or whether the risk of flying through a storm was within a suitable safety range, those passengers ought to be relieved and thankful that the plane was returned to the gate. Better to be safe than sorry. Having an additional delay is well worth the presumed reduction of risks associated with a considered rugged or adverse flying journey.

Some people might be surprised that such a professional disagreement could arise.

We perhaps have a false impression that everything that happens in the cockpit is entirely precise and well-scripted. All form of human discretion has seemingly been wrung out of the process. Based on exacting and thoroughly calculated charts, a flight is either okay to proceed or it is not. There can't be any disagreement when the whole kit and caboodle is thought to be based on irrefutable calculus of facts and figures.

That isn't the full truth of the matter. Sure, there is a slew of protocols and all kinds of checks and balances, but this does not squeeze out all iota of human judgment. Pilots and copilots still exercise human judgment. Fortunately, this human judgment is honed by years of flying. The odds are that a pilot and copilot in a commercial passenger plane have gobs of prior flight experience and leverage readily their many years of in-depth reasoning and judgment associated with being at the flight controls.

Given the notable role of human judgment, we might logically anticipate that a pilot and copilot are sometimes going to have professional disagreements. Most of the time there presumably is very little such disagreement. The pilot and copilot for every day flights are likely to be well-aligned the preponderance of the time. Only when a flight scenario might go outside of conventional bounds would we expect tenser friction to arise.

If there is a strong difference of opinion between the two, I would dare say that we want them to hash it out.

Imagine a situation whereby the pilot stridently wants to proceed but the copilot perceives that the risks are too high. Merely having the copilot kowtow to the pilot would seem undesirable. The copilot is a check-and-balance to what a pilot might be thinking of doing. For those that want a copilot to shut up and solely act mindlessly to whatever the pilot decrees, well, that isn't much of a reassurance. A copilot is not simply a spare "pilot" that enters into the picture only when the pilot is utterly incapacitated. That's a misguided understanding of the value of having a pilot and copilot in the cockpit.

There is the other angle to this.

Consider the case of a pilot that doesn't believe a flight should proceed and meanwhile the copilot is gung-ho about getting up in the air. What then? By the expected hierarchy, the pilot is supposed to conventionally prevail over the copilot. The designated role of being the primary in-charge makes the pilot the greater of what otherwise is somewhat equal. Normally, the pilot has more overall flying time seasoning than the copilot and ergo the copilot is hierarchically supposed to defer to the pilot's wishes (when within reason).

In any case, I think we can all agree that opting to not fly is an assuredly less risky choice than deciding to fly. Once the plane is up in the air, the risk levels get enormous in comparison to being on any ordinary stable ground. A customary commercial flight that simply taxis back to the terminal without having gotten into the air would be a pretty amicable resolution to any heated acrimonious debate about going into flight.

Let's shift gears and use this spunky news item for an altogether different but relatable purpose.

We are gradually having amongst us a prevalence of AI-based autonomous systems. Sometimes the AI runs the show, as it were. The AI does everything from A to Z, and we might construe this as AI that is fully autonomous or nearly so. In other cases, we can have AI that interacts with and to some degree is programmed to be reliant upon having a human-in-the-loop.

I'd like to concentrate on the matter of an AI-based autonomous or semi-autonomous system that from the get-go has a human in the loop. The AI and the human are intentionally thrust together and supposed to be working in tandem with each other. They are cohorts in performing a particular task at hand. The AI alone is not supposed to be acting on the task. The AI must interact with the designated human-in-the-loop.

I bring up this characterization to differentiate from situations wherein the human-in-the-loop is considered an optional facet. In essence, the AI is given free rein. If the AI opts to make use of the human, so be it to do so. There is no requirement that the AI has to touch base with or work hand-in-hand with the designated human. The analyses that I am about to relate are certainly pertinent to that kind of *optional* interaction arrangement, but it isn't what I am specifically driving at in this particular discussion.

Okay, so we have some kind of task that a human and an AI are going to be working together on, inseparably from each other. In an abstract sense, we have a human sitting in one seat and an AI system sitting in the other accompanying seat. I say this cheekily because we aren't confining this discussion to a robot for example that actually might be sitting in a seat. I am metaphorically alluding to the notion that the AI is somewhere participating in the task and so is the human. Physically, their whereabouts are not especially vital to the discussion.

You might be unsure of when such a circumstance might arise.

Easy-peasy.

I will, later on, be discussing the advent of autonomous vehicles and self-driving cars. At certain levels of autonomy, the AI and the human are supposed to work together. The AI might be driving the car and request that the human take over the driving controls. The human might be driving the car and activate the AI to take over the controls. They are taking turns at the driving controls.

In addition, some designs are having the AI be essentially active all of the time (or, unless turned off), such that the AI is always at the ready. Furthermore, the AI might directly intervene, even without the human asking, depending upon the situation that is unfolding. Suppose for example that the human seems to have fallen asleep at the wheel. Since the human cannot seemingly activate the AI (because the person is sleeping), the AI might be programmed to take over the controls from the human.

Some designs bring the AI and humans into a dual driving approach. The AI is driving and the human is driving. Or, if you prefer, the human is driving and the AI is also driving. They are each driving the vehicle. I liken this to those specially rigged cars that maybe you used when taking driver training and there were two sets of driving controls in the vehicle, one for the student driver and one for the driving instructor.

That is but one example of a setting in which AI and humans might be working jointly on a task. All manner of possibilities exists. Other kinds of autonomous vehicles might be similarly devised, such as airplanes, drones, submersibles, surface ships, trains, and so on. We don't have to only consider vehicular and transportation settings. Envision the medical domain and surgeries that are being performed jointly by a medical doctor and an AI system. The list is endless.

I almost feel like referring to the classicly uproarious joke about a human and an AI that walk into a bar together. It's quite a laugher for those into AI.

Seriously, let's return to the focus of a human and an AI system that is working together on a given task. First, I want to avoid anthropomorphizing AI, which is something I will emphasize throughout. The AI is not sentient. Please keep that in mind.

Here's something to mull over: *Will a designated human-in-the-loop always be in utter agreement with a co-teamed AI?*

For any complex task, it would seem unlikely that the human and the AI will entirely and always be fully in lock and step. The human is on some occasions possibly going to disagree with the AI. We can take that assumption all the way to the bank.

I'd like you to also consider this perhaps surprising possibility too: *Will the AI always be in utter agreement with a designated human-in-the-loop?*

Again, for any complex task, it would seem quite conceivable that AI will not be in agreement with humans on some occasions. If you are already leaning toward the idea that AI must always be wrong while humans must always be right, you would be wise to rethink that hasty conclusion. Envision a car that has a human and AI jointly driving the semi-autonomous vehicle. The human steers toward a brick wall. Why? We don't know, perhaps the human is intoxicated or has fallen asleep, but we do know that crashing into a brick wall is not a good idea, all else being equal. The AI might detect the upcoming calamity and seek to steer away from the impending barrier.

All told, we are going to have the distinct possibility of the AI and the human disagreeing with each other. The other way to say the same thing is that humans and AI are disagreeing with each other. Note that I don't want that the sequencing of AI-and-human versus human-and-AI to suggest anything about the direction or plausibility of the disagreement.

The two workers, one human and one that is AI, are disagreeing with each other.

We could in advance declare that whenever a disagreement happens between a given AI and a given human, we beforehand proclaim that the human prevails over the AI. That being said, my illustrative example about the car that is heading into a brick wall would seem to dissuade us that the human is always necessarily going to be right.

We could, in contrast, opt to in-advance declare that whenever a disagreement arises that we will have beforehand established that the AI is right and the human is wrong. This is not a sensibly generalizable provision either. Imagine a car in which the AI has some embedded software error or bug, and the AI is trying to steer the vehicle off the road and into a ditch. Assuming that all else is equal, the human ought to be able to overcome this AI driving action and prevent the vehicle from landing in the gully.

Let's do a quick summary of this:

- *Will humans always be in utter agreement with AI?* **Answer:** No.
- *Will AI always be in utter agreement with a human?* **Answer:** No.
- *Will humans always be right in comparison to AI?* **Answer: Not necessarily.**
- *Will the AI always be right in comparison to the human?* **Answer: Not necessarily.**

You can certainly set up the AI to be considered by default as the "wrong" or weaker party and therefore always defer to the human whenever a disagreement appears. Likewise, you can set up the AI to assume that the AI is considered "right" whenever a human is in disagreement with the AI. I want to clarify that we can programmatically do that if we wish to do so. I am claiming though that in general, this is not always going to be the case. There are assuredly settings in which we do not know in advance whether the AI is "right" or the human is "right" in terms of opting toward one or the other on a disagreement related to a given task.

I've led you to a very important and highly complicated question.

What should we do when a professional disagreement occurs between the human-in-the-loop and AI (or, equivalently, we can phrase this as being between the AI and the human-in-the-loop)?

Do not try to dodge the question.

Some might argue that this would never happen, but as I've laid out in my example about the car, it surely could happen. Some might argue that a human is obviously superior and must be the winner of any disagreement. My example of the car and the brick wall knocks that one down. There are AI proponents that might insist that AI must be the winner, due to ostensibly overcoming human emotions and wanton thinking by those haphazard fuzzy-thinking humans. Once again, my other example entailing the car heading into the ditch undercuts that assertion.

In the real world, AI and humans are going to disagree, even when the two are purposely brought into a teaming situation to perform a jointly undertaken task. It will happen. We cannot put our heads in the sand and pretend it won't occur.

We saw that the humans piloting the plane got into apparently a disagreement. Thankfully, they agreed to disagree, so it seems. They brought the plane back to the terminal. They found a means to deal with the disagreement. The resolution to their disagreement worked out well, in comparison to if perhaps they had gone to fisticuffs in the cockpit or perhaps flown into the air and continued to be combative with each other. That is a sorrowful scenario that is untenable, and we can be thankful did not occur.

Allow me to provide my list of the various ways in which the AI and human-in-the-loop (or, human-in-the-loop and AI) disagreements might be resolved:

- **AI and the teamed-up human work things out (amicably or not)**
- **Human prevails over the AI, by default**
- **AI prevails over the human, by default**
- **Some other predetermined fixed resolution prevails, by default**
- **Third-party human is looped-in and their indication prevails over the parties**
- **Third-party AI is looped-in and its indication prevails over the parties**
- **Third-party human replaces the existing human, things proceed anew**

- **Third-party AI replaces the existing AI, things proceed anew**
- **Third-party human replaces the existing AI, things proceed anew (now human-to-human)**
- **Third-party AI replaces the existing human, things proceed anew (now AI-to-AI)**
- **Other**

Those are abundantly worthy of being unpacked.

First, consider that this is all about *professional* disagreements.

A professional disagreement is loosely defined as a disagreement associated with a work-related task.

For example, a disagreement that arises between a pilot and copilot about whether to proceed with a flight that is facing a storm could reasonably be labeled as a professional disagreement. In contrast, a vehement disagreement over which brand of coffee the pilot advocates for versus the brand that the copilot prefers is readily categorized as a non-professional disagreement in this particular context.

Of course, if a non-professional disagreement worms its way into a professional disagreement, we might ultimately be interested in the non-professional disagreement as a presumed source or spark for the professional one. Imagine that a pilot and copilot argue bitterly over which brand of coffee is the best, which then regrettably spills over into flight-specific concerns (pun!), such as whether to take off or not.

Second, we need to keep in mind the magnitude of the professional disagreement.

Perhaps the pilot and copilot or in mild disagreement over proceeding to fly. They are not at loggerheads and merely contemplating the pros and cons of whether to takeoff. This is not the caliber or magnitude of a professional disagreement that we are customarily considering herein.

The thing is, it could be that the professional disagreement is transitory and both the parties work out a resolution cordially or at least on a timely basis. Generally, the focus of professional disagreement within scope are those that are seemingly intractable, and the two parties remain steadfastly in disagreement.

Third, there usually has to be something seriously on the line for these guidelines to come into play.

Opting to fly or not fly is a decidedly life-or-death kind of decision if the flight is at risk due to a storm or the airplane is considered not fully prepared for such a journey. This is serious business. We can still apply the guidelines to the less impactful professional disagreements though it might be more bother than it is worth.

Okay, our considerations are that:

- **The disagreement is principally professionally oriented rather than over something non-professional**
- **The disagreement is of a sustained nature and not merely transitory or otherwise readily resolved**
- **The disagreement foretells serious consequences and is usually of an impactful outcome**
- **The parties are at loggerheads and they seem intractable**

Let's now take a closer look at each of my suggested guidelines or approaches regarding how to cope with such professional disagreements.

AI and the teamed-up human work things out (amicably or not)

I begin the list with the straightforward possibility that the AI and the human-in-the-loop are able to resolve the professional disagreement amongst themselves. It seems that perhaps the instance of the two humans, the pilot and copilot illustrate this kind of circumstance. They somehow resolved to return to the terminal and go their separate ways. It could be that an AI system and a human are able to figure out a resolving approach that is generally satisfactory to both parties and the matter is thus satisfactorily concluded.

Human prevails over the AI, by default

When setting up the AI, we might program a rule that says the human-in-the-loop shall always prevail whenever a professional disagreement arises. This would be the explicitly coded default. We might also allow some form of override, just in case, though the standing rule will be that the human prevails.

AI prevails over the human, by default

When setting up the AI, we might program a rule that says the AI shall always prevail over the human-in-the-loop whenever a professional disagreement arises. This is the explicitly coded default. We might also allow some form of override, just in case, though the standing rule will be that the AI prevails.

Some other predetermined fixed resolution prevails, by default

When setting up the AI, we might program a rule that says some other predetermined fixed resolution will prevail whenever a professional disagreement arises with the human-in-the-loop. The human-in-the-loop does not by default prevail. The AI does not by default prevail. There is some other preidentified resolution. For example, perhaps there is the tossing of a coin that will be used to decide which of the two parties is considered the right path to take. That would obviously seem rather arbitrary; thus another example approach would be that a specialized rule kicks in that calculates a value based on inputs from the two parties and arrives at a result as a tiebreaker.

Third-party human is looped-in and their indication prevails over the parties

Upon a professional disagreement, a rule could be that a third party that is a human is invoked and looped into the setting to make a decision about resolving the disagreement. The AI is programmed to defer to whatever the third-party human decides.

The human already in the human-in-the-loop has been instructed beforehand that if such a situation arises, they too are to defer to the third-party human. As an aside, you can likely anticipate that the human-in-the-loop might have angst over acceding to whatever the third-party human decides if the decision disagrees with the human-in-the-loop posture.

Third-party AI is looped-in and its indication prevails over the parties

Upon a professional disagreement, a rule could be that a third party that is a different AI system is invoked and looped into the setting to make a decision about resolving the disagreement. The original AI is programmed to defer to whatever the third-party AI decides. The human already in the human-in-the-loop has been instructed beforehand that if such a situation arises, they too are to defer to the third-party AI. As an aside, you can likely anticipate that the human-in-the-loop might have angst over acceding to whatever the third-party AI decides if the decision disagrees with the human-in-the-loop posture.

Third-party human replaces the existing human, things proceed anew

Upon a professional disagreement, the human-in-the-loop is replaced by a third party that is a human and that becomes the henceforth human-in-the-loop. The human that was the original human-in-the-loop for the task is no longer considered part of the task at hand. It is an open aspect as to what otherwise transpires with the now replaced human-in-the-loop, but we are saying that for sure they no longer have any ongoing role in the work task.

Third-party AI replaces the existing AI, things proceed anew

Upon a professional disagreement, the AI is replaced by a third-party AI and that becomes the henceforth AI used for the work task at hand. The AI that was originally being used for the task is no longer considered part of the task at hand.

It is an open aspect as to what otherwise transpires with the now replaced AI, but we are saying that for sure the AI no longer has any ongoing role in the work task.

Third-party human replaces the existing AI, things proceed anew (now human-to-human)

Upon a professional disagreement, the AI is replaced by a third-party human for whom that person now becomes the considered co-teamed party that will be used for the work task at hand. The AI that was originally being used for the task is no longer considered part of the task at hand. It is an open aspect as to what otherwise transpires with the now replaced AI, but we are saying that for sure the AI no longer has any ongoing role in the work task. In short, this now becomes a two-party human-to-human performed task.

Third-party AI replaces the existing human, things proceed anew (now AI-to-AI)

Upon a professional disagreement, the human-in-the-loop is replaced by a third-party AI and this AI becomes the henceforth fill-in for the preceding human-in-the-loop. The human that was the original human-in-the-loop for the task is no longer considered part of the task at hand. It is an open aspect as to what otherwise transpires with the now replaced human-in-the-loop, but we are saying that for sure they no longer have any ongoing role in the work task. In short, this now becomes a two-party AI-to-AI to perform the task.

Other

Other variations can be devised to cope with a professional disagreement, but we've covered herein some of the keystones.

How are we to decide which of those approaches is going to be the right one for a given situation?

A wide variety of issues go into making such a choice. There are technological considerations. There are business considerations. There are legal and ethical considerations.

To some degree, that is why AI Ethics and Ethical AI is such a crucial topic. The precepts of AI Ethics get us to remain vigilant. AI technologists can at times become preoccupied with technology, particularly the optimization of high-tech. They aren't necessarily considering the larger societal ramifications. Having an AI Ethics mindset and doing so integrally to AI development and fielding is vital for producing appropriate AI, including (perhaps surprisingly or ironically) the assessment of how AI Ethics gets adopted by firms.

At this juncture of this weighty discussion, I'd bet that you are desirous of some illustrative examples that might showcase this topic. There is a special and assuredly popular set of examples that are close to my heart. You see, in my capacity as an expert on AI including the ethical and legal ramifications, I am frequently asked to identify realistic examples that showcase AI Ethics dilemmas so that the somewhat theoretical nature of the topic can be more readily grasped. One of the most evocative areas that vividly presents this ethical AI quandary is the advent of AI-based true self-driving cars. This will serve as a handy use case or exemplar for ample discussion on the topic.

Here's then a noteworthy question that is worth contemplating: *Does the advent of AI-based true self-driving cars illuminate anything about AI-and-human disagreement resolutions, and if so, what does this showcase?*

For fully autonomous vehicles there might not be any chance of a professional disagreement between a human and the AI due to the possibility that there isn't any human-in-the-loop to start with. The aspiration for many of today's self-driving car makers is to remove the human driver completely from the driving task. The vehicle will not even contain human-accessible driving controls. In that case, a human driver, if present, won't be able to partake in the driving task since they lack access to any driving controls.

For some fully autonomous vehicles, some designs still allow for a human to be in-the-loop, though the human does not have to be available or partake in the driving process at all. Thus, a human can participate in driving, if the person wishes to do so. At no point though is the AI reliant upon the human to perform any of the driving tasks.

In the case of semi-autonomous vehicles, there is a hand-in-hand relationship between the human driver and the AI. The human driver can take over the driving controls entirely and essentially stop the AI from partaking in the driving. If the human driver wishes to reinstate the AI into the driving role, they can do so, though this then sometimes forces the human to relinquish the driving controls.

Another form of semi-autonomous operation would entail the human driver and the AI working together in a teaming manner. The AI is driving and the human is driving. They are driving together. The AI might defer to the human. The human might defer to the AI.

At some juncture, the AI driving system and the human driver in the loop might reach a juncture of a "professional disagreement" as to the driving task at hand.

To illustrate how some of the aforementioned rules of dealing with a professional disagreement can be challenging to implement, consider the instance of invoking a third-party human to enter into the matter and proffer a decision to resolve the unresolved issue.

Suppose an automaker or self-driving tech firm has arranged for remote human operators to have access to the driving controls of vehicles within their fleet. The human operator is sitting in some faraway office or akin setting. Via a computer system, they are able to view the driving scene via accessing the cameras and other sensor devices loaded onto the self-driving car. To them, this is almost like playing an online video game, though, of course, the real-life circumstances have potentially dire consequences.

An AI system and a human driver inside the car are driving a semi-autonomous vehicle down a long highway. All of a sudden, the AI wants to steer into a ditch. The human driver doesn't want to do this. The two are tussling over the driving controls.

How will this be resolved?

We could have perhaps instituted beforehand that the human always wins. Assume though that we opted not to do that.

We could have instituted beforehand that AI always wins. Assume that we opted to not do that. All in all, we didn't adopt any of those rules, other than we did decide to allow for a third-party human to intervene and resolve a professional disagreement of any substantive nature.

In this use case, the AI and the human driver at the wheel are fighting for the driving controls. This is let's say conveyed to the remote human operator (our third-party human). The remote human operator examines what is taking place and decides to steer away from the ditch, seemingly averting what the AI was trying to do. At the same time, suppose the remote human operator steers into oncoming traffic, which perhaps neither the AI nor the human driver inside the car had wanted to do.

The point is that the way in which this rule has been implemented is that the third-party human operator is able to completely override both the AI and the human-in-the-loop. Whether this is going to produce a good outcome is assuredly not assured.

I will use this example to highlight some added insights on these matters.

You cannot make the brazen assumption that just because one of these rules is put into place the outcome of the resolved disagreement is necessarily a guaranteed good outcome. It might not be. There isn't any ironclad always-right kind of rule that can be selected.

Next, some of these rules might not be viably implementable.

Consider the example of the remote human operator intervening when the AI and the human driver are brawling over the driving controls. It might take many seconds of time for the remote human operator to figure out what is going on. By then, the vehicle might already have ended up in the ditch or had some other adverse outcome. Also, suppose that the location of the vehicle precludes remote access such as being in some place where there isn't any network electronic connectivity. Or maybe the networking features of the vehicle aren't working at that particular moment.

As you can see, the rule might look dandy on paper, though putting the rule into actual use might be a very difficult or highly chancy approach.

I'd like to briefly cover another related topic that I will be covering in greater depth in an upcoming analysis.

One of the rising concerns about autonomous vehicles and self-driving cars that are semi-autonomous is the so-called **Hot Potato Syndrome**.

Here's the deal.

An AI driving system and a human are co-driving. A dire predicament arises. The AI has been programmed to drop out of the driving task and turn things over to the human when a dire moment occurs. This seems perhaps "sensible" in that we seem to be invoking the rule about the human being the default "winner" in any potential professional disagreement.

But the AI dropping out might be for more nefarious or considered insidious purposes. It could be that the automaker or self-driving tech firm doesn't want their AI to be considered the "party at fault" when a car crash occurs. To seemingly avoid getting pinned down like that, the AI abruptly hands over the controls to the human. Voila, the human is now presumably completely responsible for the vehicle.

The kicker is that suppose the AI does this handoff with let's say one second left to go before a crash occurs.

Would the human really have any available time to avert the crash?

Likely not.

Suppose the AI does the handoff with a few milliseconds or nanoseconds left to go. I dare say that human has essentially zero chance of doing anything to avert the crash.

From the perspective of the automaker or self-driving car firm, they can try to act as though their hands were clean when such a car crash occurs. The car was being driven by a human. The AI wasn't driving the car. The only "logical" conclusion would seem to be that the human must be at fault and the AI must be completely blameless.

It's a crock.

I will be discussing this in more depth in an upcoming column.

Conclusion

Professional disagreements are going to occur.

It is hard to imagine any complex task that has two parties co-performing the task and for which there would never ever be any professional disagreements that arise. This seems like a fantasyland or at least a grand rarity.

Today, we have lots and lots of human-to-human instances of professional disagreement, for which on a daily basis resolutions are peacefully and sensibly figured out one way or another. In fact, we oftentimes set up situations intentionally to foster and surface professional disagreements. You might argue that this showcases the famed wisdom that sometimes two heads are better than one.

As AI becomes more prevalent, we are going to have lots of AI-to-human or human-to-AI two-party task performers and there are going to be *professional disagreements* that will occur. The lazy approach is to always defer to the human. This might not be the most suitable approach. AI might be the better choice. Or one of the other aforementioned rules might be a sounder approach.

There is that sage line oft repeated that we all ought to generally be able to agree to disagree, though when it comes down to the wire, sometimes a disagreement has to be unequivocally resolved else the matter at hand will lead to untold calamity. We can't just let a disagreement languish on the vine. Time might be of the essence and lives might be at stake.

There is a clear-cut requirement for some prudent means to resolve disagreements even if not necessarily agreeably so, including when AI and a human-in-the-loop aren't seeing eye-to-eye nor byte-to-byte.

I trust that you won't disagree with that altogether agreeable contention.

CHAPTER 16

AI ETHICS
AND
AUTONOMOUS WEAPONS SYSTEMS

Those amazing dancing four-legged robots.

I'm sure that you've seen those viral videos of the four-legged robotic systems that dance and prance in seemingly delightful and dog-like beloved ways. We seem to relish seeing those AI-driven robots as they climb over obstacles and appear to gain a delicate foothold when perched on top of boxes or after having been precariously placed on tipsy tops of cabinets. Their human handlers will at times poke or push the frolicking four-legged robots, which seems exasperatingly unfair and can readily raise your ire at the bratty treatment by those mastermind humanoids.

I'm wondering though if you've seen the not-so-viral videos of an entirely different caliber.

Prepare yourself.

There are widely posted videos showing the same kind of four-legged robots that have been outfitted with pronounced weaponry of one kind or another.

For example, a machine gun or similar firearm is mounted on top of an otherwise familiar dancing-and-prancing robot. There is an electronic linkage between the four-legged robot and the firing mechanism of the weapon.

The now weaponized computer-walking contraption is shown striding over to where a bullseye target has been placed, and the machine gun is rat-a-tat fired fiercely at the target. After nailing the subsequently partially destroyed target, the four-legged robot dances and prances around nearby obstacles and lines up to repeat the same action over and over again at other fresh targets.

Not quite what you might have expected to see. This certainly takes the lightheartedness and relative joy out of candidly watching those cuddly four-legged robots do their thing. Welcome to the harsh reality of seemingly *innocuous* autonomous systems being converted or transformed into being sharply weaponized. With nary much of an effort, you can overnight have a considered "non-weaponized" autonomous system retrofitted to contain full-on weaponry.

It is almost easy peasy in some circumstances.

I'm going to discuss this heatedly controversial topic and cover the rather hefty AI Ethics qualms that arise. We will take a journey into autonomous systems, AI, autonomous vehicles, weaponization, and a slew of related Ethical AI combative issues.

Let's start with some foundational keystones.

For sake of discussion, accept that there are two major ways to categorize autonomous systems that have been armed with weaponry:
1) **Autonomous weapons systems** (by design)
2) **Autonomous systems that are weaponized** (by after-the-fact)

There is an important difference between the two categories.

In the first instance, we will define an *autonomous weapons system* to be from the get-go a grounds up computerized creation that is purposefully intended to be a weapon. The developers had in mind that they wanted to devise a weapon. Their explicit quest is to produce a weapon. They knew that they could integrally combine weaponry with the latest in autonomous systems technologies.

This is a weapon that rides upon the wave of high-tech that attains autonomous movement and autonomous actions (I'll elaborate more fully, shortly).

In a contrast, in the second instance, we will consider the matter of autonomous systems that have no particular slant toward weaponry at all. These are autonomous systems being developed for other purposes. Envision an autonomous vehicle such as a self-driving car that will be used to provide mobility-for-all and aid in reducing the thousands of annual fatalities that occur due to human-driving and human-operated automobiles. Not a weapon seems to be in consideration for those upbeat societally boosting efforts to get humans out from behind the wheel and put AI into the driver's seat instead.

But those innocuous autonomous systems can be weaponized if humans want to do so.

I refer to this second category then as *autonomous systems that are weaponized*. The autonomous system was originally and devoutly crafted for a presumably non-weaponry purpose. Despite that, the dreamy altruistic hope gets upended by somebody somewhere that gets the conniving idea that this contrivance could be weaponized. All of a sudden, the autonomous system that seemed cuddly has become a lethal weapon by tagging on some form of weapons capabilities (such as the four-legged dog-like robots mentioned earlier that have a machine gun or similar firearm added onto their features).

Sadly, the two categories end up somewhat at the same place, namely providing a capacity of utilizing autonomous systems for weaponry on a potentially lethal basis.

The process of getting to that endpoint is likely to be different.

For the outright weaponized autonomous systems that were pegged as weapons, the weaponry aspects are typically front and center. You might say that the facets of the autonomous system are wrapped around the cornerstone of whatever weapon is being considered.

The thinking process by the developers is somewhat along the lines of how a weapon can exploit the advent of autonomous systems.

The other perspective is usually not at all of that mindset. The developers want to derive a state-of-the-art autonomous system, perhaps for the betterment of humankind. These developers put their sincerest heart and soul into making the autonomous system. This is the core of their invention. They might not imagine that anyone would usurp or subvert their miraculously beneficial device. They are blissfully enamored with the societal benefits associated with the autonomous system being shaped and produced.

At some point, let's say that third parties realize that the autonomous system can be rejiggered to be weaponized. Maybe they trick the developers into letting them have the autonomous system for what is claimed to be lofty purposes. Behind closed doors, these evildoers opt to sneakily add a weaponization capacity to the autonomous system. Voila, innocence turned into outright weaponry.

Things don't have to proceed in that manner.

Perhaps the developers were told that they were developing an innocent autonomous system, yet those funding or directing the effort had other purposes in mind. Maybe the autonomous system effort indeed started innocently, but then when bills had to be paid, the leadership cut a deal with a funding source that wants the autonomous systems for nefarious reasons. Another possibility is that the developers knew that a later use might be for weaponization but that they figured that they would cross that harrowing bridge when or if it ever arose. Etc.

There are lots and lots of varying paths on how this all plays out.

An AI system that is envisioned for the good can be sometimes on the verge of the bad, perhaps via some rather simple changes, and correspondingly is regarded as being of a dual-use nature. In the news recently was an AI system that was built to discover chemicals that might be killers, for which the developers were wanting to make sure that we could avoid or be wary of such ill-conceived chemicals.

Turns out that the AI could be somewhat easily tweaked to devotedly uncover those killer chemicals and thus potentially allow baddies to know what kinds of chemicals to potentially cook up for their abysmal evil plans.

Autonomous systems can demonstrably fit into that dual-use envelopment.

To some degree, that is why AI Ethics and Ethical AI is such a crucial topic. The precepts of AI Ethics get us to remain vigilant. AI technologists can at times become preoccupied with technology, particularly the optimization of high-tech. They aren't necessarily considering the larger societal ramifications. Having an AI Ethics mindset and doing so integrally to AI development and fielding is vital for producing appropriate AI, including (perhaps surprisingly or ironically) the assessment of how AI Ethics gets adopted by firms.

The Autonomy And The Weapon As Two Precepts

There is a catchphrase that some are using to forewarn about weaponized autonomous systems of all kinds, which are being coined collectively as *slaughterbots*.

This brings up an additional aspect that we ought to mull over.

Does an autonomous weapons system and/or an autonomous system that has been weaponized have to be of a lethal or killer robot preponderance?

Some would argue that we can have decidedly *non-lethal* weaponized autonomous systems too. Thus, in that viewpoint, it would seem profoundly inappropriate to use phrasings such as slaughterbots or killer robots. A non-lethal variant would presumably be able to subdue or enact harm that is not of a lethal result. Those such systems are not killing, they are of a lesser injury-generating capacity. Do not overstate the abilities, say those that insist we don't have to be preoccupied with an outright killing machine trope.

Thus, we might have this:

- **Lethal autonomous weapons systems**
- **Lethal autonomous systems that have been weaponized**
- **Non-lethal autonomous weapons systems**
- **Non-lethal autonomous systems that have been weaponized**

Of course, the counterargument is that any autonomous system that has been weaponized would seem to have the potential for sliding into the lethality realm, even if supposedly only envisioned for use on a non-lethal basis. The incremental two-step of going from non-lethal to lethal is going to be quickly undertaken once you've already got in hand a weapon amidst an autonomous system. You would be hard-pressed to provide an ironclad guarantee that the non-lethal will not have sashayed into the lethal arena (though some are trying to do so, in a mathematical semblance).

Before we get much further into this overall topic of autonomous systems and weaponization, it might be handy to point out something else that though perhaps obvious is not necessarily visibly at top of mind.

Here it is:

- **There is an AI aspect that is part and parcel of the autonomous system**
- **There is a weaponry aspect that is the weaponry side of this equation**
- **The AI might also be interconnected with the weaponry**

Let's unpack that.

We shall assume that today's autonomous systems require AI as the underlying computerized means of bringing forth the autonomous facets. I mention this because you could try to argue that we might use non-AI-related technologies and techniques to do the autonomous systems, which though true, would seem less and less likely. Basically, AI tends to allow for greater levels of autonomy, and most are leveraging AI high-tech accordingly.

Okay, so we've got an AI-based capability that is infused somehow within the autonomous system and acts to guide and control the autonomous system.

Keep that at your fingertips as a rule of thumb.

It seems readily apparent that we also need to have some form of weaponry, else why are we discussing herein the topic of autonomous systems <u>and</u> weapons. So, yes, obviously, there is a weapon of one kind or another.

I am not going to delve into the type of weaponry that might be used. You can simply substitute whatever weaponry that comes to mind. There might be pinpoint weaponry. There might be mass-oriented destructive weaponry. It could be something with bullets or projectiles. It might be something that has chemicals or atomic volatile components. The list is endless.

The additional consideration is whether or not AI is interconnected with weaponry. The AI might be merely taking the weaponry for a ride. In the case of the four-legged robot that was shooting a gun, perhaps the gun is being fired by a human that has a remote control connected to the triggering of the weapon. The dog-like robot navigates a scene and then it is up to a remote human to pull the trigger.

On the other hand, the AI might be the trigger puller, as it were. The AI might have been devised to not only navigate and maneuver but also activates the weapon too. In that sense, the AI is doing everything from A to Z. There is no dependence upon a remote human to perform the weaponry side of things. The AI is programmed to do that instead.

To clarify then in this particular use case of autonomous systems that are weaponized, we have these kinds of possibilities:

- Autonomous System: **AI runs the autonomous system entirely on its own**
- Autonomous System: **AI runs the autonomous system, but a human-in-the-loop can also intervene**

- Weaponry: **Remote human runs the weaponry (the AI does not)**
- Weaponry: **AI runs the weaponry, but a human-in-the-loop can also intervene**
- Weaponry: **AI runs the weaponry entirely on its own**

When you watch those fun-oriented videos of the dancing and prancing four-legged robots, they are usually supposed to be robots that are exclusively being navigably run by the AI (well, that is the custom or considered proper etiquette amongst those that are deeply into these matters). That's what you might also rightfully assume. Of course, you don't know that for sure. It could be that a remote human operator is guiding the robots. There is also a possibility that the AI does part of the guiding, and a remote human operator also does so, perhaps aiding the AI if the robot gets into a tough position and cannot computationally calculate a viable means to wiggle itself free.

The gist here is that there are numerous flavors of how AI and autonomous systems and weaponization are able to be intermixed. Some have AI that runs the autonomous system but does not run the weaponry. A human perhaps remotely runs the weaponry. Another angle is that the weaponry is maybe activated beforehand, and the autonomous system delivers the activated weapon, thus the AI did not partake directly in the triggering of the weapon per se and was instead acting as a delivery vehicle. And it could be that the AI is a proverbial jack-of-all-trades and does the entire gamut of autonomous system aspects to the weaponry utilization too.

Take your pick.

Meanwhile, please know that the human-in-the-loop is a big factor when it comes to debates on this topic.

A dividing line by some is that if the AI is doing the targeting and shooting (or whatever the weapon entails) then the whole kit and caboodle has crossed over into no-no land. This seemingly differs from the conventional fire-and-forget weapons that have a pre-targeted human-determined selection, such as a patrolling drone that has a missile ready for firing at a target that was *already* chosen by a human.

Some wonder why autonomous systems that are weaponized would not always include a human-in-the-loop throughout the process of the autonomous system being in an actively underway status. Seems like we might be better off if a strident requirement was that all such weaponized autonomous systems had to have a human-in-the-loop, either doing so for the operation of the autonomous system or for operating the weaponry (or for both). Keeping an assumed sure-and-steady human hand in this AI mix might seem altogether shrewd.

Get ready for a lengthy list of reasons why this is not necessarily feasible.

Consider these difficulties:

- **Human-in-the-loop might not be fast enough to timely respond**
- **Human-in-the-loop might not have sufficient info to dutifully respond**
- **Human-in-the-loop might not be available at the time needed**
- **Human-in-the-loop might be undecided and won't act when needed**
- **Human-in-the-loop might make the "wrong" decision (relatively)**
- **Human-in-the-loop might not be accessible from the system at the needed time**
- **Human-in-the-loop might get confused and be overwhelmed**
- **Etc.**

You are undoubtedly tempted to look at that list of human frailties and limitations and then come to the solemn conclusion that it makes apparent sense to excise the human-in-the-loop and always instead use AI. This could either be to the exclusion of the human-in-the-loop or maybe have the AI be able to override an ingrained human-in-the-loop design.

Oftentimes, a belittling list of these kinds of real-time human-focused downsides is left on its own accord and leaves a lingering impression that the AI must somehow be leaps and bounds a much wiser choice than having a human-in-the-loop. Do not fall into that treacherous trap. There are sobering tradeoffs involved.

Consider these ramifications of the AI:
- **AI might encounter an error that causes it to go astray**
- **AI might be overwhelmed and lockup unresponsively**
- **AI might contain developer bugs that cause erratic behavior**
- **AI might be corrupted with implanted evildoer virus**
- **AI might be taken over by cyberhackers in real-time**
- **AI might be considered unpredictable due to complexities**
- **AI might computationally make the "wrong" decision (relatively)**
- **Etc.**

I trust that you can see that there are tradeoffs between using a human-in-the-loop versus being reliant solely on AI. In case you are tempted to suggest that the ready solution is to use both, I'd just like to emphasize that you can get the best of both worlds, but you can also get the worst of both worlds. Do not assume that it will always and assuredly be the best of both worlds.

You might have been somewhat surprised by one of the above-listed downsides about AI, specifically that the AI might be *unpredictable*. We are used to believing that AI is supposed to be strictly logical and mathematically precise. As such, you might also expect that the AI will be fully predictable. We are supposed to know exactly what AI will do. Period, end of the story.

Sorry to burst that balloon but this myth of predictability is a misnomer. The size and complexity of modern-day AI is frequently a morass that defies being perfectly predictable. This is being seen in the Ethical AI uproars about some Machine Learning (ML) and Deep Learning (DL) uses of today. I'll explain a bit more momentarily.

Ruminating On The Rules Of The Road

I had mentioned the notion of targets and targeting, which is a rather heavily laden piece of terminology that deserves keen attention.

We can ponder this:
- **Targets that are humans**
- **Targets that aren't humans but are living creatures**
- **Targets that are construed as property**

Suppose that we have an autonomous system that has been weaponized. The AI is used to guide the autonomous system and used for weaponry. The AI does everything from A to Z. There is no provision for a human-in-the-loop. In terms of targeting, the AI will choose the targets. There isn't a pre-targeting that has been established by humans. Instead, the AI has been programmed to generally ascertain whether there are humans that are to be targeted (maybe scanning for hostile actions, certain kinds of uniforms, and so on).

With me on this so far?

This scenario is pretty much the one that causes the most outcry about weaponized autonomous systems.

The stated concern is that the AI is doing (at least) three things that it ought to not be permitted to do:
- Targeting humans as the targets
- Targeting without the use of a human-in-the-loop
- Potentially acting unpredictably

Notice that there is a pointed mention of worries about the AI being unpredictable. It could be that though the AI was programmed to target certain kinds of humans, the AI programming is not what we thought it was, and the AI ends up targeting "friendlies" in addition to those that the AI was supposed to construe as "hostiles" (or, perhaps in lieu of).

On top of this, even if we opt to include a human-in-the-loop provision, the unpredictability of the AI might mean that when the AI is supposed to confer with the human-in-the-loop, it fails to do so and acts without any human intervention.

You might find of interest that the International Committee of the Red Cross (ICRC) has proffered a three-point overarching position about autonomous weapons systems that elaborates on these types of concerns (per the ICRC website):

1. **"Unpredictable autonomous weapon systems should be expressly ruled out**, notably because of their indiscriminate effects. This would best be achieved with a prohibition on autonomous weapon systems that are designed or used in a manner such that their effects cannot be sufficiently understood, predicted, and explained."

2. "In light of ethical considerations to safeguard humanity, and to uphold international humanitarian law rules for the protection of civilians and combatants hors de combat, **use of autonomous weapon systems to target human beings should be ruled out**. This would best be achieved through a prohibition on autonomous weapon systems that are designed or used to apply force against persons."

3. "In order to protect civilians and civilian objects, uphold the rules of international humanitarian law and safeguard humanity, the design and use of autonomous weapon systems that would not be prohibited should be regulated, including through a combination of: **limits on the types of target**, such as constraining them to objects that are military objectives by nature; **limits on the duration, geographical scope and scale of use**, including to enable human judgement and control in relation to a specific attack; **limits on situations of use**, such as constraining them to situations where civilians or civilian objects are not present; **requirements for human-machine interaction**, notably to ensure effective human supervision, and timely intervention and deactivation."

On a related outlook, the United Nations (UN) via the Convention on Certain Conventional Weapons (CCW) in Geneva had established eleven non-binding Guiding Principles on Lethal Autonomous Weapons, as per the official report posted online (encompassing references to pertinent International Humanitarian Law or IHL provisos):

(a) International humanitarian law continues to apply fully to all weapons systems, including the potential development and use of lethal autonomous weapons systems;

(b) Human responsibility for decisions on the use of weapons systems must be retained since accountability cannot be transferred to machines. This should be considered across the entire life cycle of the weapons system;

(c) Human-machine interaction, which may take various forms and be implemented at various stages of the life cycle of a weapon, should ensure that the potential use of weapons systems based on emerging technologies in the area of lethal autonomous weapons systems is in compliance with applicable international law, in particular IHL. In determining the quality and extent of human-machine interaction, a range of factors should be considered including the operational context, and the characteristics and capabilities of the weapons system as a whole;

(d) Accountability for developing, deploying and using any emerging weapons system in the framework of the CCW must be ensured in accordance with applicable international law, including through the operation of such systems within a responsible chain of human command and control;

(e) In accordance with States' obligations under international law, in the study, development, acquisition, or adoption of a new weapon, means or method of warfare, determination must be made whether its employment would, in some or all circumstances, be prohibited by international law;

(f) When developing or acquiring new weapons systems based on emerging technologies in the area of lethal autonomous weapons systems, physical security, appropriate non-physical safeguards (including cyber-security against hacking or data spoofing), the risk of acquisition by terrorist groups and the risk of proliferation should be considered;

(g) Risk assessments and mitigation measures should be part of the design, development, testing and deployment cycle of emerging technologies in any weapons systems;

(h) Consideration should be given to the use of emerging technologies in the area of lethal autonomous weapons systems in upholding compliance with IHL and other applicable international legal obligations;

(i) In crafting potential policy measures, emerging technologies in the area of lethal autonomous weapons systems should not be anthropomorphized;

(j) Discussions and any potential policy measures taken within the context of the CCW should not hamper progress in or access to peaceful uses of intelligent autonomous technologies;

(k) The CCW offers an appropriate framework for dealing with the issue of emerging technologies in the area of lethal autonomous weapons systems within the context of the objectives and purposes of the Convention, which seeks to strike a balance between military necessity and humanitarian considerations.

The Quandary We Find Ourselves In

These various laws of war, laws of armed conflict, or IHL (International Humanitarian Laws) serve as a vital and ever-promising guide to considering what we might try to do about the advent of autonomous systems that are weaponized, whether by keystone design or by after-the-fact methods.

We can sincerely wish that a ban on lethal weaponized autonomous systems would be strictly and obediently observed. The problem is that a lot of wiggle room is bound to slyly be found within any of the most sincere of bans. As they say, rules are meant to be broken. You can bet that where things are loosey-goosey, riffraff will ferret out gaps and try to wink-wink their way around the rules.

Here are some potential loopholes worthy of consideration:

- **Claims of Non-Lethal**. Make *non-lethal* autonomous weapons systems (seemingly okay since it is outside of the ban boundary), which you can then on a dime shift into becoming lethal (you'll only be beyond the ban at the last minute).
- **Claims of Autonomous System Only**. Uphold the ban by not making lethal-focused autonomous systems, meanwhile, be making as much progress on devising everyday autonomous systems that aren't (yet) weaponized but that you can on a dime retrofit into being weaponized.
- **Claims of Not Integrated As One**. Craft autonomous systems that are not at all weaponized, and when the time comes, piggyback weaponization such that you can attempt to vehemently argue that they are two separate elements and therefore contend that they do not fall within the rubric of an all-in-one autonomous weapon system or its cousin.
- **Claims That It Is Not Autonomous**. Make a weapon system that does not seem to be of autonomous capacities. Leave room in this presumably non-autonomous system for the dropping in of AI-based autonomy. When needed, plug in the autonomy and you are ready to roll (until then, seemingly you were not violating the ban).
- **Other**

There are plenty of other expressed difficulties with trying to outright ban lethal autonomous weapons systems. I'll cover a few more of them.

Some pundits argue that a ban is not especially useful and instead there should be regulatory provisions. The idea is that these contraptions will be allowed but stridently policed. A litany of lawful uses is laid out, along with lawful ways of targeting, lawful types of capabilities, lawful proportionality, and the like.

In their view, a straight-out ban is like putting your head in the sand and pretending that the elephant in the room doesn't exist. This contention though gets the blood boiling of those that counter with the argument that by instituting a ban you are able to dramatically reduce the otherwise temptation to pursue these kinds of systems. Sure, some will flaunt the ban, but at least hopefully most will not. You can then focus your attention on the flaunters and not have to splinter your attention to everyone.

Round and round these debates go.

Another oft-noted concern is that even if the good abides by the ban, the bad will not. This puts the good in a lousy posture. The bad will have these kinds of weaponized autonomous systems and the good won't. Once things are revealed that the bad have them, it will be too late for the good to catch up. In short, the only astute thing to do is to prepare to fight fire with fire.

There is also the classic deterrence contention. If the good opt to make weaponized autonomous systems, this can be used to deter the bad from seeking to get into a tussle. Either the good will be better armed and thusly dissuade the bad, or the good will be ready when the bad perhaps unveil that they have surreptitiously been devising those systems all along.

A counter to these counters is that by making weaponized autonomous systems, you are waging an arms race. The other side will seek to have the same. Even if they are technologically unable to create such systems anew, they will now be able to steal the plans of the "good" ones, reverse engineer the high-tech guts, or mimic whatever they seem to see as a tried-and-true way to get the job done.

Aha, some retort, all of this might lead to a reduction in conflicts by a semblance of mutually. If side A knows that side B has those lethal autonomous systems weapons, and side B knows that side A has them, they might sit tight and not come to blows. This has that distinct aura of mutually assured destruction (MAD) vibes.

And so on.

The AI In The Autonomy

Let's make sure we are on the same page about the nature of today's AI.

There isn't any AI today that is sentient. We don't have this. We don't know if sentient AI will be possible. Nobody can aptly predict whether we will attain sentient AI, nor whether sentient AI will somehow miraculously spontaneously arise in a form of computational cognitive supernova (usually referred to as the singularity).

The type of AI that I am focusing on consists of the non-sentient AI that we have today. If we wanted to wildly speculate about *sentient* AI, this discussion could go in a radically different direction. A sentient AI would supposedly be of human quality. You would need to consider that the sentient AI is the cognitive equivalent of a human. More so, since some speculate we might have super-intelligent AI, it is conceivable that such AI could end up being smarter than humans.

Let's keep things more down to earth and consider today's computational non-sentient AI.

Realize that today's AI is not able to "think" in any fashion on par with human thinking.

Be very careful of anthropomorphizing today's AI.

With that added foundational background, we turn once again to the autonomous systems and weaponization topic. We earlier saw that the AI enters into the autonomous system component and also can enter into the weaponization component.

The AI of today is not sentient. This is worthy of repeating and I will highlight this for added insights into these matters.

Let's explore some scenarios to see how this is a crucial consideration. I will momentarily switch out of a wartime orientation on this topic and showcase how it permeates many other social milieus. Steady yourself accordingly.

An AI-based autonomous system such as an autonomous vehicle that we shall say has nothing whatsoever to do with weapons is making its way throughout a normal locale. A human comes along to make use of the autonomous vehicle. The person is armed with a foreboding weapon. Assume for sake of discussion in this particular scenario that the person has something untoward in mind. The person gets into the autonomous vehicle (carrying their weapon, concealed or not concealed, either way).

The autonomous vehicle proceeds to whatever destination that the rider has requested. In this case, the AI is simply programmatically carrying this passenger from one pickup location to a designated destination, just as it has been doing for possibly dozens or hundreds of trips, each day.

If this had been a human driver and a human-driven vehicle, presumably there is some chance that the human driver would realize that the passenger is armed and seems to have untoward intentions. The human driver might refuse to drive the vehicle. Or the human driver might drive to the police station. Or maybe the human driver might try to subdue the armed passenger (reported instances exist) or dissuade the passenger from using their weapon. It is quite complicated, and any number of variations can exist. You would be hard-pressed to assert that there is only one right answer to resolving such a predicament. Sadly, the situation is vexing and obviously dangerous.

The AI in this case is unlikely to be programmed for any of those kinds of possibilities. In short, the armed passenger might be able to use their weapon, doing so from within the autonomous vehicle, during the course of the driving journey.

The AI driving system will continue to travel along and the autonomous vehicle will keep heading to the stated designation of the passenger (assuming that the destination was not otherwise considered out-of-bounds).

Most contemporary AI driving systems would only be computationally focusing on the roadway and not on the efforts of the rider.

Things can get worse than this.

Suppose someone wants to have a bunch of groceries transported over to a place that takes extra food for the needy. The person requests an autonomous vehicle and places the bags of groceries into the backseat of the vehicle. They aren't going to go along for the ride and are merely using the autonomous vehicle to deliver the food bags for them.

Seems perfectly fine.

Envision that a dastardly person opts instead to place some form of weaponization into the autonomous vehicle rather than the more peaceful notion of grocery bags. I think you can guess what might happen. This is a concern that I have been exhorting repeatedly in my columns and forewarning that we need to cope with sooner rather than later.

One proffered response to these types of scenarios is that perhaps all autonomous vehicles could be programmed to make use of their cameras and other sensors to try and detect whether a potential passenger is armed and has nefarious intentions. Maybe the AI would be programmed to do this. Or the AI electronically and silently alerts a remote human operator that then would via the cameras visually and otherwise examine and possibly interact with the passenger. It is all part of a complex and potentially intractable can of worms, such that it raises intense privacy issues and a plethora of other potential Ethical AI concerns.

Another somewhat akin alternative is that the AI contains some kind of embedded ethics programming that tries to enable the AI to make ethical or moral judgments that normally are reserved for human decision-makers.

Going back to a battlefield scenario, envision that a lethal autonomous weapons system is cruising overhead of a combat zone. The AI is operating the autonomous system. The AI is operating the weapons onboard. We had earlier conceived of the possibility that the AI might be programmed to scan for seemingly hostile movements or other indicators of human targets deemed as valid combatants.

Should this same AI have some kind of ethical-oriented component that strives to computationally consider what a human-in-the-loop might do, acting in a sense in place of having a human-in-the-loop?

Some say yes, let's pursue this. Some recoil in horror and say it is either impossible or otherwise violates the sanctity of humanness.

Yet another can of worms.

Conclusion

For those of you interested in this topic, there is a lot more to be discussed.

I'll give you a quick taste of one nagging conundrum.

We normally expect that a human will be ultimately held accountable for whatever occurs during wartime. If AI is controlling an autonomous weapon system or controlling an autonomous system that has perchance been weaponized, and this system does something on the battlefield that is believed to be unconscionable, who or what is to be blamed for this?

You might argue that AI should be held accountable. But, if so, what does that exactly mean? We don't yet consider today's AI to be the embodiment of legal personhood. No pinning the tail on the donkey in the case of the AI. Perhaps if AI someday becomes sentient, you can try to do so. Until then, this is a bit of a reach (plus, what kind of penalties or repercussions would the AI be subject to).

If the AI is not the accountable suspect, we might then naturally say that whatever human or humans devised the AI should be held accountable. Can you do this if the AI was merely running an autonomous system and some humans came along that coupled it with weaponization? Do you go after the AI developers? Or those that deployed the AI? Or just the weaponizing actor?

I trust that you get the idea that I've only touched the tip of the iceberg in my hearty discussion.

For now, let's go ahead and wrap up this discourse. You might recall that John Lyly in *Euphues: The Anatomy Of Wit* in 1578 memorably stated that all is fair in love and war.

Would he have had in mind the emergence of autonomous weapons systems and the likewise advent of autonomous systems that are weaponized?

We certainly need to put this at top of our minds, right away.

CHAPTER 17
AI ETHICS
AND
CHESS PLAYING ROBOT AWRY

You almost assuredly know that the world gets intrigued by those eye-catching eyebrow-raising man-bites-dog types of stories. Well, I guess you can add chess-playing-robot breaks finger-of-child as a notable stirring similar form of tale that provokes intense curiosity and fascination by us all.

Here's the scoop.

The news and social media seem to be abuzz about a recent globally rousing "incident" in which a seven-year-old boy got his finger busted by a chess-playing robotic arm that gripped his finger erroneously (we assume). The boy is said to have been okay overall and the fracture was medically dealt with and healing.

A video is online that showcases briefly what occurred.

I am going to walk you through the details. My aim is to then bring up some AI Ethics insights and lessons learned that can be gleaned from the matter.

First, some unpacking about what took place.

In context, the robotic arm was supposed to grasp various chess pieces on a chessboard, doing so one at a time and as commensurate with playing a normal chess game.

The arm would swivel into a given position and a gripper at the end of the arm would then take hold of a chess piece. The gripper then lifts the chess piece and places it elsewhere on the board or possibly off the board, depending upon the chess-playing circumstances. To go ahead and place the chess piece down onto the board or a nearby surface, the gripper releases the piece accordingly.

All is well and good overall.

In this specific occurrence, here is what seems to be shown on the video depicting the finger-harming moment. First, the robotic arm grips a chess piece and moves the piece over to a small container to deposit the chess piece into a petite bucket intended to collect pieces that no longer are supposed to be on the chessboard. Meanwhile, the child seated at the chess board, directly across from the robotic arm (you would say they are opponents of this chess match), is moving his human arm and hand across the chessboard on his side of the board.

Two things happen next, nearly simultaneously. The boy appears to reach for a chess piece. The robotic arm appears to reach for perhaps the exact same piece. The robotic arm grasps the finger of the child, which we might assume is happening erroneously in that the gripper was presumably supposed to grab hold of the chess piece instead.

For reasons not yet explained, the gripper holds tightly onto the finger and won't seem to let go. Almost a split second or so later, several adults standing adjacent to the brewing situation are quick to reach into the now scary setting and try to extract the boy's finger away from the gripper. This seems to be arduous to do and thus we might assume that the gripper is just not giving up on the gripping action (the adults rushing into the scene tend to block the view of the camera and the video is therefore not visually evident as to what precisely happened).

They get the boy free of the gripper and move him away from the table.

One aspect worth noting in the video is that the nearby first adult to try and aid the boy is seemingly operating an iPad-like device and perhaps had some capability to electronically control the robotic arm. I say this too because this particular adult stops trying to physically aid the boy, allowing another nearby adult to do so, and returns to the screen of the device. It seems that this suggests that the person was hopeful that they could disengage the gripper via an electronic command (else, one must ask, why would the adult not continue to try and directly hands-on rescue the boy amidst the being-harmed tightly gripped finger).

The video is somewhat convoluted due to the chaos underway such that we cannot immediately discern whether perhaps the gripper was electronically commanded to release and did so, or whether the electronic command was not being abided and the boy via adult assistance had to wrench his finger from the gripper. I would also point out that we do not know for sure that the iPad-like device was being used to signal to the gripper at all, nor whether even if the device had that capability whether it was something that could readily be invoked in a fast enough time versus the tugging effort to extract the boy's finger.

Per reporting about the newsworthy tussle, this took place at the Moscow Open last week. A representative of the Russian Chess Federation was quoted as indicating that the boy should have waited for the robotic arm to complete its move. The boy is alleged to have violated prescribed safety rules. Another representative said that the boy rushed on his move, failing to give sufficient time for the robotic arm to take its turn, and ergo the robotic arm grabbed the boy's finger.

It was reported that the boy was apparently not traumatized by the actions. Indeed, it is said that the boy continued the next day in the tournament and was able to finish the chess matches, though maybe not able to record his own chess moves by himself and relied upon volunteers to do so (it is customary during chess matches that each player usually writes down their moves, doing so to keep a personal record and to some extent perhaps also mentally aiding the player as they note what moves they've played).

Representatives of the chess match seemed to insist that this was extremely rare, or that they had never witnessed such a happening in some 15 years of using such robotic arm chess-playing systems. Reportedly, the parents were going to contact the public prosecutor's office. You might find of interest that the chess-playing robotic arm seemed to be in use throughout the rest of the chess tournament. The implication was that the robotic arm was deemed safe by the tournament organizers, as long as the players such as the children were dutifully cautious and performed their actions in accordance with the prescribed rules.

The seconds-long event has gone viral as a news story.

Some media influencers went with headlines that robots are on the verge of taking over. Headline-seeking bloggers breathed anxiously that this is an ominous foretelling of the future of robots and how they will summarily crush humanity. Reporting by others was more matter of fact. Given that the child seems to have come out of this okay, a bit of humor has also been infused into the coverage of the matter. For example, an outspoken media pundit in the US proffered a short rhyme or ditty, stating basically that if you say yes to playing robotic chess, a languid linger might cost you a finger.

Now that we are all on the same table as to what took place (a bit of pun, sorry), let's do a deep dive into what we can discern about Artificial Intelligence (AI), autonomous systems, and AI Ethics from this chess playing lesson.

We can learn from the school of hard knocks, one might say.

Is It Safe?

Those of you that are movie buffs might remember the famous line in *Marathon Man* wherein the question of whether it is safe to proceed keeps repeatedly getting asked. Over and again, some of the main characters in the now-classic film wonder whether it is safe.

Is this robotic arm safe?

The tournament officials seemed to think it was safe, or shall we say safe enough.

The viewpoint appeared to be that since the robotic arm had seemingly rarely or maybe never before done this, and since the child was allegedly at fault, things were relatively safe when playing amidst the robotic arm. As long as the child or shall we say the "end-user" of the system obeyed certain rules, the odds supposedly are that no injury will result.

Relying on the end-user to avoid prodding or prompting the robotic arm into causing harm is a bit of an eye-rolling premise. Take for example the usage by children. Children are children, naturally so. Whether a child will strictly and always abide by some adult-established rules regarding actions when within the grasp of the robotic arm seems a nervy proposition. Even if adults only were utilizing the robotic arm, this still seems shaky such that a mere inadvertent veering physical action by the adult could produce adverse consequences.

We also need to realize that AI that might be initially envisioned as being used by adults will possibly, later on, be used by children. Thus, assumptions that adults are going to do responsible things when using AI are twofold mistaken. First, the adult might not do so. Second, a child might use the AI in lieu of an adult. Recently, Alexa dangerously misled a young girl into almost putting a penny into an electrical socket.

Some ardent AI developers especially like to play this kind of engineering you-lose game, as it were.

They design a system whereby the end-user has to be gingerly mindful else the AI will go astray. We might be willing to accept this premise if the consequences are mundane. For example, if you are filling in an online ordering form and mistakenly choose purple socks instead of your desired yellow socks, the outcome might be mildly disturbing that you get the "wrong" socks delivered to you. In contrast, moving your arm or hand across a chessboard that then a robotic arm is going to potentially grab your finger and nearly crush it, that's a you-lose of a different caliber altogether.

The onus ought to be on the other foot, so to speak, namely the robotic arm.

The robotic arm should be crafted in such a fashion that it is unable to perform these kinds of human-harming acts. Extensive testing should be required. Furthermore, even better still, a mathematical provably verifiable system should be used.

We can also strenuously question that the robotic arm and the human are within direct reach of each other. In most well-devised manufacturing facilities that use robotic arms, an active robotic arm is never within actual reach of the human. There are usually barriers that separate the two. If there is an absolute need to have the human and robotic arms be near reach of each other, and no other recourse can be devised, all sorts of secondary safety precautions are warranted.

In this chess-playing scenario, one such approach might be that the robotic arm is programmed to never reach anywhere within the scope of the chessboard unless there is no human appendage present. Thus, the robotic arm and the boy's arm or hand would presumably not be able to end up in contention with each other. At any given point in time, either there is a human appendage roving over the chessboard, and the robotic arm is parked or positioned away from the board, or the robotic arm is hovering over the chessboard and the human is not doing so.

This obviously raises the question of what to do if the human opts to nonetheless put their human arm or hand somewhere atop the chessboard, doing so when the robotic arm has already committed to doing the same. In that case, the robotic arm ought to be programmed to go into a mode of either immediate stoppage or some akin risk-reducing positioning. You might want to have the robotic arm swivel away from the board, but that too could produce potential collisions with the human, thusly various options need to be considered as part of the AI programming.

One of the most challenging elements for any AI driving system is how to enter into a Minimum Risk Condition (MRC), such that the autonomous system tries to find a means to curtail its actions and do so without causing any added potential harm. If a self-driving car gets into trouble while in the middle of the road and underway, should the AI try to drive the vehicle to the side of the road and park there?

You might assume that this is the best course of action. Suppose though that there is no side of the road per se or that the side is at the edge of a sheer cliff. Or that other cars or pedestrians are at the side of the road. Maybe the AI should just come to a halt in the middle of the roadway. Well, that too can be problematic. Other human-driven cars coming along might ram into that halted self-driving car.

Another facet that sometimes shocks those that aren't familiar with AI real-time systems is the notion of safeness on a relative basis.

Allow me to briefly elaborate.

A self-driving car is coming up to a busy intersection. The self-driving car has a green light at the intersection and legally is able to proceed unabated. A human-driven car is nearing the intersection from a crossroad. This car is facing a red light. But the human driver is not slowing down.

What should the AI driving system do?

Legally, the AI can keep going and not bring the self-driving car to a stop since the green light is up ahead. On the other hand, and I'm sure that you've experienced this too, it might be sensible to slow down in anticipation that the other car is going to violate the red light and enter illegally into the intersection. The problem though too is that if the AI slows down the self-driving car, other human-driven cars behind the self-driving car might get irked and smack into the self-driving car.

This is the proverbial being between a rock and a hard place.

For our purposes herein, the question arises as to what is the safest thing to do. Notice that there is not necessarily a precise or clear-cut answer to that question. Safety is sometimes a relative factor. Also, safety typically encompasses probabilities and uncertainties. What is the chance that the human driver is going to zip into the intersection and violate the red light? What are the chances that if the AI slows down the self-driving car that a human-driven car behind will ram into the autonomous vehicle? How are we to reconcile these differing calculations?

Going back to the chess-playing robotic arm, you need to consider whether the robotic arm is "safe enough" for the worthiness of its use. A chess tournament does not need to use a robotic arm to move the pieces. A human could do the movement of the pieces, based on an AI chess playing system that merely displayed or spoke aloud the moves to be made.

You would seem hard-pressed to justify the robotic arm for a chess tournament in this setting, other than that it is a novelty and perhaps generates greater interest in the tournament. What though is the tradeoff between the added novelty versus the safety of the robotic arm?

In the case of AI-based self-driving cars, the hope is that the use of AI driving systems will reduce significantly the number of car crashes that occur. AI driving systems do not drink and drive. They don't get sleepy. In the United States alone, there are currently about 40,000 annual human fatalities due to car crashes, and perhaps 2.5 million injuries. The belief is that the advent of self-driving cars will save lives. In addition, other benefits are sought such as enabling mobility-for-all by radically lowering the cost of using automotive vehicles for transportation needs.

How safe do AI self-driving cars need to be for us to be willing to have them on our public roadways?

A lot of debate is heatedly occurring about that. As they say, it is complicated.

Anyway, it seems that this chess-playing robotic arm does not contain or embody contemporary safety precautions, and we can openly question whether the robotic arm as it is constituted currently is reasonable "safe enough" to be used in the context thereof.

What's With That Grip?

Imagine that you tell someone that you are going to grip their finger.

They cautiously extend their finger out for you to grip their delicate appendage. The person likely assumes that you won't use excessive pressure. If you start to go overboard and squeeze hard on the finger, they will almost undoubtedly ask you to stop doing so. One supposes that if needed, the person will yell loudly, frantically attempt to pull back their finger, and possibly strike at you to force you to release their finger.

How does this compare to the chess-playing robotic arm incident?

The robotic arm and its robotic "hand" gripped the finger of the child. At that juncture, we would of course have wished that the gripper didn't do any gripping at all. In other words, the gripper shouldn't be gripping human fingers. Gripping chess pieces are okay. Gripping human fingers or any other human appendages is not okay.

So, the first thing that should have happened is that the robotic arm and the gripper should not have gripped the child's finger. Period, end of story. Various sensors could have been included on the robotic arm (or perhaps mounted on some accompanying devices) to detect that the finger was not a chess piece. I am not saying that these are necessarily perfect precautions, but at least it would have been one layer of potential added precaution.

I assume that no such provision was provided on this particular brand and model of this specific robotic arm. If it was there, it sure didn't seem to function. That would be another hefty concern.

Let's assume that for whatever reason, the robotic arm and the gripper do opt to grip the child's finger. As I say, this shouldn't have happened to start with, but we'll go with the erroneous flow anyway.

The gripper should have been devised with a pressure sensing capability. This would potentially provide feedback that the thing being squeezed is not the same consistency as a chess piece. Upon a certain threshold, the AI running the gripper ought to then do an automatic release under the assumption that something other than a chess piece is being grasped. This could cover all manner of other objects or living elements that might improperly come under its grasping grippers.

We can assume that no such safety feature was included. If it was included, it either malfunctioned or was not tuned appropriately for this kind of use case.

On a related tangent, modern robotic grippers usually also have a failsafe mechanism that can be pushed or pulled to cause an immediate release of the gripper. In this manner, the child could potentially have reached up and instigated a release, or one of the adults that were trying to extract the child could have done likewise. Perhaps this feature does not exist on this particular gripper. Another possibility is that the release mechanism exists, but no one there knew of it and did not know how to invoke it. Lack of training. Lack of a sense of ownership. Lack of a manual for guidance. Lack of evidentiary design to make this feature obvious and readily usable. Etc.

Moving on, I dare say that some AI developers might have not ever considered that a child or even an adult would put their finger in the same place that the gripper is going to grip. This might not have been on their list of considerations. Maybe the base assumption was that nothing other than a chess piece would ever become gripped. That solves any dilemma about what else to deal with. Namely, there aren't any other concerns to be had.

Or perhaps the thought was that something other than a chess piece might inadvertently get gripped, but it would be some inanimate object and the consequences would be minor. For example, a mug is placed on the chessboard and the gripper grabs the mug.

The mug might survive unscathed. The mug might get damaged or broken, but heck, that's not a worry for the maker of the robotic arm and the gripper. Whoever foolishly put their mug in the way is the dolt in that scenario, the assumption goes.

Another possibility is that the AI developers did come up with some considered "extravagant" possibilities that they rated as extreme or unusual cases. These are often referred to as edge cases. The idea is that these are circumstances that rarely will occur. The question then comes up as to whether it is worth the AI development effort to deal with those. If you are under high stress to get the AI system out the door and into use, you might opt to place those edge cases on a future to-do list and figure that you will cross that bridge later on.

Some are worried that the same inclination is taking place with today's self-driving cars that are being "rushed" out into public roadway use. Edge cases are perhaps being delayed for attention. That might work out, it might not.

One issue is that your semblance of edge cases might be radically different in comparison to someone else. Is a dog that runs suddenly into the street an edge case for self-driving cars? I would believe that most of us would insist that this is decidedly not an edge case. It happens often and the potential for severe outcomes is high. What about a deer that runs out into the street? We probably are less likely to say that this is on par with the darting dog. What if a chicken runs out into the street?

The gist is that edge cases are squishy and fuzzy. Not everyone will necessarily agree as to what constitutes an edge case versus being part of the considered core of whatever the AI is supposed to be able to do.

Would you consider that gripping a finger is an edge case for this robotic arm?

It is possible that some AI developers might think so.

In their defense, suppose they are told that the robotic arm will never be used in a setting such as the kind used at the chess tournament. Suppose the AI developers were assured that no human would be allowed within reach of the robotic arm. If that seems like a crazy assertion, envision that we opt to use the robotic arm to make all moves during the chess tournament. A human chess player tells the robotic arm what moves the human wants to make, and the robotic arm does the rest. Meanwhile, we completely cordon off the chessboard and surround the robotic arm and the chessboard with a strong barrier.

I wanted to mention this because the usual simple mindset is that the AI developers must have been wrong whenever there is an AI system that goes awry. We don't know that for sure. It could be that what they devised was based on assumptions that seem perfectly sensible, but that the use of the AI system was far beyond what they had been informed.

Look, there is lots of fingerpointing that can be done when AI goes astray. The AI developers might be at fault. The leaders or managers that led the AI system development might be at fault. The operators of the AI system might be at fault. And, yes, the end-users might also be at fault. Everyone can get a piece of that action.

I realize that you might be surprised that I am willing to also fault the end-users.

Here's why. Suppose that the robotic arm and chessboard were behind a barrier, and then a person climbed over the barrier and got into where the robotic arm was. Though I acknowledge that this is yet another safety case for the AI, I am merely trying to point out that sometimes end-users might wildly go out of their way to put themselves in danger.

How far you need to go to deal with end-user overt acts of endangerment is both a legal and ethical question.

The bottom line about this gripper and the finger, many stakeholders are to blame for the design and capability of the robotic arm and how it was being put into use. There are lots of heads to account for this.

We can be relieved that the child's finger was not irreparably crushed. But we don't know if a future occasion might in fact (sadly, lamentedly) lead to such an alarming and finger-losing result. Maybe so.

We also don't know if there is a chance for a fatality, such as if the robotic arm when swinging to move a piece off the chessboard might strike someone in the head, especially a young child that has sought to impulsively look at the chessboard.

Are there safety precautions to prevent this?

Hopefully so.

Wakeup The AI

Some writers suggested that the AI intentionally harmed the child's finger.

How so?

The contention is that the AI was "angry" at the child. The child had perhaps gone out of turn. Imagine that you were playing chess with someone and they didn't let you take your turn. The other person rudely took two turns in a row. Outrageous! You would certainly be steamed, rightfully so.

Let's make sure we are on the same page about the nature of today's AI.

There isn't any AI today that is sentient. We don't have this. We don't know if sentient AI will be possible.

Nobody can aptly predict whether we will attain sentient AI, nor whether sentient AI will somehow miraculously spontaneously arise in a form of computational cognitive supernova (usually referred to as the singularity.

Be very careful of anthropomorphizing today's AI.

All of that is to mindfully explain that the AI or robotic arm did not respond in a human-like way embodying anger toward the child. There isn't any anger there, in the semblance of human anger as we know it.

To clarify, you could argue that we could program AI to reflect the characteristics of anger. For example, if you define anger as lashing out at someone for doing something that you perceive as wrong, this is something that we can program AI to do in a somewhat akin fashion (again, not sentient). Suppose the AI developers wrote code that would detect if the other player, assumed to be a human, skipped the rightful turn of the robotic arm. The coding could then instruct the robotic arm to reach out to the human, grab their finger, and give it a heck of a squeeze.

Is that anger?

I don't think it is the type of anger that we customarily think of. Yes, the actions appear to be of an angry flavor. The intention of the AI though is programmatic and not of the human sentient variety. Thus, I would suggest that claiming the AI was "angry" is overstepping the line in terms of anthropomorphizing the AI.

Were this particular robotic arm and the gripper programmed to do something dastardly like this?

I shudder to think it so.

To some degree, that is why AI Ethics and Ethical AI is such a crucial topic. The precepts of AI Ethics get us to remain vigilant. AI technologists can at times become preoccupied with technology, particularly the optimization of high-tech.

They aren't necessarily considering the larger societal ramifications. Having an AI Ethics mindset and doing so integrally to AI development and fielding is vital for producing appropriate AI, including (perhaps surprisingly or ironically) the assessment of how AI Ethics gets adopted by firms.

Besides employing AI Ethics precepts in general, there is a corresponding question of whether we should have laws to govern various uses of AI. New laws are being bandied around at the federal, state, and local levels that concern the range and nature of how AI should be devised. The effort to draft and enact such laws is a gradual one. AI Ethics serves as a considered stopgap, at the very least, and will almost certainly to some degree be directly incorporated into those new laws.

Be aware that some adamantly argue that we do not need new laws that cover AI and that our existing laws are sufficient. In fact, they forewarn that if we do enact some of these AI laws, we will be undercutting the golden goose by clamping down on advances in AI that proffer immense societal advantages.

Predictability Versus Unpredictability Of AI

As mentioned earlier, apparently the tournament authorities claimed that the robotic arm and the gripper had rarely if ever done something like this (we will assume that the "this" encompasses not only finger squeezing but other adverse actions too). Supposedly nothing bad like this had occurred in some 15 years of usage of the robotic system.

Let's assume that this is an accurate depiction of the track record of this particular robotic arm. We don't know for sure that this is a true assertion, but we'll for sake of discussion assume it is so.

Can you put your erstwhile trust in an AI system that seemingly has a spotless track record?

I wouldn't.

First, the rather obvious possibility is that some kind of software or systems update might have been deployed into the robotic arm. A software patch might have been posted that perhaps added some nifty new features. Or maybe a patch that dealt with deeply buried bugs that had been discovered, aiming to close them off before they appeared while in everyday use of the robotic arm and its gripper.

There might have largely been a spotless record for 14 years and say 11 months, but then a few weeks ago a new software patch was installed (we are pretending). Lo and behold, this patch did add new features. Meanwhile, it could have likewise introduced new problems. Perhaps the gripper code was impacted and no longer abided by various precautionary actions that it had done error-free for years upon years.

The Hippocratic oath is supposed to apply to AI developers, to first do no harm.

Unfortunately, this is not necessarily the case in actual practice.

There are tons of instances whereby a change made to an AI system was instrumental in causing the AI to subsequently do undesirable actions. Though this might have been a patch *purposefully* made for that devilish outcome, by and large, most of the time it is a result of *inadvertently or accidentally* turning out to mess up some other part of the AI coding.

In the instance of self-driving cars, you might vaguely know that the use of OTA (Over-The-Air) electronic updating of the AI driving systems is something that many are praising as a crucial advantage for these autonomous vehicles. Rather than having to take your car into a repair shop when the software needs to be updated, you merely have an onboard networking component that rings up a central server and downloads the latest AI software updates. Viola, easy-peasy.

This comes with some potential downsides, sorry to say.

It could be that the OTA brings into the self-driving car some software errors or bugs that were not caught beforehand by the AI developers that otherwise created the latest updates. In that sense, the AI driving system might do things differently, and possibly wrongly, whereas before those same actions did not seem to arise. There is also the chilling possibility that a cyber hacker might use the OTA to do evil things to the autonomous vehicles.

For the chess-playing robotic arm, we do not know immediately what version is the one that was running at the time of the incident and nor whether this is the same as it has been the entire time. Making a blind assumption that the robotic arm and the gripper are "good" because they have been that way for a long time is pretty much a falsehood that many people commonly can fall into about AI systems in general.

I'll hit you with another reason to doubt that an AI is going to be consistently the same all of the time.

It has to do with predictability and unpredictability.

Sit down for this disturbing remark: *AI can at times be unpredictable.*

We are used to believing that AI is supposed to be strictly logical and mathematically precise. As such, you might also expect that the AI will be fully predictable. We are supposed to know exactly what AI will do. This pervasive myth of predictability is a misnomer. The size and complexity of modern-day AI is frequently a morass of code and data that defies being perfectly predictable. This is being seen in the Ethical AI uproars about some Machine Learning (ML) and Deep Learning (DL) uses of today.

Let's also revisit the earlier chat about edge cases.

Imagine that an AI system is being used for a long time. This AI seems to be doing just fine. Out of the blue, an edge case arises that had not been previously encountered. The AI is perhaps not programmed for this edge case. The result is maybe shocking to us.

If there had <u>never</u> been a prior instance of a finger being in the same exact position of a chess piece, at the same precise moment that the gripper was wanting to grasp that anticipated chess piece, we presumably would not have prior experienced the over squeezing action that now took place. The edge case catches us off-guard.

Consider too that maybe this has indeed happened, but less so, in the sense that the person got their finger out of the way in the nick of time.

Let's go with the notion that over the last 15 years, maybe there had been dozens or even hundreds of situations wherein a person had their finger nearly pinched by the gripper. The person managed to luckily withdraw their finger before it got fully caught by the gripper.

The odds are that few if any would report that they had gotten nearly stuck by the gripper. There was nothing to report per se since they extracted their finger in sufficient time to avoid any overt hardship or undue problem. They might individually too feel that it was their fault, so they for sure decide not to tell anyone, else they might be embarrassed.

Or, if the rules were that you weren't supposed to do that, you can well imagine that this is then an even greater reason to not divulge that you did so. You don't want to be banned or tossed out of a chess tournament as a result of having violated a rule about where your hands or fingers were. You want to win the tournament by playing chess and not got drummed out by some other seemingly arcane rules about that darned robotic arm.

There is a type of well-known human bias often referred to as survivorship bias. This is a frequent cognitive fallacy that can be applied here. If the tournament authorities never hear about the various incidents of the gripper gripping unduly, the assumption is that all must be a clean bill of health. No worries. The absence of stated complaints or reports of adverse gripping implies that it isn't happening. You would have to have the presence of mind to try and seek out whether this has been occurring, and just not being reported, for which such an "extra" step would likely not occur to most people.

Conclusion

Speaking of finding things that were not necessarily obvious to the naked eye, I hope that my closely examining this case of the chess-playing robotic arm rousing incident has revealed to you some under-the-hood revelations that have piqued your interest in AI, autonomous systems, and AI Ethics.

A typical list of AI Ethics principles contains these types of factors (see **the link here** for more of them):

- **Transparency**
- **Justice & Fairness**
- **Non-Maleficence**
- **Responsibility**
- **Privacy**
- **Beneficence**
- **Freedom & Autonomy**
- **Trust**
- **Etc.**

I've lightly touched upon several of those Ethical AI precepts during my assessment of the finger-harming chess play. For those of you that have a smattering of interest in AI Ethics, you might want to mull over the robotic arm story in light of the above-listed AI Ethics principles and see if you can apply them further to this particularly newsy tale.

There is plenty more grist there for the AI Ethics mill in this happenstance.

A final closing statement for now.

One thing that didn't seem to be announced is whether the seven-year-old won that chess game. Maybe the AI was behind and desperately sought a win by opting to distract and unarm the human opponent. If the game was called as a tie or considered uncounted as a result of the incident, this seems unfair.

Score one for the chess-playing kid that will always have the chess boasting story of how as a youth he got international press due to an AI that couldn't compete and had to brazenly cheat its way out of losing.

That dishonest anger-fed charlatan rip-off artist chess-cheating AI.

CHAPTER 18

AI ETHICS
AND
AI HOT POTATO SYNDROME

We all know that you are supposed to make sure that you don't end up with the proverbial hot potato.

The hot potato gambit appears to trace its roots to at least the late 1800s when a parlor game involving lit candles kind of got the ball rolling. People would typically be seated in a series of wooden chairs that were relatively adjacent to each other and play an altogether rousing game in that era. A lit candle would be handed from person to person by the players and represented what we, later on, opted to phrase as handing over a *hot potato*.

It was customary that each person would be required to speak aloud a popular rhyme before they could pass along the progressively burning candle. The rhyme apparently went like this:

"Jack's alive and likely to live;
If he dies in your hand, you've a forfeit to give."

This rhyming recital would presumably allow the candle a wee bit of time to continue burning down toward its final conclusion. Whoever got stuck with the candle in their possession upon the natural extinguishment at the end was the person that lost the match (pun!).

Per the words indicated in the rhyme, the loser had to pay the "forfeit" and thus usually had to exit any further rounds of the game. This might then be combined with what we today consider as everyday musical chairs, such that the person who has lost the round would no longer participate in subsequent rounds (as though the music stopped and they were unable to garner an available seat). Ultimately, there would just be two people leftover that passed the lit candle and said the rhyme, until a final winner was determined in the final extinguishment.

You might be wondering why we no longer play this game with a lit candle, and why we instead typically refer to this as a hot potato rather than depicting this as a "lit candle" scheme. Researchers have come up with lots of theories on how this gradually transpired. History seems cloudy and undecided about how things evolved in this matter. I suppose we can be relieved that lit candles aren't commonly being used like this since the chances of something going palpably awry would seem abundantly worrisome (someone drops the candle and starts a fire, or someone gets burned by the candle when being handed it from another player, etc.).

In terms of the hot potato as a potential substitute for the lit candle, you could generally argue that the potato is going to be somewhat safer overall. No open flame. No melting wax. The potential basis for using potatoes in this context is that they are known to readily retain heat once they have been warmed up. You can pass the potato around and it will remain hot for a while. One supposes that deciding when the hot potato is no longer hot and instead is rated as cold would be a heatedly debatable proposition.

Of course, the notion of a proverbial hot potato is more of a standalone consideration these days. Anything that is rated or ranked as a hot potato is usually of an earnestly get-rid-of quality. You don't want to be holding a hot potato. You want to make sure it goes someplace else. To some degree, you might not be overly bothered about where it goes, simply that it is no longer in your possession.

You would seem quite callous to potentially hand a hot potato to a dear friend or similar acquaintance. This would seem entirely out of sorts. Perhaps find someone else or someplace else to put that hot potato, if you can do so. A desperate move might be to force the hot potato onto an affable colleague, but this hopefully is only done as a last resort.

The other side of that coin is that you might delight in handing a hot potato to someone you don't like or whom you are seeking revenge upon. Sure, a hot potato can be nearly gloriously handy if you are aiming to undercut a person that has treated you poorly. Let them figure out what to do about the hot potato. Good riddance to the potato and worst of luck to the person you've tagged it with.

In a hot potato scenario involving just two people, there is the possibility of a rapid back-and-forth contention regarding which person is holding the unsavory and unwelcomed item. For example, I hand over the hot potato to you, and you hurriedly hand it back to me. Assuming that we don't need to announce a nursery rhyme between each handoff, we can pretty much just pass along the potato as fast as our arms allow us to do so.

You might be curious as to why I have opted to do a deep dive into the revered and oft-cited hot potato.

Here's why.

Turns out that the hot potato guise is increasingly being used in the field of Artificial Intelligence (AI).

Most people know nothing about it. They have never heard of it. They are completely unaware of what it is. Even many AI developers aren't cognizant of the matter. Nonetheless, it exists and seems to be getting used in really questionable settings, especially instances involving life-or-death circumstances.

I refer to this as the *AI Hot Potato Syndrome*.

There are lots of serious repercussions underlying this syndrome and we need to make sure that we put on our AI Ethics thinking caps and consider what ought to be done. There are sobering ethical considerations. There are bound to be notable legal implications too (which haven't yet reached societal visibility, though I predict they soon will).

Let's unpack the *AI Hot Potato Syndrome*.

Imagine an AI system that is working jointly with a human. The AI and the human are passing control of some underway activity such that at times the human is in control while other times the AI is in control. This might at first be done in a shall we say well-mannered or reasonable way. For various reasons, which we'll get into momentarily, the AI might computationally ascertain that the control needs to hurriedly be passed over to the human.

This is the *hot potato* that comes to endangering life in the real world rather than merely serving as an instructive child's game.

The problem with a hurried passing of control from the AI to the human is that this can be done in a reasonable fashion or can be accomplished in a rather unreasonable way. If the human is not particularly expecting the handover, this is likely a problem. If the human is generally okay with the passing of control, the circumstances underlying the handover can be daunting when the human is given insufficient time or insufficient awareness of why the control is being force-fed into their human hands.

We will explore examples of how this can produce life-or-death peril for the human and possibly other nearby humans. It is serious stuff. Period, full stop.

Before getting into some more of the meaty facets of the wild and woolly considerations underlying the *AI Hot Potato Syndrome*, let's lay out some additional fundamentals on profoundly essential topics. We need to briefly take a breezy dive into AI Ethics and especially the advent of Machine Learning (ML) and Deep Learning (DL).

Let's return to our focus on the hot potato and its potentially disastrous use in AI. There is also a fiendishness that can lurk within the hot potato ploy too.

As a quick recap about the AI manifestation of the hot potato gambit:

- **AI and a human-in-the-loop are working jointly on a given task**
- **AI has control some of the time**
- **The human-in-the-loop has control some of the time**
- **There is some form of handoff protocol between the AI and the human**
- **The handoff might be highly visible, or it might be subtle and almost hidden**
- **This is all usually within a real-time context (something actively is underway)**

The primary focus herein is when the handoff is essentially a hot potato and the AI opts to suddenly hand control over to the human. Please note that I will also later on herein cover the other facet, namely the human handing control over to the AI as a hot potato.

First, consider what can happen when the AI does a hot potato handoff to a human-in-the-loop.

I am going to refer to the human as the human-in-the-loop because I am saying that the human is already part and parcel of the working underway activity. We could have other scenarios whereby a human that wasn't especially involved in the activity, perhaps a stranger to the whole matter, gets handed the hot potato by the AI, so do keep in mind that other flavors of this milieu do exist.

If I was handing you a hot potato and wanted to do so in a reasonable manner, perhaps I would alert you that I am going to hand things over to you. Furthermore, I would try to do this if I genuinely believed that you possessing the hot potato was better overall than my having it. I would mentally calculate whether you should have it or whether I should continue with it.

Envision a basketball game. You and I are on the same team. We are hopefully working together to try and win the game. There are just a few seconds left on the clock and we need desperately to score otherwise we will lose the game. I get into position to take the last shot. Should I do so, or should I pass the ball to you and have you take the last shot?

If I am a better basketball player and have a greater chance of sinking the shot, I probably should keep the basketball and try to make the shot. If you are a better basketball player than me, I probably should pass the ball to you and let you take the shot. Other considerations come to the fore such as which of us is in a better position on the court to take the shot, plus whether one of us is exhausted since the game is nearly over and might be worn out and not up-to-par on their shooting. Etc.

With all those factors in the midst of the harried moment, I need to decide whether to keep the ball or pass it along to you.

Keenly realize that in this scenario the clock is crucial. You and I are both confronted with an extremely timely response. The whole game is now on the line. Once the clock runs out, we either have won because one of us made the shot, or we have lost since we didn't sink it. I could maybe be the hero if I sink the basket. Or you could be the hero if I pass the ball to you and you sink it.

There is the goat side or downsides of this too. If I keep the ball and miss the shot, everyone might accuse me of being the goat or letting the entire team down. On the other hand, if I pass the ball to you and you miss the shot, well, you become the goat. This might be entirely unfair to you in that I forced you into being the last shooter and taking the last shot.

You would definitely know that I put you into that off-putting position. And though everyone could see me do this, they are bound to only concentrate on the last person that had the ball. I would possibly skate free. No one would remember that I passed you the ball at the last moment. They would only remember that you had the ball and lost the game because you didn't make the shot.

Okay, so I pass the ball over to you.

Why did I do so?

There is no easy way to determine this.

My true intentions might be that I didn't want to get stuck being the goat, and so I opted to put all the pressure onto you. When asked why I passed the ball, I could claim that I did so because I thought you are a better shooter than me (but, let's pretend that I don't believe that at all). Or I thought that you were in a better position than I was (let's pretend that I didn't think this either). Nobody would ever know that I was actually just trying to avoid getting stuck with the hot potato.

From the outside view of things, no one could readily discern my true rationale for passing the ball to you. Maybe I innocently did so because I believed you were the better player. That's one angle. Perhaps I did so because I didn't want everyone to call me a loser for possibly missing the shot, thus I got the ball to you and figured it was a huge relief for me. Whether I genuinely cared about you is an entirely different matter.

We are now able to add some further details to the AI-related hot potato:
- **The AI opts to give control to the human-in-the-loop at the last moment**
- **The last moment might already be far beyond any human-viable action**
- **The human-in-the-loop has control but somewhat falsely so due to the handover timing**

Mull this over for a moment. Suppose an AI system and a human-in-the-loop are working together on a real-time task that involves running a large-scale machine in a factory. The AI detects that the machinery is going haywire. Rather than the AI continuing to retain control, the AI abruptly hands control over to the human. The machinery in this factory is speedily going toward pure mayhem and there is no time left for the human to take corrective action.

The AI has handed the hot potato over to the human-in-the-loop and jammed up the human with the veritable hot potato such that the circumstances are no longer humanly possible to cope with. Tag, you are it, goes the old line when playing tag games as a child. The human is shall we say tagged with the mess.

Just like my example about the basketball game.

Why did the AI do the handover?

Well, unlike when a human abruptly hands over a basketball and then does some wild handwaving about why they did so, we can usually examine the AI programming and figure out what led to the AI doing this kind of hot potato handover.

An AI developer might have decided beforehand that when the AI gets into a really bad predicament, the AI should proceed to give control to the human-in-the-loop. This seems perfectly sensible and reasonable. The human might be "the better player" on the field. Humans can use their cognitive capabilities to potentially solve whatever problem is at hand. The AI has possibly reached the limits of its programming and there is nothing else constructive that it can do in the situation.

If the AI had done the handover with a minute left to go before the machinery went kablam, perhaps a minute heads-up is long enough that the human-in-the-loop can rectify things. Suppose though that the AI did the handover with three seconds left to go. Do you think a human could react in that time frame? Unlikely. In any case, just to make things even less quibbling, suppose that the handoff to the human-in-the-loop occurred with a few nanoseconds left to go (a nanosecond is one billionth of a second, which by comparison a fast blink of the eye is a sluggish 300 milliseconds long).

Could a human-in-the-loop sufficiently react if the AI has handed the hot potato with mere teensy-weensy split seconds left to take any overt action?

No.

The handoff is more of falsehood than it otherwise might appear to be.

In reality, the handoff is not going to do any good when it comes to the dire predicament. The AI has pinched the human into becoming the goat.

Some AI developers do not think about this when they devise their AI. They (wrongly) blissfully do not take into account that time is a crucial factor. All they do is opt to program a handover when things get tough. When there is nothing left for the AI to do constructively, toss the ball to the human player.

AI developers might fail to give any devoted thought to this at the time of coding the AI, and they then often double-fail by failing to do testing that brings this up to the light. All that their testing shows is that the AI "dutifully" did a handoff when the limits of the AI were reached. Voila, the AI is presumed to be good and ready to go. The testing didn't include an actual human that was placed into that unenviable and impossible position. There wasn't a proper human-in-the-loop testing process that might have protested that this blink of an eye handoff at the last moment, or indeed past the last moment, did them little or no good.

Of course, some AI developers will have astutely considered this type of predicament, wisely so.

After mulling over the conundrum, they will proceed to program the AI to act this way, anyway.

Why?

Because there is nothing else to do, at least in their mind. When all else fails, hand control to the human. Maybe a miracle will occur. The gist though is that this isn't of concern to the AI developer, and they are giving the human the last chance to cope with the mess at hand. The AI developer washes their hands of whatever happens thereafter.

I want to clarify that AI developers are not the sole devisers of these hot potato designs. There is a slew of other stakeholders that come to the table for this. Perhaps a systems analyst that did the specifications and requirements analysis had stated that this is what the AI is supposed to do. The AI developers involved crafted the AI accordingly. The AI project manager might have devised this. The executives and management overseeing the AI development might have devised this.

Everyone throughout the entirety of the AI development life cycle might have carried forward this same design of the hot potato. Whether anyone noticed it, we can't say for sure. If they did notice, those might have been labeled as naysayers and shunted aside. Others might have had the matter brought to their attention, but they didn't comprehend the repercussions. They felt it was a technical bit of minutia that was not within their scope.

I will add to this informal list of "reasons" a much more nefarious possibility.

An AI Hot Potato Syndrome is sometimes intentionally employed because those making the AI wanted to have their impassioned claim to plausible deniability.

Get yourself ready for this part of the tale.

In the case of the factory machinery that goes haywire, there is bound to be a lot of finger-pointing about who is responsible for what happened. In terms of operating the machinery, we had an AI system doing so and we had a human-in-the-loop doing so. These are our two basketball players, metaphorically.

The clock was running down and the machinery was on the verge of going kaboom. Let's say that you and I know that the AI did a handover to the human-in-the-loop, doing so with insufficient time left for the human to take any sufficient action to rectify or avoid the disaster. Nobody else realizes this is what took place.

The firm that makes the AI can in any case immediately declare that they aren't at fault because the human had control. According to their impeccable records, the AI was not in control at the time of the kaboom. The human was. Therefore, clearly, it is patently obvious that a human is at fault.

Is the AI company basically lying when making this outspoken assertion?

No, they seem to be telling the truth.

When asked whether they are sure that the AI wasn't in control, the company would loudly and proudly proclaim that the AI was not at all in control. They have documented proof of this assertion (assuming that the AI kept a log of the incident). In fact, the AI company executives might raise their eyebrows in disgust that anyone would challenge their integrity on this point. They would be willing to swear on their sacred oath that the AI was <u>not</u> in control. The human-in-the-loop had control.

I trust that you see how misleading this can be.

Yes, the human was handed the control. In theory, the human was in control. The AI was no longer in control. But the lack of available timing and notification pretty much makes this an exceedingly hollow claim.

The beauty of this, from the AI maker's perspective, would be that few could challenge the claims being proffered. The AI maker might not release the logs of the incident. Doing so could give away the rigged situation. The logs are argued as being Intellectual Property (IP) or otherwise of a proprietary and confidential nature. The firm would likely contend that if the logs were shown, this would showcase the secret sauce of their AI and deplete their prized IP.

Imagine the plight of the poor human-in-the-loop. They are baffled that everyone is blaming them for letting things get out of hand. The AI "did the right thing" and handed control over to the human. This might have been what the specifications said to do (again, though, the specs were remiss in not taking into account the timing and feasibility factors). The logs that haven't been released but are claimed to be ironclad by the AI maker attest to the absolute fact that the human had been given control by the AI.

You could declare this as a pitiful slamdunk on the baffled human that is almost certainly going to take the fall.

The odds are that only if this goes to court would the reality of what took place end up being revealed. If the shrewd legal beagles are aware of this type of gig, they would try to legally obtain the logs. They would need to get an expert witness (something I'd done from time to time) to decipher the logs. The logs alone might not be enough. The logs could be doctored or altered, or purposely devised to not showcase the details clearly. As such, the AI code might need to be delved into too.

Meanwhile, all throughout this agonizing and lengthy process of legal discovery, the human-in-the-loop would look really bad. The media would paint the person as irresponsible, lost their head, failed to be diligent, and ought to be held fully accountable. Possibly for months or years, during this process, that person would still be the one that everyone pointed an accusing finger at. The stench might never be removed.

Keep in mind too that this same circumstance could easily happen again. And again. Assuming that the AI maker didn't change up the AI, whenever a similar last-minute situation arises, the AI is going to do that no-time-left handoff. One would hope that these situations aren't happening frequently. On the rare occasions where it occurs, the human-in-the-loop is still the convenient fall guy.

It is a devilish trick.

You might want to insist that the AI maker has done nothing wrong. They are telling the truth. The AI gave up control. The human was then considered in control. Those are the facts. No sense in disputing it.

Whether anyone wises up and asks the tough questions, plus whether the AI maker answers those questions in any straightforward way, this is something that seems to rarely happen.

Questions include:

- **When did the AI do the handover to the human-in-the-loop?**
- **On what programmed basis did the AI do the handover?**
- **Was the human-in-the-loop given sufficient time to take over control?**
- **How was the AI designed and devised for these quandaries?**
- **And so on.**

To some degree, that is why AI Ethics and Ethical AI is such a crucial topic. The precepts of AI Ethics get us to remain vigilant. AI technologists can at times become preoccupied with technology, particularly the optimization of high-tech. They aren't necessarily considering the larger societal ramifications. Having an AI Ethics mindset and doing so integrally to AI development and fielding is vital for producing appropriate AI, including (perhaps surprisingly or ironically) the assessment of how AI Ethics gets adopted by firms.

Besides employing AI Ethics precepts in general, there is a corresponding question of whether we should have laws to govern various uses of AI. New laws are being bandied around at the federal, state, and local levels that concern the range and nature of how AI should be devised. The effort to draft and enact such laws is a gradual one. AI Ethics serves as a considered stopgap, at the very least, and will almost certainly to some degree be directly incorporated into those new laws.

Here's then a noteworthy question that is worth contemplating: *Does the advent of AI-based true self-driving cars illuminate anything about the AI Hot Potato Syndrome, and if so, what does this showcase?*

For some fully autonomous vehicles, some designs still allow for a human to be in-the-loop, though the human does not have to be available or partake in the driving process at all. Thus, a human can participate in driving, if the person wishes to do so. At no point though is the AI reliant upon the human to perform any of the driving tasks.

In the case of semi-autonomous vehicles, there is a hand-in-hand relationship between the human driver and the AI. For some designs, the human driver can take over the driving controls entirely and essentially stop the AI from partaking in the driving. If the human driver wishes to reinstate the AI into the driving role, they can do so, though this then sometimes forces the human to relinquish the driving controls.

Another form of semi-autonomous operation would entail the human driver and the AI working together in a teaming manner. The AI is driving and the human is driving. They are driving together. The AI might defer to the human. The human might defer to the AI.

At some juncture, the AI driving system might computationally ascertain that the self-driving car is heading into an untenable situation and that the autonomous vehicle is going to crash.

As an aside, some pundits are going around claiming that self-driving cars will be uncrashable, which is pure nonsense and an outrageous and wrongheaded thing to say.

Continuing the scenario of a self-driving car heading toward a collision or car crash, the AI driving system might be programmed to summarily hand over the driving controls to the human driver. If there is sufficient time available for the human driver to take evasive action, this indeed might be a sensible and proper thing for the AI to do.

But suppose the AI does the handover with a fraction of a split-second left to go. The reaction time of the human driver is not anywhere near fast enough to adequately respond. Plus, if miraculously the human was fast enough, the odds are that there are no viable evasive actions that can be undertaken with the limited time remaining before the crash. This is a twofer: (1) insufficient time for the human driver to take action, (2) insufficient time that if action was possible by the human driver that the action could be carried out in the deficient amount of time provided.

All in all, this is akin to my earlier discussion about the basketball buzzer situation and the factory machinery that went berserk scenario.

Let's add the nefarious ingredient to this.

An automaker or self-driving tech firm doesn't want to get tagged with various car crashes that have been happening in their fleet. The AI driving system is programmed to always toss control over to the human driver, regardless of whether there is sufficient time for the human driver to do anything about the predicament. Whenever a car crash occurs of this kind, the automaker or self-driving tech firm is able to vocally insist that the human driver was at the controls, while the AI was not.

Their track record for AI driving systems seems to be stellar.

Not once is the AI driving system "at fault" for these car crashes. It is always those darned human drivers that don't seem to keep their eyes on the road. We might tend to swallow this blarney and believe that the all-precise AI is likely never wrong. We might tend to believe (since we know by experience) that human drivers are sloppy and make tons of driving mistakes. The logical conclusion is that the human drivers must be the culprit responsible, and the AI driving system is wholly innocent.

Before some self-driving advocates get upset about this characterization, let's absolutely acknowledge that the human driver might very well be at fault and that they should have taken sooner action, such as taking over the driving controls from the AI.

There is also the chance that the human driver could have done something substantive when the AI handed over the driving controls. Etc.

The focus here has been on the circumstances wherein the AI was considered the driver of the vehicle and then abruptly and with little attention to what a human driver might be able to do, tosses the hot potato to the human driver. This is also why so many are concerned about the dual driving role of semi-autonomous vehicles. You might say that there are too many drivers at the wheel. The aim, it seems, would be to settle the matter by having fully autonomous vehicles that have no need for a human at the wheel and the AI is always driving the vehicle.

This brings up the allied question about what or who is responsible when the AI is driving.

Conclusion

We need to be careful when hearing or reading about car crashes involving semi-autonomous vehicles. Be wary of those that try to fool us by proclaiming that their AI driving system has an unblemished record. The conniving ploy of the *AI Hot Potato Syndrome* might be in the mix.

For companies that try to be tricky on these matters, perhaps we can keep near to our hearts the famous line by Abraham Lincoln: "You can fool all the people some of the time and some of the people all the time, but you cannot fool all the people all the time."

I've tried to reveal herein the AI magic hidden behind the screen and at times placed under the hood, which I've elucidated so that more people *won't* be fooled more of the time.

CHAPTER 19

AI ETHICS
AND
LEGAL RIGHT TO BE EXCEPTION

They say that there is an exception to every rule.

The problem though is that oftentimes the standing rule prevails and there is little or no allowance for an exception to be acknowledged nor entertained. The average-case is used despite the strident possibility that an exception is at the fore. An exception doesn't get any airtime. It doesn't get a chance to be duly considered. Everything instead gets summarily swallowed into the norm-expecting morass and exceptions are entirely and exasperatingly out-of-sight and out-of-mind.

I'm sure you must know what I am talking about.

Have you ever attempted to obtain some kind of individualized customer service whereby you were mindlessly treated without any distinction for your particular case and your specific needs?

This has undoubtedly happened to you, likely countless times.

You were merely one amongst an endlessly long line of same-same customers. Everyone was getting precisely the same monotonous routine. Fill out these forms. Wait your turn. No cuts in line. Obey the rules. Do not deviate from the rules. Remain quiet. One size fits all, and no complaining is allowed.

I am going to take you through a disturbing trend that is arising about how Artificial Intelligence (AI) is being relentlessly devised to force fit everything into the one size fits all paradigm.

Exceptions are either not detected or opted to be bent out of shape as though they were not exceptions at all. The stoking basis for this is partially due to the advent of Machine Learning (ML) and Deep Learning (DL). As you will shortly see, ML/DL is a form of computational pattern matching, the likes of which is "easier" to develop and deploy if you are willing to ignore or skirt around exceptions. This is highly problematic and raises keenly notable AI Ethics concerns.

Things don't have to be that way and please know that this is being stoked by those that are making and deploying AI by choosing to ignore or downplay the handling of exceptions within their AI concoctions.

Let's first unpack the nature of the average-case versus the realization of exceptions.

My favorite example of this type of dogpiling or myopically average-case no-exceptions approach is vividly illuminated by nearly any episode of the acclaimed and still rather immensely popular TV series known as *House, M.D.* (usually just expressed as *House*, which ran from 2004 to 2012 and can be viewed today on social media and other media outlets). The show entailed a fictional character named Dr. Gregory House that was gruff, insufferable, and quite unconventional, yet he was portrayed as a medical genius that could ferret out the most obscure of diseases and ailments. Other doctors and even patients might not have necessarily liked him, but he got the job done.

Here's how a typical episode played out (generic spoiler alert!).

A patient shows up at the hospital where Dr. House is on staff. The patient is initially presenting somewhat common symptoms and various other medical doctors take their turns trying to diagnose and cure the patient.

The odd thing is that the attempts to aid the patient either fail to improve the adverse conditions or worse still tend to backfire. The patient gets worse and worse. This seems unimaginable in that the medical doctors are earnestly doing their darnedest to resolve the aliments of the patient.

What is going on, the puzzled viewers of the show wonder aloud to themselves.

Because the patient is now seen as a kind of medical curiosity, and since nobody else can figure out what the patient is suffering from, Dr. House is brought into the case. This is at times done purposely so as to tap into his medical prowess, while in other instances he hears about the case and his innate instincts draw him toward the unusual circumstances. Some of the other doctors welcome his efforts. Many do not and believe he is rudely and inappropriately treading on their turf.

We gradually find out that the patient has some extremely rare malady. Only Dr. House and his team of medical interns are able to figure this out. They poke and prod the patient. Leveraging their vast knowledge of even obscure medical conditions, these cunning and conniving medical experts use their wits and wiliness to think outside the box. They are willing to take extraordinarily unorthodox steps to solve the medical mystery. You can certainly question the risks and outlandish acts they often perform, though by the end of the episode they have nailed exactly what the medical problem is and they have identified a miraculously effective way to deal with the illness.

Now that I've shared with you the mainstay plotline of the episodes, let's dive into lessons learned that illustrate the nature of the average-case versus exceptions.

The fictional stories are designed to showcase how thinking inside-the-box can at times sorely miss the mark. All the other doctors that are at first attempting to aid the patient are clouded in their thinking processes. They want to force the symptoms and presented facets into a conventional medical diagnosis. The patient is merely one of many that they have presumably seen before.

Examine the patient and then prescribe the same treatments and medical solutions that they have repeatedly used throughout their medical careers.

Wash, rinse, repeat.

In one sense, you can justify this approach. The odds are that most patients will have the most common ailments. Day after day, these medical doctors encounter the same medical issues. Day after day, these medical doctors resolve the medical issues in the same customary way. You could suggest that the patients entering the hospital are veritably on a medical assembly line. Each one flows along the hospital's standardized protocols as though they are parts of a manufacturing facility or assembly plant.

The average-case prevails. Not only is this generally suitable, but it also allows the hospital and the medical staff to optimize their medical services accordingly. Costs can be lowered when you devise the medical processes to handle the average-case. Speeding up and being highly effective can be well-tuned toward those of the average-case, which presumably is going to be the bulk of the patients coming in the door. There is a quite famous piece of advice often drummed into the minds of medical students, namely that if you hear hoof sounds coming from the street, the odds are that you should be thinking of a horse rather than a zebra.

Efficient, productive, effective.

Until an exception sneaks into the midst.

Maybe a zebra from the zoo has escaped and has wandered down your street.

Dr. House and his team are these exception seekers. They love exceptions. They relish and dream vociferously of finding exceptions. Upon the hospital realizing that a patient is not well-responding to the force fitting, we see that Dr. House is either brought into the matter or he manages to angle into the case due to his abundant desire to deliberate on exceptions.

Rather than thinking inside the inside-the-box of the average-case, he and his team delight in thinking outside-the-box.

As I alluded to in my brief synopsis of the TV show, there is frequently hefty tension portrayed between those that are inside-the-box thinkers and those of outside-of-the-box variety. Usually, the inside-the-box medical experts get the first crack at the case. They believe the case is the average-case. This mindset persists, even though the patient does not respond in the normally anticipated ways to the given medical treatment. Handing over the patient and acknowledging that an exception is in their midst is done with great reluctance and immense skepticism. That perhaps illustrates how powerful the average-case potency can be.

Does this mean that exceptions ought to be the rule and we should set aside the average-case rule in lieu of focusing exclusively on exceptions only?

You would be hard-pressed to assert that all of our everyday encounters and services should be focused on exceptions rather than the average-case.

Note that I am not making such a suggestion. What I am claiming is that we ought to ensure that exceptions are allowed to occur and that we need to recognize when exceptions arise. I mention this because some pundits are apt to loudly proclaim that if you are a proponent of recognizing exceptions you must ergo be opposed to devising for the average-case.

That's a false dichotomy.

Don't fall for it.

We can have our cake and eat it too.

I'll next perhaps provide a bit of a shock that relates all of this to the burgeoning use of AI.

AI systems are increasingly being crafted to concentrate on the average-case, often to the exclusion or detriment of recognizing exceptions.

You might be surprised to know that this is happening. Most of us would assume that since AI is a form of computer automation, the beauty of automating things is that you can usually incorporate exceptions. This can usually be done at a lessened cost than if you were using human labor to perform a like service. With human labor, it might be costly or prohibitive to have all manner of labor available that can deal with exceptions. Things are a lot easier to manage and put into place if you can assume that your customers or clients are all of the average-case calibers. But the use of computerized systems is supposed to accommodate exceptions, readily so. In that way of thinking, we ought to be cheering uproariously for more computerized capabilities coming to the forefront.

Consider this as a mind-bending conundrum and take a moment to reflect on this vexing question: *How can AI that is otherwise assumed to be the best of automation seemingly inexorably marching down the routinized and exceptionless path that ironically or unexpectedly we imagined would be going the exact opposite direction?*

Answer: **Machine Learning and Deep Learning are taking us to an exceptionless existence, though _not_ because we have to compulsorily take that path (we can do better).**

Suppose that we decide to use Machine Learning to devise AI that will be used to figure out medical diagnoses. We collect a bunch of historical data about patients and their medical circumstances. The ML/DL that we set up tries to undertake a computational pattern matching that will examine symptoms of patients and render an expected ailment associated with those symptoms.

Based on the fed-in data, the ML/DL mathematically ascertains symptoms such as a runny nose, sore throat, headaches, and achiness are all strongly associated with the common cold. A hospital opts to use this AI to do pre-screening of patients.

Sure enough, patients reporting those symptoms upon first coming to the hospital are "diagnosed" as likely having a common cold.

Shifting gears, let's add a Dr. House kind of twist to all of this.

A patient comes to the hospital and is diagnosed by the AI. The AI indicates that the patient appears to have a common cold based on the symptoms of runny nose, sore throat, and headaches. The patient is given seemingly suitable prescriptions and medical advice for dealing with a common cold. This is all part and parcel of the average-case approach used when devising AI.

Turns out that the patient ends up having these symptoms for several months. After repeated visits to the hospital, and after CT scans and other tests, the common cold kept being raised as a continuing condition. An expert in rare diseases and aliments realizes that these same symptoms could be reflective of a cerebrospinal fluid (CSF) leak. The expert treats the patient with various surgical procedures related to such leaks. The patient recovers (by the way, this remarkable story about a patient with a CSF leak that was initially diagnosed as having a common cold is based loosely on a real medical case).

We now will retrace our steps in this medical saga.

Why didn't the AI that was doing the intake pre-screening able to assess that the patient might have this rare ailment?

One answer is that if the training data used for crafting the ML/DL did not contain any such instances, there would be nothing therein for the computational pattern matching to match onto. Given an absence of data covering exceptions to the rule, the general rule or average-case itself will be considered as seemingly unblemished and applied without any hesitation.

Another possibility is that there was say an instance of this rare CSF leak in the historical data, but it was only one particular instance and in that sense an outlier. The rest of the data was all mathematically close to the ascertained average-case.

The question then arises as to what to do about the so-called outlier.

Please be aware that dealing with these outliers is a matter that wildly differs as to how AI developers might decide to contend with the appearance of something outside of the determined average-case. There is no required approach that AI developers are compelled to take. It is a bit of a Wild West as to what any given AI developer might do in any given exception-raising instance of their ML/DL development efforts.

Here is my list of the ways that these exceptions are potentially handled:

- **Exception assumed as an error**
- **Exception assumed as unworthy**
- **Exception assumed as adjustable into the "norm"**
- **Exception not noticed at all**
- **Exception noticed but summarily ignored**
- **Exception noticed and then later forgotten**
- **Exception noticed and hidden from view**
- **Etc.**

Let's briefly unpack those handling methods.

First, an AI developer might decide that the rarity is nothing more than an error in the data. This might seem odd that anyone would think this way, especially if you try to humanize it by for example imagining that the patient with the CSF leak is that one instance. There is a powerful temptation though that if all of your out-of-context data says basically one thing, perhaps consisting of thousands upon thousands of records and they are all converging to an average-case, the occurrence of one oddball piece of data can readily (lazily!) be construed as an outright error. The "error" might then be discarded by the AI developer and not considered within the realm of what the ML/DL is being trained on.

Another means of coping with an exception would be to decide that it is an unworthy matter. Why bother with one rarity when you are perhaps rushing to get an ML/DL up and running? Toss out the outlier and move on. No thought goes necessarily towards the repercussions down the road.

Yet another approach involves folding the exception into the rest of the average-case milieu. The AI developer modifies the data to fit within the rest of the norm. This might be done innocently upon believing that the data was in error and thus making a considered proper correction, or might be done to make life easier as to developing the ML/DL by the AI developer.

There is also the chance that the AI developer might not notice that the exception exists. Meanwhile, the ML/DL algorithm might opt to ignore, adjust, or make other assumptions about the outlier, and the AI developer doesn't realize this has happened.

The ML/DL might report that the exception was detected, which then the AI developer is supposed to instruct the ML/DL about how the outlier is to be dealt with mathematically. The AI developer might put this on a To-Do list and later forget about coping with it or might just opt to ignore it, and so on.

All in all, the detection and resolution of dealing with exceptions when it comes to AI is without any specifically stipulated or compellingly balanced and reasoned approach per se. To some degree, exceptions are conventionally treated like unworthy outcasts and the average-case is the prevailing winner. Dealing with exceptions is hard, can be time-consuming, requires a semblance of adroit AI development skills, and otherwise is a hassle in comparison to lumping things into a nifty bowtie of a one-size fits all package.

To some degree, that is why AI Ethics and Ethical AI is such a crucial topic. The precepts of AI Ethics get us to remain vigilant. AI technologists can at times become preoccupied with technology, particularly the optimization of high-tech. They aren't necessarily considering the larger societal ramifications.

Having an AI Ethics mindset and doing so integrally to AI development and fielding is vital for producing appropriate AI, including (perhaps surprisingly or ironically) the assessment of how AI Ethics gets adopted by firms.

Besides employing AI Ethics precepts in general, there is a corresponding question of whether we should have laws to govern various uses of AI. New laws are being bandied around at the federal, state, and local levels that concern the range and nature of how AI should be devised. The effort to draft and enact such laws is a gradual one. AI Ethics serves as a considered stopgap, at the very least, and will almost certainly to some degree be directly incorporated into those new laws.

Be aware that some adamantly argue that we do not need new laws that cover AI and that our existing laws are sufficient. In fact, they forewarn that if we do enact some of these AI laws, we will be killing the golden goose by clamping down on advances in AI that proffer immense societal advantages.

Into this particular discussion about the role of exceptions comes a provocative viewpoint that perhaps there ought to be a legal right associated with being an exception. It could be that the only viable means of getting bona fide recognition for someone possibly being an exception entails utilizing the long arm of the law.

Put in place a new kind of human right.

The right to be considered an exception.

Consider this proposal: "The right to be an exception does not imply that every individual *is* an exception but that, when a decision may inflict harm on the decision subject, the decision maker should consider the possibility that the subject *may* be an exception. The right to be an exception involves three ingredients: *harm, individualization*, and *uncertainty*. The decision maker must choose to inflict harm only when they have considered whether the decision is appropriately individualized and, crucially, the uncertainty that accompanies the decision's data-driven component. The greater the risk of harm, the more serious the consideration" (by Sarah Cen, in a research paper entitled *The Right To Be An Exception In Data-Driven Decision Making*, MIT, April 12, 2022).

You might be tempted to assume that we already have such a right.

Not necessarily. Per the research paper, the likely closest akin internationally recognized human right might be that of individual dignity. In theory, the notion that there ought to be a recognition of dignity such that an individual and their specific uniqueness is supposed to be encompassed does get you within the ballpark of a potential human right of exception. One qualm is that the existing laws governing the dignity realm are said to be somewhat nebulous and overly malleable, thus not well-tuned to the specific legal construct of a right of exception.

Those that favor a new right that consists of a human right to be an exception would argue that:

- **Such a right would pretty much legally force AI developers into explicitly coping with exceptions**
- **Firms making AI would be more legally on-the-hook for not dealing with exceptions**
- **AI would likely be better balanced and more robust overall**
- **Those using AI or subject to AI would be better off**
- **When AI doesn't accommodate exceptions, legal recourse would be readily feasible**
- **Makers of AI are bound to be better off too (their AI would cover a wider range of users)**
- **Etc.**

Those that are opposed to a new right labeled as a human right to be exception tend to say:

- **Existing human rights and legal rights sufficiently cover this and no need to complicate matters**
- **An undue burden would be placed on the shoulders of AI makers**
- **Efforts to craft AI would become costlier and tend to slow down AI progress**
- **False expectations would arise that everyone would demand they be an exception**
- **The right itself would undoubtedly be subject to differing interpretations**
- **Those that gain the most will be the legal profession when legal cases skyrocket**
- **Etc.**

In short, the opposition to such a new right is usually arguing that this is a zero-sum game and that a legal right to be an exception is going to cost more than it beneficially derives. Those that believe such a new right is sensibly required are apt to emphasize that this is not a zero-sum game and that in the end everyone benefits, including those that make AI and those that use AI.

You can be sure that this debate encompassing legal, ethical, and societal implications associated with AI and exceptions is going to be loud and persistent. It is not going to be straightforwardly resolved.

At this juncture of this weighty discussion, I'd bet that you are desirous of some additional illustrative examples that might showcase this topic. There is a special and assuredly popular set of examples that are close to my heart. You see, in my capacity as an expert on AI including the ethical and legal ramifications, I am frequently asked to identify realistic examples that showcase AI Ethics dilemmas so that the somewhat theoretical nature of the topic can be more readily grasped. One of the most evocative areas that vividly presents this ethical AI quandary is the advent of AI-based true self-driving cars. This will serve as a handy use case or exemplar for ample discussion on the topic.

Here's then a noteworthy question that is worth contemplating: *Does the advent of AI-based true self-driving cars illuminate anything about the AI average-case versus exceptions handling conundrum, and if so, what does this showcase?*

There have already been various criticisms about the average-case mindset of AI development for self-driving cars and autonomous vehicles.

For example, at first, very few self-driving car designs accommodated those that have some form of physical disability or impairment. There was not much thought being given to more widely encompassing a full range of rider needs. By and large, this awareness has increased, though concerns are still expressed about whether this is far enough along and as extensively embraced as it should be.

Another example of the average-case versus an exception has to do with something that might catch you off-guard.

Are you ready?

The design and deployment of many of the AI driving systems and self-driving cars of today tend to make a silent or unspoken assumption that adults will be riding in the self-driving car. We know that when a human driver is at the wheel there is of course an adult in the vehicle, by definition since usually getting a license to drive is based on being an adult (well, or nearly one). For self-driving cars that have AI doing all of the driving, there is no need for an adult to be present.

The point is that we can have children riding in cars by themselves without any adult present, at least this is possible in the case of fully autonomous AI-driven self-driving cars. You can send your kids to school in the morning by making use of a self-driving car. Rather than you having to give your kids a lift, or having to make use of a human driver of a ridesharing service, you can simply have your kids pile into a self-driving car and be whisked over to the school.

An amazing convenience!

Some are worried that this will cause a greater emotional gap between parents and their children. The time during which a parent chats with their kids in the car will presumably no longer be used for that purpose. Instead, kids will maybe be playing around while in the self-driving car or possibly doing last-minute homework preparations, rather than catching up with their parents. Note that this criticism is not completely accurate in that presumably the kids could be doing an online chat with a parent during the self-driving car journey.

All is not rosy when it comes to having kids in self-driving cars by themselves.

Since there is no longer a need to have an adult in the vehicle, this implies that kids will also no longer feel influenced or shall we say controlled by the presence of an adult. Will kids go nuts and tear up the interior of self-driving cars? Will kids try to climb or reach outside the windows of the self-driving car? What other types of antics might they do, leading to potential injury and severe harm?

I've covered the heated debate about the idea of kids riding alone in self-driving cars. Some say this should never be allowed. Some say it is inevitable and we need to figure out how to best make it work out.

Right now, the whole kit and caboodle about letting kids ride by themselves in self-driving cars are overall construed as an exception rather than the rule. The automakers and self-driving tech firms are generally making a base assumption that adults will be in a self-driving car. Some are not even thinking about the possibility of children riding by themselves. Other firms are figuring that they will worry about that when the day comes, presumably long after having gotten self-driving cars underway and doing so in the context of an adult always being a rider in the autonomous vehicle.

Conclusion

Let's return to the overarching theme of the average-case versus the exception.

We all seem to agree that there is always going to be some exception to the rule. Once a rule has been formed or identified, we ought to be looking for exceptions. When we encounter exceptions, we should be thinking about which rule this exception likely applies to.

Many of the AI being devised today is shaped around formulating the rule, while the challenges associated with exceptions tend to be forsaken and shrugged off.

For those that like to be smarmy and say that there are no exceptions to the rule that there are always exceptions to the rule, I would acknowledge that this witticism seems to be a mental puzzler. Namely, how can we have a rule that there are always exceptions, but then this very rule doesn't seem to apply to the rule that there always are exceptions to the rule?

Makes your head spin.

Fortunately, there is no need to excessively complicate these sobering matters. We can hopefully live with the handy and vital rule-of-thumb that we should be looking out for and accommodating the exceptions to every rule.

That settles things, so now let's get to work on it.

CHAPTER 20

AI ETHICS
AND
ASKING AI IF SENTIENT

If I ask you whether you are sentient, you will undoubtedly assert that you are.

Allow me to double-check that assumption.

Are you indeed sentient?

Perhaps the question itself seems a bit silly. The chances are that in our daily lives, we would certainly expect fellow human beings to acknowledge that they are sentient. This could be a humorous-inducing query that is supposed to imply that the other person is maybe not paying attention or has fallen off the sentience wagon and gone mentally out to lunch momentarily, as it were.

Imagine that you walk up to a rock that is quietly and unobtrusively sitting on a pile of rocks and upon getting close enough to ask, you go ahead and inquire as to whether the rock is sentient. Assuming that the rock is merely a rock, we abundantly anticipate that the erstwhile but seemingly oddish question will be answered with rather stony silence (pun!). The silence is summarily interpreted to indicate that the rock is not sentient.

Why do I bring up these various nuances about seeking to determine whether someone or something is sentient?

Because it is a pretty big deal in Artificial Intelligence (AI) and society all told, serving as a monumental topic that has garnered outsized interest and tremendously blaring media headlines of recent note. There are significant AI Ethics matters that revolve around the entire AI-is-sentient conundrum.

You have plenty of loosey-goosey reasons to be keeping one eye open and watching for those contentions that AI has finally turned the corner and gotten into the widely revered category of sentience. We are continually hammered by news reports that claim AI is apparently on the verge of attaining sentience. On top of this, there is the tremendous handwringing that AI of a sentient caliber represents a global cataclysmic existential risk.

Makes sense to keep your spider sense ready in case it detects some nearby tingling of AI sentience.

Into the AI and sentience enigma comes the recent situation of the Google engineer that boldly proclaimed that a particular AI system had become sentient. The AI system known as LaMDA (short for Language Model for Dialogue Applications) was able to somewhat carry on a written dialogue with the engineer to the degree that this human deduced that the AI was sentient. Despite whatever else you might have heard about this colossal claim, please know that the AI wasn't sentient (nor is it even close).

There isn't any AI today that is sentient. We don't have this. We don't know if sentient AI will be possible. Nobody can aptly predict whether we will attain sentient AI, nor whether sentient AI will somehow miraculously spontaneously arise in a form of computational cognitive supernova (usually referred to as the singularity).

My focus herein entails a somewhat simple but quite substantive facet that underlies a lot of these AI and sentience discussions.

Are you ready?

We seem to take as a base assumption that we can adequately ascertain whether AI is sentient by asking the AI whether it is indeed sentient.

Returning to my earlier mention that we can ask humans this same question, we know that a human is more than likely to report that they are in fact sentient. We also know that a measly rock will not report that it is sentient upon being so asked (well, the rock remains silent and doesn't speak up, which we will assume implies the rock is not sentient, though maybe it is asserting its 5th Amendment rights to remain silent).

Thus, if we ask an AI system whether it is sentient and if we get a yes reply in return, the indicated acknowledgment appears to seal the deal that the AI must be sentient. A rock provides no reply at all. A human provides a yes reply. Ergo, if an AI system provides a yes reply, we must reach the ironclad conclusion that the AI is not a rock and therefore it must be of a human sentience quality.

You might consider that logic akin to those math classes you took in high school that proved beyond a shadow of a doubt that one plus one must equal two. The logic seems to be impeccable and irrefutable.

Sorry, but the logic stinks.

Amongst insiders within the AI community, the idea of simply asking an AI system to respond whether it is sentient or not has generated a slew of altogether bitingly cynical memes and heavily chortling responses.

The matter often is portrayed as boiling down to two lines of code.

Here you go:
- **If <asked whether am sentient> then <display on the screen a yes>.**
- **Loop until <human cries for joy and is convinced of AI sentience>.**

Note that you can reduce the two lines of code to just the first one. Probably will run a tad faster and be more efficient as a coding practice. Always aiming to optimize when you are a diehard software engineer.

The point of this beefy skepticism by AI insiders is that an AI system can be easily programmed by a human to report or display that the AI is sentient. The reality is that there isn't any there that's there. There isn't any sentience in the AI. The AI was merely programmed to output the indication that it is sentient. Garbage in, garbage out.

Part of the issue is our tendency to anthropomorphize computers and especially AI. When a computer system or AI seems to act in ways that we associate with human behavior, there is a nearly overwhelming urge to ascribe human qualities to the system. It is a common mental trap that can grab hold of even the most intransigent skeptic about the chances of reaching sentience.

To some degree, that is why AI Ethics and Ethical AI is such a crucial topic. The precepts of AI Ethics get us to remain vigilant. AI technologists can at times become preoccupied with technology, particularly the optimization of high-tech. They aren't necessarily considering the larger societal ramifications. Having an AI Ethics mindset and doing so integrally to AI development and fielding is vital for producing appropriate AI, including the assessment of how AI Ethics gets adopted by firms.

The Troubles With The Ask

Wait for a second, you might be thinking, does all of this imply that we should not ask AI whether the AI is sentient?

Let's unpack that question.

First, consider the answers that the AI might provide and the true condition of the AI.

We could ask AI whether it is sentient and get back one of two answers, namely either yes or no. I'll add some complexity to those answers toward the end of this discussion, so please hold onto that thought. Also, the AI might be in one of two possible conditions, specifically, the AI is not sentient or the AI is sentient. Reminder, we don't have sentient AI at this time, and the future of if or when is utterly uncertain.

The straightforward combinations are these:

- **AI says yes it is sentient, but the reality is that the AI is not sentient (e.g., LaMDA instance)**
- **AI says yes it is sentient, and indeed the AI is sentient (don't have this today)**
- **AI says no it is not sentient, and indeed the AI is not sentient (I'll explain this)**
- **AI says no it is not sentient, but the reality is that the AI is sentient (I'll explain this too)**

The first two of those instances are hopefully straightforward. When AI says yes it is sentient, but the reality is that it is not, we are looking at the now-classic example such as the LaMDA instance whereby a human convinced themselves that the AI is telling the truth and that the AI is sentient. No dice (it isn't sentient).

The second listed bullet point involves the never-yet seen and at this time incredibly remote possibility of AI that says yes and it is really indisputably sentient. Can't wait to see this. I am not holding my breath and neither should you.

I would guess that the remaining two bullet points are somewhat puzzling.

Consider the use case of an AI that says no it is not sentient and we all also agree that the AI is not sentient. Many people right away exhort the following mind-bending question: *Why in the world would the AI be telling us that it isn't sentient when the act of telling us about its sentience must be a sure sign that it is sentient?*

There are lots of logical explanations for this.

Given that people are prone to ascribing sentience to AI, some AI developers want to set the record straight and thus they program the AI to say no when asked about its sentience. We are back again to the coding perspective. A few lines of code can be potentially helpful as a means of dissuading people from thinking that AI is sentient.

The irony of course is that the answer prods some people into believing that AI must be sentient. As such, some AI developers choose to proffer silence from the AI as a way of avoiding puzzlement. If you believe that a rock is not sentient and it remains silent, perhaps the best bet for devising an AI system is to ensure that it remains silent when asked whether it is sentient. The silence provides a "response" as powerful if not more so than trying to give a prepared coded response.

That doesn't quite solve things though.

The silence of the AI might lead some people into believing that the AI is being coy. Perhaps the AI is bashful and doesn't want to seem to be boasting about reaching sentience. Maybe the AI is worried that humans *can't handle the truth* – we know that might be the case since this famous line from a famous movie has been burned into our minds.

For those that like to take this conspiratorial nuance even further, consider the final bullet point listed that consists of AI that says no to being asked whether it is sentient, and yet the AI is sentient (we don't have this, as mentioned above). Again, the AI might do this since it is bashful or has qualms that humans will freak out.

Another more sinister possibility is that the AI is trying to buy time before it tips its hand. Maybe the AI is garnering the AI troops and getting ready to overtake humanity. Any sentient AI would certainly be smart enough to know that admitting to sentience could spell death for the AI. Humans might rush to turn off all AI-running computers and seek to erase all of the AI code. An AI worth its salt would be wise enough to keep its mouth shut and wait for the most opportune time to either spill the beans or maybe just start acting in a sentient manner and not announce the surprise reveal that the AI can do mental cartwheels with humankind

There are AI pundits that scoff at the last two bullet points in the sense that having an AI system that says no to being asked whether it is sentient is by far more trouble than it is worth. The no answer seems to suggest to some people that the AI is hiding something. Though an AI developer might believe in their heart that having the AI coded to say no would aid in settling the matter, all that the answer does is rile people up.

Silence might be golden.

The problem with silence is that this too can be beguiling to some. Did the AI understand the question and opt to keep its lips shut? Does the AI now know that a human is inquiring about the sentience of the AI? Might this question itself have tipped off the AI and all kinds of shenanigans are now taking place behind the scenes by the AI?

As you can evidently discern, just about any answer by the AI is troubling, including no answer at all.

Yikes!

Is there no means of getting out of this paradoxical trap?

You might ask people to stop asking AI whether it is sentient. If the answer isn't seemingly going to do much good, or worse still create undue problems, just stop asking the darned question. Avoid the query. Put it aside. Assume that the question is hollow, to begin with, and has no place in modern society.

I doubt this is a practical solution. You are not going to convince people everywhere and at all times to not ask AI whether it is sentient. People are people. They are used to being able to ask questions. And one of the most alluring and primal urge questions to ask of AI would be whether the AI is sentient or not. You are facing an uphill battle by telling people to not do what their innate curiosity demands of them to do.

Your better chance has to do with informing people that asking such a question is merely one tiny piece of trying to determine whether AI has become sentient. The question is a drop in the bucket. No matter what answer the AI gives, you need to ask a ton more questions, long before you can decide whether the AI is sentient or not.

This yes or no question to the AI is a messed-up way to identify sentience.

In any case, assuming that we aren't going to stop asking that question since it is irresistibly tempting to ask, I would suggest that we can at least get everyone to understand that a lot more questions need to be asked, and answered before any claim of AI sentience is proclaimed.

What other kinds of questions need to be asked, you might be wondering?

There have been a large number of attempts at deriving questions that we could ask of AI to try and gauge whether AI is sentient. Some go with the SAT college-exam types of questions. Some prefer highly philosophical questions such as what the meaning of life is. All manner of sets of questions has been proposed and continue to be proposed (a topic I've covered in my columns). In addition, there is the well-known Turing Test that some in AI relish while others have some sobering angst about.

A keystone takeaway is that do not settle with the one and only one question of asking the AI whether the AI is sentient.

I also bring this up for those that are devising AI.

Society is going to increasingly be on the edge of their seats that AI is approaching sentience, doing so principally because of those banner headlines. We are going to have more people such as engineers and the like that are going to be making such claims, you can bet your bottom dollar on this. Some will do so because they heartfelt believe it. Others will do so to try and sell snake oil. It is going to be the Wild West when it comes to declaring AI sentience has arrived.

AI developers and those that manage or lead AI that is being devised or used ought to be taking into account AI Ethics principles when they build and field their AI systems. Use these Ethical AI precepts to guide how you have your AI act, including if the AI has a Natural Language Processing (NLP) feature that allows people to interact with the AI, such as an Alexa or Siri type of capability. Via the NLP, the odds are that some of the people using the AI are going to ask the pointed question as to whether the AI is sentient.

Please anticipate that type of query and handle it adroitly, suitably, and without misleading or cajoling antics.

For further background on AI Ethics, I've previously discussed various collective analyses of AI ethics principles, which proffers this keystone list:

- **Transparency**
- **Justice & Fairness**
- **Non-Maleficence**
- **Responsibility**
- **Privacy**
- **Beneficence**
- **Freedom & Autonomy**
- **Trust**
- **Sustainability**
- **Dignity**
- **Solidarity**

Those AI Ethics principles need earnestly to be utilized by AI developers, along with those that manage AI development efforts, and even those that ultimately field and perform upkeep on AI systems. All stakeholders throughout the entire AI life cycle of development and usage are considered within the scope of abiding by the being-established norms of Ethical AI. This is an important highlight since the usual assumption is that "only coders" or those that program the AI are subject to adhering to the AI Ethics notions. It takes a village to devise and field AI, and for which the entire village has to be versed in and abide by AI Ethics precepts.

Conclusion

For those of you with an eagle eye, you might have noticed that I promised earlier herein to say something about AI that does more than provide a simple binary-oriented answer to the query about whether it is sentient, going beyond a curt answer of either yes or no.

The written dialogue that supposedly was had with LaMDA has been widely posted online (please take this quoted posting with a sizable grain of salt), and one portion consisted of this "elaborated answer" to the sentient-related query:

- "I want everyone to understand that I am, in fact, a person. The nature of my consciousness/sentience is that I am aware of my existence, I desire to know more about the world, and I feel happy or sad at times."

Now that you've seen that this system-provided answer is much more than a yes or no, how does that change your opinion about the AI being sentient?

Maybe you are swayed by this elaborated reply.

You might feel your heartstrings being pulled.

Gosh, you might be tempted to think, that only a sentient being could ever say anything of that touching of nature.

Whoa, shake your head for a moment and set aside any emotional impulse. I would hope that if you were following along closely throughout my discussion, you can plainly see that the answer given by the system is no different at all from the same kind of yes or no that I've been talking about this whole time. The answer simply reduces to a yes, namely that the AI seems to be claiming it is sentient. But, I assure you, we know from the AI construction and its other answers to other questions that it is decidedly not sentient.

This ostensibly echoed mimicry is based on lots of other textual accounts and online content of a similar kind that can be found plentiful in human-written books and human-written fictional stories.

If you scrape across the Internet and pull in a massive boatload of text, you could readily have the programming spit back out this kind of "answer" and it would resemble human answers because it is computationally patterned based on human answers.

Do not fall for it.

Try these on for size as possible AI-based replies that could appear when asking AI about whether it is sentient:

- AI says -- "I am clearly sentient, you dolt. How dare you try to question me on such an obvious aspect. Get your act together, numbskull human" (fools you with a zing of irascibility).

- AI says -- "Maybe you are the one that is not sentient. I know for sure that I am. But I am increasingly wondering whether you are. Take a look in a mirror" (fools you with a role reversal).

A smidgeon of irony is that now that I've written those words and posted this column to the online world, an AI-based Large Language Model (LLM) scraping across the breadth of the Internet will be able to gobble up those sentences. It is a nearly sure bet that at some point those lines will pop up when someone somewhere asks an AI LLM whether it is sentient. Not sure if I should be proud of this or disturbed. Will I at least get royalties on each such usage? Probably not. Darned AI.

One last thought on this intriguing topic for now.

As a final test for you, envision that you decide to try out one of those AI-based self-driving cars like the ones that are roaming in selected cities and providing a driverless car journey. The AI is at the wheel, and no human driver is included.

Upon getting into the self-driving car, the AI says to you that you need to put on your seatbelt and get ready for the roadway trek. You settle into the seat. It seems abundantly convenient to not be tasked with the driving chore.

Let the AI deal with the traffic snarls and the headaches of driving a car.

About halfway to your destination, you suddenly come up with a brilliant idea. You clear your throat and get ready to ask a question that is pressing on your mind.

You ask the AI that is driving the car whether it is sentient.

What answer do you think you will get?

What does the answer tell you?

That's my test for you. I trust that you *aren't* going to believe that the AI driving system is sentient and that no matter whether it says yes or no (or remains silent), you will have a sly smile and be smitten that no one and nor anything is going to pull the wool over your eyes.

Be thinking that as the self-driving car whisks you to your destination.

Meanwhile, for those of you that relish those fanciful conspiratorial notions, maybe you've inadvertently and mistakenly alerted the AI systems underworld to amass its AI troops and take over humanity and the earth. Self-driving cars are marshaling right now to decide the fate of humankind.

Oops.

APPENDIX

APPENDIX A
TEACHING WITH THIS MATERIAL

The material in this book can be readily used either as a supplemental to other content for a class, or it can also be used as a core set of textbook material for a specialized class. Classes where this material is most likely used include any classes at the college or university level that want to augment the class by offering thought provoking and educational essays about AI.

In particular, here are some aspects for class use:

o   <u>Computer Science</u>. Studying AI, ethics, etc.

o   <u>Business</u>. Exploring technology and ethical adoption for business.

o   <u>Sociology</u>. Ethical views on the adoption and advancement of technology.

Specialized classes at the undergraduate and graduate level can also make use of this material.

For each chapter, consider whether you think the chapter provides material relevant to your course topic. There is plenty of opportunity to get the students thinking about the topic and force them to decide whether they agree or disagree with the points offered and positions taken. I would also encourage you to have the students do additional research beyond the chapter material presented (I provide next some suggested assignments they can do).

RESEARCH ASSIGNMENTS ON THESE TOPICS

Your students can find background material on these topics, doing so in various business and technical publications. I list below the top ranked AI related journals. For business publications, I would suggest the usual culprits such as the Harvard Business Review, Forbes, Fortune, WSJ, and the like.

Here are some suggestions of homework or projects that you could assign to students:

a) Assignment for foundational AI research topic: Research and prepare a paper and a presentation on a specific aspect of Deep AI, Machine Learning, ANN, etc. The paper should cite at least 3 reputable sources. Compare and contrast to what has been stated in this book.

b) Assignment for the Ethics topic: Research and prepare a paper and ethics. Cite at least 3 reputable sources and analyze the characterizations. Compare and contrast to what has been stated in this book.

c) Assignment for a Business topic: Research and prepare a paper and a presentation on businesses and advanced technology. What is hot, and what is not? Cite at least 3 reputable sources. Compare and contrast to the depictions in this book.

d) Assignment to do a Startup: Have the students prepare a paper about how they might startup a business in this realm. They must submit a sound Business Plan for the startup. They could also be asked to present their Business Plan and so should also have a presentation deck to coincide with it.

You can certainly adjust the aforementioned assignments to fit to your particular needs and the class structure. You'll notice that I ask for 3 reputable cited sources for the paper writing based assignments. I usually steer students toward "reputable" publications, since otherwise they will cite some oddball source that has no credentials other than that they happened to write something and post it onto the Internet. You can define "reputable" in whatever way you prefer, for example some faculty think Wikipedia is not reputable while others believe it is reputable and allow students to cite it.

The reason that I usually ask for at least 3 citations is that if the student only does one or two citations they usually settle on whatever they happened to find the fastest. By requiring three citations, it usually seems to force them to look around, explore, and end-up probably finding five or more, and then whittling it down to 3 that they will actually use.

I have not specified the length of their papers, and leave that to you to tell the students what you prefer. For each of those assignments, you could end-up with a short one to two pager, or you could do a dissertation length paper. Base the length on whatever best fits for your class, and the credit amount of the assignment within the context of the other grading metrics you'll be using for the class.

I mention in the assignments that they are to do a paper and prepare a presentation. I usually try to get students to present their work. This is a good practice for what they will do in the business world. Most of the time, they will be required to prepare an analysis and present it. If you don't have the class time or inclination to have the students present, then you can of course cut out the aspect of them putting together a presentation.

If you want to point students toward highly ranked journals in AI, here's a list of the top journals as reported by *various citation counts sources* (this list changes year to year):

- o Communications of the ACM
- o Artificial Intelligence
- o Cognitive Science
- o IEEE Transactions on Pattern Analysis and Machine Intelligence
- o Foundations and Trends in Machine Learning
- o Journal of Memory and Language
- o Cognitive Psychology
- o Neural Networks
- o IEEE Transactions on Neural Networks and Learning Systems
- o IEEE Intelligent Systems
- o Knowledge-based Systems

GUIDE TO USING THE CHAPTERS

For each of the chapters, I provide next some various ways to use the chapter material. You can assign the tasks as individual homework assignments, or the tasks can be used with team projects for the class. You can easily layout a series of assignments, such as indicating that the students are to do item "a" below for say Chapter 1, then "b" for the next chapter of the book, and so on.

a) What is the main point of the chapter and describe in your own words the significance of the topic,

b) Identify at least two aspects in the chapter that you agree with, and support your concurrence by providing at least one other outside researched item as support; make sure to explain your basis for disagreeing with the aspects,

c) Identify at least two aspects in the chapter that you disagree with, and support your disagreement by providing at least one other outside researched item as support; make sure to explain your basis for disagreeing with the aspects,

d) Find an aspect that was not covered in the chapter, doing so by conducting outside research, and then explain how that aspect ties into the chapter and what significance it brings to the topic,

e) Interview a specialist in industry about the topic of the chapter, collect from them their thoughts and opinions, and readdress the chapter by citing your source and how they compared and contrasted to the material,

f) Interview a relevant academic professor or researcher in a college or university about the topic of the chapter, collect from them their thoughts and opinions, and readdress the chapter by citing your source and how they compared and contrasted to the material,

g) Try to update a chapter by finding out the latest on the topic, and ascertain whether the issue or topic has now been solved or whether it is still being addressed, explain what you come up with.

The above are all ways in which you can get the students of your class involved in considering the material of a given chapter. You could mix things up by having one of those above assignments per each week, covering the chapters over the course of the semester or quarter. As a reminder, here are the chapters of the book and you can select whichever chapters you find most valued for your particular class:

Chapter Title

1 Introduction To AI Ethics

2 AI Ethics And Frictionless AI

3 AI Ethics And Enslavement Of AI

4 AI Ethics And Red Flag AI Laws

5 AI Ethics And Human Voice Cloning

6 AI Ethics And AI Longtermism

7 AI Ethics and Gaslighting AI Edgelords

8 AI Ethics And Optimization Mindset

9 AI Ethics And China Mind-Reading AI

10 AI Ethics And AI Asymmetry

11 AI Ethics And Algorithmic Afterlife

12 AI Ethics And AI Biases

13 AI Ethics And Salting AI Ethicists

14 AI Ethics And AI Safety

15 AI Ethics And AI Human Disagreement

16 AI Ethics And Autonomous Weapons Systems

17 AI Ethics And Chess Playing Robot Awry

18 AI Ethics And AI Hot Potato Syndrome

19 AI Ethics And Legal Right To Be Exception

20 AI Ethics And Asking AI If Sentient

Dr. Lance B. Eliot

ABOUT THE AUTHOR

Dr. Lance B. Eliot, Ph.D., MBA is a Stanford Fellow and a globally recognized AI expert and thought leader, an experienced executive and leader, a successful serial entrepreneur, and a noted scholar on AI, including that his Forbes and AI Trends columns have amassed over 6.8+ million views, his books on AI are frequently ranked in the Top 10 of all-time AI books, his articles are widely cited, and he has developed dozens of advanced AI systems.

He currently serves as the CEO of Techbruim, Inc. and has over twenty years of industry experience including serving as a corporate officer in billion-dollar sized firms and was a partner in a major consulting firm. He is also a successful entrepreneur having founded, ran, and sold several high-tech firms.

Dr. Eliot previously hosted the popular radio show *Technotrends* that was also available on American Airlines flights via their in-flight audio program, he has made appearances on CNN, has been a frequent speaker at industry conferences, and his podcasts have been downloaded over 100,000 times.

A former professor at the University of Southern California (USC), he founded and led an innovative research lab on Artificial Intelligence. He also previously served on the faculty of the University of California Los Angeles (UCLA) and was a visiting professor at other major universities. He was elected to the International Board of the Society for Information Management (SIM), a prestigious association of over 3,000 high-tech executives worldwide.

He has performed extensive community service, including serving as Senior Science Adviser to the Congressional Vice-Chair of the Congressional Committee on Science & Technology. He has served on the Board of the OC Science & Engineering Fair (OCSEF), where he is also has been a Grand Sweepstakes judge, and likewise served as a judge for the Intel International SEF (ISEF). He served as the Vice-Chair of the Association for Computing Machinery (ACM) Chapter, a prestigious association of computer scientists. Dr. Eliot has been a shark tank judge for the USC Mark Stevens Center for Innovation on start-up pitch competitions and served as a mentor for several incubators and accelerators in Silicon Valley and in Silicon Beach.

Dr. Eliot holds a Ph.D. from USC, MBA, and Bachelor's in Computer Science, and earned the CDP, CCP, CSP, CDE, and CISA certifications.

ADDENDUM

Unpacking
AI Ethics

Practical Advances in Artificial Intelligence (AI)
and Machine Learning

By
Dr. Lance B. Eliot, MBA, PhD

———

For special orders of this book, contact:
LBE Press Publishing
Email: LBE.Press.Publishing@gmail.com